"Engaging an impressive range of literary and cultural texts spanning centuries and continents, Losambe celebrates a 'postcolonial agency' that – at times counter-intuitively – unites decoloniality and ambivalence, in a studied meditation on the politics of interstitiality."
— **Laura T. Murphy,** *Professor of Human Rights and Contemporary Slavery, Helena Kennedy Centre for International Justice, Sheffield Hallam University, UK*

"An expansive and illuminating study of figures who disrupted colonial and other dehumanizing agendas from within the establishment, not as alienated collaborators but as mindful yet subversive insiders. This book invites us to redefine the notion of anti-/postcolonial agency in its unending dialogue with and against Western modernity."
— **Moradewun Adejunmobi,** *Professor of African American and African Studies, University of California, Davis, USA*

"This book raises crucial questions to rethink African modernity: 'How did we get here?' 'Why are we still witnessing class, racial, ethnic, gender, sexual and religious hostilities and injustices?' 'What conditions would allow for the possibility of a new humanity that promotes and celebrates multiculturalism, mutualism, biodiversity, and conviviality?' The author approaches these questions through readings of major cultural producers who have profoundly shaped the historical, political, and philosophical map of knowledge. His subtle and complex analysis of these rich texts is a tour de force and a unique contribution that will enrich the African Archive."
— **Frieda Ekotto,** *Lorna Goodison Professor of Afroamerican and African Studies, The University of Michigan, USA*

"The breadth and depth of Lokangaka Losambe's literary research resulting in this book is very impressive. Losambe opens our eyes and minds to the crisscrossing and integrative experiences of Africans in the Home Continent and Diaspora and, instead of lamenting the European disruption of others with colonialism, picks on the agency exercised by the people of African descent. In the book's three sections consisting of a total of six chapters and a concluding coda, Losambe distills from fiction, autobiography, plays, and other forms of 'letters' the essence of the African people's postcolonial agency through their imaginative writings to affirm the fecund African imagination at home and in the diaspora. This book is meticulous, profound, and groundbreaking. With it Losambe restores a measure of classicism to the criticism of African literature today."
— **Tanure Ojaide,** *PhD, Frank Porter Graham Professor of Africana Studies, University of North Carolina at Charlotte, USA*

"This is a rewarding book: expansive in its coverage, valuable in its contemporaneity. Reading widely from the eighteenth century to the twenty-first, Lokangaka Losambe explores the contributions of a multiracial gathering that includes missionaries, memoirists, novelists, and filmmakers. In doing so, he brings out the incisive visions that a long tradition of African and African Diasporic intellectual work makes available. This book surely enriches our conversations in African and Black Diasporic cultural criticism."
— **Olakunle George,** *Professor of English, Brown University, USA*

Postcolonial Agency in African and Diasporic Literature and Film

This book chronicles the rise and the development of postcolonial agency since Africa's encounter with Western modernity through African and African diasporic literature and film.

Using African and African diasporic imaginaries (creative writings, autobiographies, polemical writings, and filmic media), the author shows how African subjects have resisted enslavement and colonial domination over the past centuries, and how they have sought to reshape "global modernity." Authors and film makers whose works are examined in detail include Olaudah Equiano, Haile Gerima, Amma Asante, George Washington Williams, William Sheppard, Wole Soyinka, Dani Kouyaté, Chris Abani, Chimamanda Adichie, and Leila Aboulela.

Providing a critical study of nativism, hybridity, and post-hybrid conjunctive consciousness, this book will be of interest to students and scholars of African and African diasporic literature, history, and cultural studies.

Lokangaka Losambe is the Frederick M. and Fannie C.P. Corse Professor of English at the University of Vermont, USA. His numerous publications include *Borderline Movements in African Fiction*; *An introduction to the African Prose Narrative*; *Literature, the Visual Arts and Globalization in Africa and Its Diaspora* (edited with Maureen Eke*)*; and *Pre-colonial and Post-colonial Drama and Theatre in Africa* (edited with Devi Sarinjeive).

Routledge Contemporary Africa Series

Implementing the Sustainable Development Goals in Nigeria
Barriers, Prospects and Strategies
Edited by Eghosa O. Ekhator, Servel Miller and Etinosa Igbinosa

Cultures of Change in Contemporary Zimbabwe
Socio-Political Transition from Mugabe to Mnangagwa
Edited by Oliver Nyambi, Tendai Mangena and Gibson Ncube

Indigenous Elites in Africa
The Case of Kenya's Maasai
Serah Shani

Media and Communication in Nigeria
Conceptual Connections, Crossroads and Constraints
Edited by Bruce Mutsvairo and Nnamdi T Ekeanyanwu

The Zimbabwean Crisis after Mugabe
Multidisciplinary Perspectives
Edited by Tendai Mangena, Oliver Nyambi and Gibson Ncube

Postcolonial Agency in African and Diasporic Literature and Film
A Study in Globalectics
Lokangaka Losambe

Inequality in Zambia
Edited by Caesar Cheelo, Marja Hinfelaar and Manenga Ndulo

For more information about this series, please visit: https://www.routledge.com/Routledge-Contemporary-Africa/book-series/RCAFR

Postcolonial Agency in African and Diasporic Literature and Film
A Study in Globalectics

Lokangaka Losambe

LONDON AND NEW YORK

First published 2022
by Routledge
2 Park Square, Milton Park, Abingdon, Oxon OX14 4RN

and by Routledge
605 Third Avenue, New York, NY 10158

Routledge is an imprint of the Taylor & Francis Group, an informa business

© 2022 Lokangaka Losambe

The right of Lokangaka Losambe to be identified as author of this work has been asserted in accordance with sections 77 and 78 of the Copyright, Designs and Patents Act 1988.

All rights reserved. No part of this book may be reprinted or reproduced or utilised in any form or by any electronic, mechanical, or other means, now known or hereafter invented, including photocopying and recording, or in any information storage or retrieval system, without permission in writing from the publishers.

Trademark notice: Product or corporate names may be trademarks or registered trademarks and are used only for identification and explanation without intent to infringe.

British Library Cataloguing-in-Publication Data
A catalogue record for this book is available from the British Library

Library of Congress Cataloging-in-Publication Data
A catalog record has been requested for this book

ISBN: 978-0-367-33638-7 (hbk)
ISBN: 978-1-032-19573-5 (pbk)
ISBN: 978-0-429-32242-6 (ebk)

DOI: 10.4324/9780429322426

Typeset in Times New Roman
by codeMantra

For Bibi and all our grandchildren

Contents

Acknowledgments   xi

Introduction   1

I
The enslaved African and postcolonial agency   9

1. Olaudah Equiano's *The Interesting Narrative of the Life of Olaudah Equiano, or Gustavus Vassa, the African, written by himself;* Haile Gerima's *Sankofa* (film); Amma Asante's *Belle* (film)   11

II
The Black American stranger and postcolonial agency in Africa: the Congo narrative   35

2. The anti-enslavement/-colonial activist: George Washington Williams (1849–1891)   37

3. The postcolonial pragmatist: William Henry Sheppard (1865–1927)   54

4. The other allies   107

III
Articulations of postcolonial agency in contemporary African literature   129

5. The colonial encounter and postcolonial agency in Wole Soyinka's *Death and the King's Horseman* and Dani Kouyaté's *Keita! l'héritage du Griot* (film)   131

x Contents

6 Postcolonial conjunctive consciousness in the literature
   of the new African diaspora: Chris Abani's *The Virgin
   of Flames,* Chimamanda Ngozi Adichie's *Americanah,*
   Leila Aboulela's *The Translator*   147

   CODA: Francis Abiola Irele and the
   African imagination   170

   Bibliography   177
   Index   187

Acknowledgments

In shaping the ideas contained in this book, I have benefitted from comments made by colleagues and friends on my critical assumptions about the worldliness of the literary art. Amongst those generous individuals, I wish to mention Moradewun Adejunmobi, Tanure Ojaide, Kasongo Kapanga, Olakunle George, Aliko Songolo, Chiwengo Ngwarsungu, Emily Bernard, Anthony Bradley, Andrew Barnaby, Vicki Brennan, John Gennari, Libby Miles, Dan Fogel, Mary Lou Kete, Eric Lindstrom, Todd McGowan, Hilary Neroni, Valerie Rohy, Lisa Schnell, Helen Scott, Major Jackson, Jinny Huh, Hyon Joo Yoo and Lori Holiff. Special thanks to my research assistant Katherine Fischer for carefully proofreading the entire manuscript and compiling the index.

I owe a debt of gratitude to the University of Vermont College of Arts and Sciences for granting me the sabbatical time (Spring 2017) and financial assistance that I needed in order to carry out archival research at Hampton University, Virginia, and Mercer University in Atlanta, Georgia. For their generosity and hospitality, I thank Donzella D. Maupin and the entire staff of Hampton University Archives, as well as Priscilla Eppinger and her staff at the American Baptist Historical Society archives (Mercer University).

As always, I am deeply grateful to my life-partner Bibi and our children for their love and moral support. Many thanks also to my brothers-in-law Louis Okitohambe Okoka, Adam Matala, and Victor Lundja Okoka for their interest in my research work.

Finally, I wish to thank the following publishers for permission to reuse portions of my previously published materials: Wiley Blackwell for a portion from Losambe, L (2021), "Post-Hybrid Conjunctive Consciousness in the Literature of the New African Diaspora," in Olakunle George, ed., *A Companion to African Literatures.* Hoboken, N.J., 367–380.; Routledge for a portion from Losambe, L (2020), "The Local and the Global in Francis Abiola Irele's Critical Thought." *Journal of the African Literature Association* 14:1, 58–71.; Routledge for a portion from Losambe, L. (2017), "The Colonial Stranger and Postcolonial Agency." *Interventions: International Journal of Postcolonial Studies* 19: 6, 837–854.; Oxford University Press for a portion from Losambe, L (2010), "Patrice Lumumba," in Abiola Irele and Biodun Jeyifo, eds., *Oxford Encyclopedia of African Thought*. New York: OUP, 79–81.; and Sage for a portion from Losambe, L. (2007), "Death, Power and Cultural Translation in Wole Soyinka's *Death and the King's Horseman*." *Journal of Commonwealth Literature* 42: 1, 21–31.

Introduction

> Globalectics combines the global and the dialectical to describe a mutually affecting dialogue, or multi-logue, in the phenomena of nature and nurture in a global space that's rapidly transcending that of the artificially bounded, as nation and region. The global is that which humans in spaceships or on the international space see: the dialectical is the internal dynamics that they do not see. Globalectics embraces wholeness, interconnectedness, equality of potentiality of parts, tension, and motion. It is a way of thinking and relating to the world, particularly in the era of globalism and globalization.
> Ngugi wa Thiong'o, *Globalectics*

Assessing the state of world postcoloniality in 1993, in his book *Culture and Imperialism*, the late Palestinian American cultural analyst and literary critic Edward Said rightly affirmed that: "[P]artly because of empire, all cultures are involved in one another; none is single and pure, all are hybrid, heterogeneous, extraordinarily differentiated, and unmonolithic" (1993:xxv–xxvi). The Kenyan writer Ngugi wa Thiong'o made a similar point at the same time, stating: "[S]lavery, colonialism, and the whole web of neocolonial relationships so well analyzed by Frantz Fanon, were as much part of the emergence of the modern West as they were of modern Africa" (Ngugi 1993:10). And stretching further Said and Ngugi's point, a few years after the end of apartheid in South Africa and at the dawn of the 21st century, Michael Hardt and Antonio Negri (2000) proclaimed the end of imperialism (as far as it is defined by extensions of sovereignties) and celebrated contemporary world's transition to a new centerless global empire. According to them, the new "Empire can only be conceived as universal republic, a network of powers and counterpowers structured in a boundless and inclusive architecture" (166–167). The new empire is therefore sustained by a constant liberating tension between, on the one hand, its normalizing socioeconomic, political, and cultural forces shaped by modern, capitalist institutions like IMF, WTO, World Bank, multinational corporations, and nation-states, and, on the other hand, its subversive, deterritorizing forces made of multitudes like "Occupy Wall Street," "Black Lives Matter," public square movements, the

DOI: 10.4324/9780429322426-1

2 *Introduction*

Arab Spring, Women's March, and workers' mass protests catalyzed and facilitated by global social networks, videography, audio-visual arts, public murals, music, and transnational literary production.

In order to understand the working of this global network of normalizing powers and subversive, deterritorizing counterpowers which shape and reshape contemporary subjectivities within and across national boundaries, a number of postcolonial scholars have suggested trans-disciplinary critical approaches such as planetarity or planetary humanism (Gayatri Spivak 2003 and Paul Gilroy 2005), tidalectics (Kamau Brathwaite 1999 and Elizabeth DeLoughrey 2007), globalectics (Ngugi wa Thiong'o 2014), critical regionalism (Spivak 2008), and decolonialism (Walter Mignolo 2013). Among the questions that these approaches seek to answer are: how did we get here? Why are we still witnessing class, racial, ethnic, gender, sexual, and religious hostilities and injustices?[1] What are the conditions of possibility of a new humanity that promotes and celebrates multiculturalism, mutualism, bio-diversity, and conviviality? These global issues have also become the main themes not only of the literature of the new African diaspora but also of other diasporic constellations in America and Europe. As noted by Kavita Daiya, this

> [G]rowing archive of writing explodes our traditional national frames of American literature, British literature, and even world literature. This new literature offers us postcolonial stories unconstrained by national boundaries and often undone by nationalism. They are American and Nigerian, Pakistani and British, Sri Lankan and Canadian, Indian and Bangladeshi, Dominican and American.
>
> (2017:154)

Specifically, with reference to the African and African diasporic context, which is the main concern of this book, to search for answers to the above questions is to chronicle the rise and the development of postcolonial agency since Africa's encounter with Western modernity. And here, I believe, African and African diasporic letters (creative writings, autobiographies, polemical writings, and filmic media) provide useful insights into not only how African and African diasporic subjects have resisted enslavement and colonial domination in the past four centuries, but also how they have sought to reshape "global modernity." Thus, through a critical study of postcolonial concepts like nativism, hybridity, and post-hybrid conjunctive consciousness as articulated in a representative selection of early modern and contemporary African and diasporic letters, this book chronicles the rise and the development of postcolonial agency in Africa and its diaspora. Authors and filmmakers whose works are examined in detail include Olaudah Equiano, George Washington Williams, William Sheppard, Haile Gerima, Wole Soyinka, Dani Kouyaté, Chris Abani, Chimamanda Adichie, Leila Aboulela, and Amma Asante.

Introduction 3

In his book entitled *Inventing Ireland: The Literature of the Modern Nation*, the Irish critic Declan Kiberd has argued that "postcolonial writing does not begin only when the occupier withdraws: rather it is initiated at that very moment when a native writer formulates a text committed to cultural resistance" (1997:6).[2] While I agree with Kiberd that postcolonialism cannot be said to be synonymous with post-independence, I would like to extend his formulation by adding the sympathizing radical activist within the colonizing order as another subversive initiator of the postcolonial moment. For as Simone Bignall has pointedly remarked:

> Because postcolonial theory most commonly addresses the revitalization and recognition of the agency of colonized peoples through their acts of resistance and decolonization, it often reinforces a colonized / colonizing dichotomy, which positions the colonized class as the active or resisting force chiefly responsible for postcolonization and neglects to attribute an equal responsibility and transformative capacity to formerly colonizing subjects.
>
> (2010:4; see also Elleke Boehmer 2005a)

This view contrasts with Achille Mbembe's position. In his examination of the concept of "commandement" as deployed in the colonial context, Mbembe (2001) blurs the distinction between the colonizer and the colonial (the official and the civil), and lumps all the colonial settlers into two types, the ruthless Hegelian and the shrewd Bergsonian. He then leaves out in the cold the uncanny radical or liberal activist who frequently assumes the position of the oppressed native's ally. For the Hegelian type, as described by Mbembe:

> [T]he native subjected to power and to the colonial state could in no way be another 'myself.' As an animal, he/she was even totally alien to me. His/her manner of seeing the world, his/her manner of being, was not mine. In him/her, it was impossible to discern any power of transcendence. Encapsulated in himself or herself, he/she was a bundle of drives, but not of capacities. In such circumstances, the only possible relationship with him/her was one of violence and domination. At the heart of that relationship, the colonized could only be envisaged as the property and thing of power.
>
> (2001:26–27)

In the view of the Bergsonian type, however:

> [O]ne could, as with an animal sympathize with the colonized, even 'love' him or her; thus, one was sad when he/she died because he/she belonged, up to a point, to the familiar world [....]. In the Bergsonian tradition of colonialism, familiarity and domestication thus became the dominant trope of servitude.
>
> (Mbembe 2001:27)

Mbembe's analysis of the relationship between the colonial and the native is somewhat flawed because it appears to be solely based on Frantz Fanon's theory of Manichaeism, while ignoring his idea of post-violence "dis-alienation" (see Gilroy 2005:42) and reconciliation. It also negates Spinoza's progressive concept of "common notions" (Bignall 2010:151) and forecloses any possibility of what Judith Butler has called "shared orientation toward the material world" (1987:57, see also Bignall 2010:39 and Young 2015). This approach represses the existence of subversive, albeit sometimes ambivalent, anti-/postcolonial constellations within the imperial order as depicted in a number of African historical novels such as Sembene Ousmane's *God's Bits of Wood* (1960) and Mariama Bâ's *So Long a Letter* (1980) as well as in what I call the Congo narrative of the 19th and early 20th centuries (Losambe 2017).

In *God's Bits of Wood*, for example, Deune, one of the railway workers involved in the 1947 anti-colonial strike in French West Africa, is surprised and puzzled by the support of the French workers' unions for their struggle. Contrary to his previously normative, binary understanding of the Senegalese workers' strike as the struggle between Europeans and Africans, whites and blacks, he now starts the process of deconstructing the colonizing order, saying:

> This business of the help we've been getting from outside. I don't understand it. The support from the French unions, for instance. You have Europeans who have come all the way from up there, just to break the strike, and then there are other Europeans who send us money to go on with it. Don't you think it's odd?
>
> (Ousmane 1960:38)

Deune's confusion here, I would suggest, disrupts the logic of oppositional Manichean totality and points to the presence of a kindred subversive, postcolonial agency within the colonizing French empire. Mariama Bâ also acknowledges the presence of postcolonial agency among the colonizing subjects when Ramatoulaye, the main character of her epistolary novel *So Long a Letter*, proudly reminds her friend Aissatou:

> Aissatou, I will never forget the white woman who was the first to desire for us an 'uncommon' destiny. [...] To lift us out of the bog of tradition, superstition and custom, to make us appreciate a multitude of civilizations without renouncing our own, to raise our vision of the world, cultivate our personalities, strengthen our qualities, to make up for our inadequacies, to develop universal moral values in us: these were the aims of our admirable headmistress. The word 'love' had a particular resonance in her. **She loved us without patronizing us, with our plaits either standing on end or bent down, with our loose blouses, our wrappers. She knew how to discover and appreciate our qualities.**
>
> (1980:15–16, emphasis added)

By their "uncommon" anti-colonial vision and action, both the French headmistress and trade unionists in these two novels deploy themselves as strangers to their country's colonial desire, on the one hand, and the colonized Africans' anxious desire to retain or reclaim cultural purity following their encounter with Western modernity, on the other hand. Here, Ousmane and Bâ effectively give a voice to the often-silenced anti-/postcolonial minority within the imperial order.

The importance of such constellations of anti-/postcolonial agents within the imperial order was prominent in the case of a number of American missionaries and liberal writers who rose against King Leopold's brutal invasion of the Congo in the 19th and early 20th centuries. The critical presence of these uncannily disruptive modern voices in the Congo space during the European powers' scramble for Africa has recently been highlighted by scholars and filmmakers such as Adam Hochschild (1998), Tim Jeal (2007), Mathew Standard (2011), and Joel Calmettes (2010). What these studies have shown is that revisiting this colonial memory is indeed necessary for a sustained, productive realignment of global decolonial multitudes against oppressive forces (whether corporate or cultural) in the 21st century. As Paul Gilroy has argued, in the 21st century, "Repudiation of those dualistic pairing—black/white, settler/native, colonizer/colonized—has become an urgent political and moral task. Like the related work of repairing the damage they have so evidently done, it can be accomplished via a concept of *relation*" (2005:42).

Western modernity's self-contradiction as it implemented its African colonial project outlined in the Berlin treaty of 1885 engendered its alternative counter-narrative produced by alienated missionaries, radical public intellectuals, and a number of creative writers within imperial centers. For instance, outraged by Belgian King Leopold's systematic, selfish, brutal violation of almost all the provisions of the treaty, especially those guaranteeing the welfare of the indigenous population, freedom of religion, and free access to commercial activities in 19th-century Congo Free State, protestant missionaries like George Washington Williams and William Sheppard and radical writers like Mark Twain started questioning the self-professed ethical validity of European colonialism and American postcoloniality as projects of Western modernity. In so doing, they became strangers to Western modernity's normative, intolerant, exclusive order, on the one hand, and the knowable unknown indigenous life-worlds, on the other. In creating and occupying a liminal positioning between the two enemies, the colonizer and the colonized, the modern Western and the knowable unknown African other, these strangers can be described, to use Derrida's term, as supplemental "undecidables" (Bauman 1991:55) who deployed themselves as ambivalent, globalist agents. As Zygmunt Bauman has pointed out:

> Undecidables are all *neither/nor*; which is to say that they militate against the *either/or*. Their underdetermination is their potency: because they

are nothing, they may be all. They put paid to the ordering power of the opposition, and so to the ordering powers of the narrators of the opposition. Oppositions enable knowledge and action; undecidables paralyse them. Undecidables brutally expose the artifice, the fragility, the sham of the most vital of separations. They bring the outside into the inside, and poison the comfort of order with suspicion of chaos. This is exactly what the strangers do.

(Bauman 1991:56)

With reference to the Congo narrative emerging from the writings mentioned above, one can discern two types of modern strangers: the anticolonial strangers like George Washington Williams and Mark Twain, and the pragmatic postcolonial strangers like William Sheppard, Samuel Lapsley, and William Morrison. The African American journalist, politician, and explorer George Washington Williams traveled to the Congo Free State on January 30, 1890. After a few months there, he decried the inhumane treatment of the Congolese people by the cruel colonial regime of King Leopold II in a protest "Open Letter to Leopold II." The letter caused a major stir in Europe as he called for an international commission to investigate atrocities committed by the Belgian King's regime in the Congo. Williams' letter was the first decisive protest against colonial brutality in Africa, and its tenor expanded the corrective narrative of modernity enunciated earlier by Equiano. The radical tone of Williams' letter was, many years later, reiterated satirically by the anti-imperialist American writer Mark Twain in his polemical work entitled *King Leopold's Soliloquy*, originally published in 1905.

Following in the footsteps of Williams, the Black Presbyterian missionary William Sheppard and his Irish American coworker Samuel Lapsley went on missionary work to the Congo and also reported on the atrocities committed by King Leopold's regime against the indigenous people while expressing their admiration for the latter's humanity and the rich diversity of their land's flora and fauna. Because Sheppard, his wife Lucy, and other Black American missionaries enabled the indigenous population to develop a subjective, postcolonial agency in the interstitial space between the encroaching Western modernity and their African local traditional practices, they positioned themselves as postcolonial pragmatists. This trend is reflected in their letters and autobiographical writings examined at length in Part 2 of this book.

This interstitial space between Western modernity and African life-worlds envisioned by Black American missionaries as the location of postcolonial African subjectivities later on became the dominant theme or a contested ground in the writings of African writers from the Negritude movement (of L.S. Senghor, Aimé Césaire, Léon Damas, David Diop, and others) to the realist tradition of authors like Chinua Achebe, Wole Soyinka, Es'kia Mphahlele, Buchi Emecheta, Ngugi wa Thiong'o, Ayi Kwei Armah, Ama

Ata Aidoo, Tayeb Salih, Nuruddin Farah, Mongo Beti, Bernard Dadié, Sembene Ousmane, Cheikh Hamidou Kane, Camara Laye, Mariama Bâ, Tsitsi Dangarembga, V.Y. Mudimbe, and Georges Ngal, to mention but a few. I have extensively dealt with this tradition in a previous book (Losambe 2005). In Part 3 of this book, I examine Soyinka's play *Death and the King's Horseman* and Dani Kouyaté's film *Keita* as representative creative articulations of the trend in drama and film.

The conjunctive, transnational consciousness articulated in the writings of the so-called third-generation African writers (Adesanmi 2014 and Ojaide 2015), now commonly referred to as Afropolitans (Selasi 2005, Mbembe 2007, and Gikandi 2011a), further foregrounds the importance of the same interstitial space mentioned above as the location of contemporary, postcolonial African and new African Diasporic subjectivities. Afropolitan writers like Chimamanda Adichie, Chris Abani, Leila Aboulela, Teju Cole, Helen Oyeyemi, Taiye Selasi, Imbolo Mbue, Abdulrazak Gurnah, Alain Mabanckou, Fatou Diome, Marie Ndiaye, Noviolet Bulawayo, Frieda Ekotto, Abdourahman Waberi, and a host of others position themselves as African new humanists (Huggan 2013) who occupy a postcolonial third space from where they cast a critical gaze upon three life-worlds: African societies they originate from, Western societies they currently reside in, and diasporic communities they are part of. Their decolonial, transformative works are discussed in the last chapter of the book.

I end this book with a coda in honor of Francis Abiola Irele. Through his extensive critical work on African literature and thought, Irele has chronicled the rise and the development of postcolonial agency in Africa and its diaspora. In these reflections, I argue that Irele's critical discourse is a construct of double entendre, the introvert and the extrovert, crystallized in his concept of the African Imagination. I briefly examine the development of this discourse from his engagement with early African diasporic writings, through the Negritude movement, to contemporary African literature while foregrounding his insightful critical legacy.

Notes

1 See, for example, recent protests against police violence in Ferguson, New York, Maryland, and Minneapolis, the solidarity marches that followed the murder of French cartoonist Charlie Hebdo in Paris and the "free our girls" protest that followed the kidnapping of more than 200 girls by the religious extremist movement "Boko Haram" in Nigeria.
2 See also Edward Said's notion of writing from a "strategic location" (1978), Gayatri Spivak's idea of "strategic essentialism" (1996), and Walter Mignolo's idea of "border thinking" (2012).

I
The enslaved African and postcolonial agency

1 Olaudah Equiano's *The Interesting Narrative of the Life of Olaudah Equiano, or Gustavus Vassa, the African, written by himself;* Haile Gerima's *Sankofa* (film); Amma Asante's *Belle* (film)

When Equiano's *Narrative* was first published in 1789, he had already bought his freedom from his last master, Robert King, back in 1766, and subsequently became a staunch activist against enslavement. Having personally experienced the inhumanity of enslavement and Western negative views of Africans, and having undergone cultural translation as he acquired literacy, learned the English language, and lived amongst the British people, Equiano put these experiences into writing in order to articulate the kinship of humanity that the Western world had been repressing because of its greed. That way, his *Narrative*, together with numerous protest letters he wrote against the enslavement of Africans from his hybrid positioning as Anglo-African, anticipated and should be regarded as a foundational part of the postcolonial discursive formation.

As rightly stated by Abiola Irele, "Equiano's *Narrative* looks forward to the existential themes of Camara Laye, Cheikh Hamidou Kane, and most of all, Chinua Achebe, who has recognized in Equiano a primary literary ancestor" (Irele 2001:49). Although autobiographical, Equiano's project is at the same time personal and collective, local (African) and global (humanity). It is a project that seeks to re-member a fragmented humanity, and as such, it can be said to be emancipatory and postcolonial. I would like to argue that the concept of "re-membering," which simultaneously signifies "reminiscing" and "reconnecting," is central to his vision of what the dehumanized and dehumanizing modern world should be. The act of reminiscing in this context means reinvesting Africa for the Western or Western-influenced mind with its original sense of humanity, while that of reconnecting implies a rebuilding of the black people's subjectivity and a sense of self-appreciation in a hostile modern world. As Irele has rightly put it, for "the Black intellectual in Africa and the African Diaspora, severed from a sense of immediate connection with the original community, an appeal to the background of African traditional life and history represents a form of spiritual homecoming, a *nostos*" (Irele 2001:71). Thus, reading Equiano's *The Interesting Narrative* (1995) against this background, I agree with Irele's view and further argue that both in his representation of Africa and

DOI: 10.4324/9780429322426-3

his redefinition of African subjectivity, Equiano can be said to be the pioneering initiator of what I have called "the postcolonial narrative corrective tradition" in black people's writings (Losambe and Eke: xii).

At the beginning of *The Interesting Narrative*, Equiano foregrounds the humanistic purpose of his creative project when he states that, rather than praise anybody or any society, his account seeks to promote "the interest of humanity" (Equiano 1995:32). His narrative is therefore "the history of neither a saint, a hero, nor a tyrant" (32), but that of human beings with a capacity to do good or evil. It is with this view that Equiano impartially reconstructs in his book three sites of memory: the African memory, the Western memory, and the middle-passage memory. The narrative itself is a complex construct blending together history, memory, and fiction, and it invites the reader to approach it simultaneously from these different disciplinary standpoints. When approached this way, the current debate about the historical or factual accuracy of Equiano's narrative (as expressed, e.g., by Carretta 2005) becomes less important, especially given the positive impact it had on the 18th-century anti-enslavement abolitionist movement.

The first part of Equiano's narrative presents an image of Africa that is crafted to refute the negative and dehumanizing representation of black Africans that dominated various Western discursive formations and iconography in the 18th century. James Houston, a physician for the Royal Africa Company on the West African coast, for example, echoed the European generalized stereotypical view of Africa when he wrote in 1725 that

> Their [Black Africans'] natural Temper is barbarously cruel, selfish and deceitful, and their Government equally barbarous and uncivil, and consequently the Men of greatest Eminence among them are those who are most capable of being the greatest Rogues.... As for their customs they exactly resemble their Fellow Creatures and Natives, the Monkeys.
> (qtd. in Pieterse 1992:40)

David Hume, who wrote during Equiano's time and later served in the British Colonial Office, also upheld the same negative image of Africans:

> I am apt to suspect the negroes, and in general all the other species of men (for there are four or five different kinds) to be naturally inferior to the whites. There never was a civilized nation of any other complexion than white, nor even any individual eminent in action or speculation. No ingenious manufactures among them, no arts, no sciences.
> (Hume 1997:33)

Countering this negative representation of Africa, on which colonial and imperialist logic has depended, from an African native's "strategic location" (Said 1978:20), Equiano restores the humanity of the African people in his narrative by showing that their lives were regulated by rational social, political, cultural, and economic systems. He particularly describes with the detail of a travel guide the Ibo culture in which he was raised up until his capture, relating aspects of their art, technology, economy, governance, and belief system from a perspective that treats the Ibo people as thinking subjects. Writing from his hybrid space (as a Westernized literate Christian and an African), Equiano avoids idealizing the Ibo culture and breaks down the colonial, binary separation of Africa and the West. He emphasizes a common kinship amongst human beings by comparing and pointing out many similarities between African customs and those of the Jews. Equiano argues that like the government of the Israelites at the time they reached the Promised Land, chiefs and elders, who doubled as judges, administered the semi-autonomous provinces which made up the kingdom of Benin. They settled disputes and punished crime using the law of retaliation like the Jews. The head of the family in Equiano's African society enjoyed a type of authority over the household akin to that ascribed to Abraham and other patriarchs. Like the Jews, Africans named their children after significant events or circumstances, practiced circumcision, and made sacrifices and burnt offerings to their gods and ancestors. The similarities between the practices of Africans and the Jews lead Equiano to conclude in his narrative that one could say: "one people had sprung from the other" (44).

Furthermore, by stating that the Ibos "never polluted the name of the object of our adoration; on the contrary, it was always mentioned with the greatest reverence; and we were totally unacquainted with swearing" (34), that "[b]efore we taste food, we always wash our hands: indeed our cleanliness on all occasions is extreme" (34), and that "we are almost a nation of dancers, musicians, and poets" (34), Equiano subverts the argument of savagery that European enslavers and colonizers advanced to justify their imperialist, colonial drive, and sense of superiority over Africans. Equiano also reinvests his African society with dignity when he describes in detail their garment technology and dressing manners, their marriage ceremonies, their housing, their iron work, and their commercial activities. This deployment of cultural comparison as an assertive self-affirmation strategy is later used by Chinua Achebe in *Things Fall Apart* in the dialogue between an Ibo elder Akunna and the Christian missionary Mr. Brown. In order to counteract the latter's colonial, assimilationist drive and negative attitude to the beliefs of the Ibo people, Akunna educates him this way: "You say that there is one supreme God who made heaven and earth [...] We also believe in Him and call Him Chukwu. He made all the world and the other gods" (Achebe 1958:126).

However, in spite of his largely positive representation of Africans in his narrative, Equiano refrains from idealizing their society. Like the European invaders, some local chiefs and their followers were often overcome by greed, captured innocent people from neighboring ethnic groups, and sold them to slave traders. Equiano, who was also captured by such cruel and corrupted Africans, and who was at one point during his enslavement in

Africa hunted like a deer (50), calls them "those sable destroyers of human rights" (51). It is his realization of the universal nature of evil manifested in this case by human beings' avarice that enables Equiano to maintain that:

> I will not suppose that the dealers in slaves are born worse than other men—No! it is the fatality of this mistaken avarice, that it corrupts the milk of human kindness, and turns it into gall. And, had the pursuits of those men been different, they might have been as generous, as tender-hearted, and just, as they are unfeeling, rapacious, and cruel.
>
> (111)

In the course of his story, Equiano deploys the trope of the child figure to denounce slavery and emphasize the common kinship of human beings. Comparing the natural treatment he received at the hands of an African child and an English child while a captive in Africa and England, respectively, Equiano notes:

> My master lodged at the house of a gentleman in Falmouth, who had a fine little daughter about six or seven years of age, and she grew prodigiously fond of me; in so much that we used to eat together, and had servants to wait on us. I was so much caressed by this family that it often reminded me of the treatment I had received from my little noble African master.
>
> (68)

Equiano also contrasts the innocent, humane world of children with the racially prejudiced, corrupted world of adults when describing his friendship with Richard Baker, the fifteen-year-old boy from America he met on board a slave ship. Baker was the first person to introduce Equiano to literacy and, by so doing, became his first postcolonial ally. Grieving over the death of Baker, Equiano laments in his narrative:

> I lost at once a kind interpreter, an agreeable companion, and a faithful friend; who at the age of fifteen, discovered a mind superior to prejudice; and who was not ashamed to notice, to associate with, and to be the friend and instructor of one who was ignorant, a stranger, of a different complexion, and a slave!
>
> (65)

Though Equiano notes the differences in their social situations, himself a slave while Baker owns slaves, he also presents their common trials, fears, and mutually comforting bodily touches on a slave ship as a humanizing, equalizing force. Through their bond, Equiano is introduced to two of the most distinctive strategies of postcoloniality and cultural hybridity: physical contact and literacy. Though the relationship between Equiano and Baker is not erotic, Equiano does note that their friendship is solidified as both go through "many sufferings together on shipboard" and spend "many nights lain in each other's bosoms when we were in great distress" (65).

This trope of childhood innocence as a moral center and the cross-color line bodily bonding as a symbol of a shared kinship of humanity are later used by Harlem Renaissance writers like Countee Cullen and Langston Hughes. For example, in his poem "Tableau" Cullen subverts American society's racial ordering by presenting a black boy and a white boy defiantly walking hand in hand against their society's normativity, as Equiano and Baker do in *The Narrative*. Here is how Cullen presents the boys in the poem that I quote in full:

> Locked arm in arm they cross the way,
> The black boy and the white,
> The golden splendor of the day,
> The Sable pride of night.
> From lowered blinds the dark folk stare,
> And here the fair folk talk,
> Indignant that these two should dare
> In unison to walk.
> Oblivious to look and word
> They pass, and see no wonder
> That lightning brilliant as a sword
> Should blaze the path of thunder. (Cullen 2004:1341)

As in his depiction of Africa, Equiano impartially describes England as another pole of humanity with its own cultural peculiarities (see Gikandi 2011b:90). In spite of the inhumane sufferings that he and other enslaved Africans experience during the middle passage, Equiano keeps an open mind and is ready to appreciate with a cool head his new environment and its possibilities. So, when he first lands in Falmouth in the spring of 1757, he says: "I was very much struck with the buildings and the pavement of the streets in Falmouth; and, indeed, any object I saw filled me with new surprise" (67). Soon, his observation moves from the attractive external beauty of England (its architecture) to the English peoples' life-world, which he constantly compares to the African one:

> [I]n seeing these white people did not sell one another, as we did, I was much pleased; and in this I thought they were much happier than we Africans. I was astonished at the wisdom of the white people in all things I saw; but was amazed at their not sacrificing, or making any offerings, and eating with unwashed hands, and touching the dead.
> (68)

This is the world of benevolent people such as the Guerin sisters and Mary's mother, who further teach him reading, writing, the English language, and

Christian religion, all of which he later on turns into instruments of liberation for himself and other slaves. As represented in the text, white liberals like Daniel Queen, Mr. Guerin and his sisters, Dr. Irving, and a number of Equiano's shipmates (those who promise and unsuccessfully try to rescue him from further enslavement after he has been betrayed by his trusted master Captain Pascal) constitute a subversive postcolonial constellation within the imperial order (see also Byrne 2014:223). Although not revolutionary (and somewhat tainted by the generalized, unbridled consumption of sugar, tea, and tobacco—products of slaves' forced labor—in 18th-century Britain),[1] the humane dispositions they show in their treatment of the enslaved Equiano contrast with the cruel attitudes of the dehumanized pro-slavery agents who have turned the Atlantic Ocean and its islands into a jungle of brutality and a graveyard for humankind. It is because of the kindred spirit he finds amongst these liberal-minded English that Equiano calls them his "new countrymen," aspires to be integrated into their society and allows himself to be baptized into Christianity: "I could now speak English tolerably well, and I perfectly understood everything that was said. I now not only felt myself quite easy with these new countrymen, but relished their society and manners. I no longer looked upon them as spirits [....]" (77–78).

However, in spite of the overwhelming attraction that the values of the new society have for him, Equiano acknowledges that they have never been able to erase those of his African society, which, according to him, "have been implanted in me with great care, and which time could not erase, and which all the adversity and variety of fortune I have since experienced served only to rivet and record" (46). Within this context, Equiano's deployment of "the trope of the talking book" (Gates 1988:152) as a site of cultural translation between African orality and Western literacy, his incorporation of the thoughts of English poets such as Milton and Sir Thomas Denham into the structure of his narrative discourse and his view of the Bible as a book that has also codified African customs and practices (as they share them with the Jews) affirm his new hybrid identity as Anglo-African. Despite Equiano's deliberate effort to learn English, his ambition to succeed in Western professions, and frequent reference to his gratitude toward his white fellows, he does not entirely surrender his African roots, as demonstrated, in part, by the fondness with which he recollects his homeland's cultural practices. Contrary to certain contemporary criticism, which argues that Equiano has been wholly absorbed into the hierarchy of colonial authority, I agree with Robin Sabino and Jennifer Hall's point that his strong denouncement of European slavery represents his subjective drive to affirm the enslaved Africans' humanity and his identification with Africa (1999:8).

Equiano's hybrid, Anglo-African identity validates Africa and England as representing two poles of humanity from which the world of the middle passage is disconnected and to which it has to be reconnected simultaneously for its redemption. The middle passage memory brings into focus all that is evil in human beings. The world of the sea and its islands are polluted by human beings' anarchic desires, and Equiano notes this at his first encounter with merciless, dehumanized white slave traders and their African victims on the first ship that is to take him to the Western world:

> the white people looked and acted, as I thought, in so savage a manner; for I had never seen among any people such instances of brutal cruelty; and this is not only shewn towards us blacks, but also to some of the whites themselves.
>
> (57)

Not believing that these brutal and debauched whites could have come from a country or a human community, Equiano mythologizes and casts them out of the world of human beings. As he states in his narrative, "I was now persuaded that I had gotten into a world of bad spirits and that they were going to kill me" (55). However, in spite of the many tortuous episodes Equiano goes through at sea on different ships and in West Indian islands, it is here that he develops his agency with the assistance of liberal-minded people like Daniel Queen, who teaches him "to shave and dress hair a little, and also to read in the Bible, explaining many passages to me, which I did not comprehend" (92); Captain Thomas Farmer, who teaches him navigation; and Robert King, who provides him with opportunities to nurture his agency as a builder of a harmonious humanity and to finally buy his freedom from slavery. Equiano articulates what a new humanity should be when he takes over the command of a ship from an ailing white captain (Captain Thomas), rescues whites and blacks from a shipwreck in the Bahama Islands, invokes Christ's gospel of love in his interactions with other races and cultures (like the Musquito Indians, the Turks and Spaniards), and marries Miss Cullen, a British woman.

Even after his manumission and freedom from enslavement, Equiano still feels the collective oppression of his African "countrymen" and calls himself "The oppressed Ethiopian" in a petition to the Queen (232). As he launches a crusade against slavery from his hybrid positioning as a literate Anglo-African Christian, Equiano says: "I hope to have the satisfaction of seeing the renovation of liberty and justice, resting on the British government, to vindicate the honour of our common nature" (232). While denouncing the dehumanizing enslavement of Africans, Equiano also makes a case for Africa's full entry into modernity with its human and natural resources. And far from encouraging European colonization of Africa, another form of enslavement that takes place in the 19th century, after his time, Equiano anticipates the industrialization of Africa to be beneficial to Africans, the British, and the whole humanity. Here is how he envisions what Africa's contribution to modernity should be:

> Population, the bowels and surface of Africa, abound in valuable and useful returns; the hidden treasures of centuries will be brought to light and into circulation. Industry, enterprize, and mining, will have their full scope, proportionably as they civilize [modernize]. In a word, it

lays open an endless field of commerce to the British manufacturers and merchant adventurers. The manufacturing interest and the general interests are synonymous. The abolition of slavery would be in reality an universal good.

(234)

Here, Equiano envisages the rise of African agency to be central in the industrial development of the continent, and his ideas are clearly articulated and given a sound expression at the beginning of the colonial period in Africa by Black Christian missionaries and thinkers like Edward Wilmot Blyden and Samuel Lewis. In his introduction to the second edition of Blyden's landmark book entitled *Christianity, Islam and the Negro Race* (1888), Samuel Lewis emphasizes the need to recognize the centrality of the African subject's role in Africa's encounter with Western modernity:

> Foreign influence may—indeed it must—for sometime to come do much for Africa, but not least, by recognising the fundamental fact that when all has been said and done by Europeans and Americans that they can either say or do, **the African himself is, and must always remain, the fittest instrument for the development of his country.** He it is who can best be trained to utilise the vast resources of Africa, not only for her own good, but for the benefit of the human race.
>
> (xii–xiii, emphasis added)

With this view in mind, Blyden proceeds by a careful observation and analysis of Africans' cultural translation of Christianity, Islam, and African beliefs and develops a social vision of Christianity crystalized in his concept of a syncretic "African personality." His syncretism will later influence the rise of anti-colonial, "messianic" spiritual movements like Kimbanguism in the Congo in the 20th century. As Irele remarks, Blyden

> came to posit an 'African personality' with an objective correlative (to use T.S. Eliot's term) in the configuration of social arrangements and communal values that, as he maintained, gave coherence to African life and established its validity on its own terms.
>
> (Irele 2001:51)

This "African life" and "its validity on its own terms" will later be the subject of African imaginaries and thoughts in the various black literary and intellectual movements.

Sankofa

The 1993 film *Sankofa*, directed by Ethiopian-born filmmaker Haile Gerima, is a part of the narrative progression within imaginative literature on the topic of Africans' enslavement and their entry into modernity. The film is to a certain extent a contemporary re-articulation of Equiano's narrative. Like Equiano, Gerima re-examines the conjunction of African cultural memory with Western modernity in the formation of the African diasporic modern subject. Gerima's articulation shies away from nativistic cultural essentialism and the Western colonial notion of cultural assimilation and emphasizes how hybrid African and African diasporic identities have become. Both authors, to use Henry Giroux's words, articulate the postcolonial

> notion of border identity that challenges any essentialized notion of subjectivity while simultaneously demonstrating that the self as a historical and cultural formation is shaped in complex, related, and multiple ways through their interaction with numerous and diverse communities.
> (Giroux 1993:10)

Like Equiano's narrative, the film *Sankofa* extensively portrays the brutal conditions of chattel slavery. The comparison between a fictional film and the primary source testimony of a living person about his own life can be fraught at times, but, nonetheless, Gerima and Equiano both share across centuries the desire to debunk European negative constructions of blackness and Africanness. The rise of Enlightenment thinking and the empirical tradition in the Western sciences served to systematize racist ideas veiled as an authoritative, objective framework of scientific discovery. For example, the Swedish botanist Carl Linnaeus' contributions to biological classification of species are tainted by his fallacious and harmful views regarding race. In the revised edition of his *Systema Naturae* (1758), he othered Africans as a separate species from Europeans and assigned them a variety of unfavorable characteristics which then served to justify black people's oppression in the eyes of Western multitudes who respected him as an authority on biological matters. Here is how Linnaeus negatively characterized "Homo Africanus" in contrast to the Europeans: "black, phlegmatic, lax; black curly hair; silky skin, apelike nose, swollen lips; the bosoms of the women are distended; their breasts give milk copiously; crafty, slothful, careless, he smears himself with fat. He is ruled by authority" (qtd. in Pieterse 1992:40). The fact that well-respected institutions at the forefront of European academia in the 18th, 19th, and early 20th centuries ubiquitously maintained these racist theses (see Eze 1997) proved their complicitous subvention of Western imperialism and colonialism in other parts of the world.

The African site of the film *Sankofa*'s action is an old slave castle overlooking the Atlantic Ocean in Cape Coast in present-day Ghana. It stands as a reminder of Africa's brutal, tragic encounter with Western modernity. From an Afrocentric perspective, this castle (like Elmina and other castles along the Atlantic coast in Ghana) is a sacred, historical site that Sankofa, the Devine Drummer (played by Kofi Ghanaba), determinedly seeks to protect against those (in contemporary Ghana and the Western world) who have pathetically turned it into an exotic commodity for tourism and photo-shoots. As the film starts, viewers are welcomed by the solemn, melancholic sounds of Sankofa's drum and a reverent voice invoking the spirits of the dead enslaved Africans who were humiliated, treated with contempt, and dehumanized by the whites in Surinam, Brazil, Jamaica, Mississippi, Louisiana, Florida, and Alabama. Ritualistically smearing his body with white clay, Sankofa goes daily to the gate of the final exit at the castle to communicate with "the lingering spirits" of the dead Africans in the black diasporas, exhorting them to "rise up and claim their bird of passage" (Gerima 1993). Unlike the official tour guide at the castle who calls him a "self-appointed guardian of the castle" and the armed Ghanaian security men who treat him as a hindrance to the material gain that results from the commodification of the site, Sankofa regards himself as a dutiful griot whose mission is to keep and transmit the memory of Africans' brutal encounter with Western modernity to younger generations to come so that they can know who they are. The meaning of the Akan word "Sankofa," which is also the name of the Devine Drummer and the title of Gerima's film, projects the lesson that both the traditionalist and the filmmaker want to teach disconnected contemporary diasporic individuals like Mona, "to go back, look for, and gain wisdom, power and hope" (Cooper 2014:1). Sankofa's invocation of the spirits of the dead has echoes of Senghor's reverent prayer to ancestors in his poem "Prayer to the Masks" (Senghor 1985:134). In both cases, the ancestors are called upon to protect and guide their children as they negotiate a subjective identity in the intersection of Western modernity and African cultural memory.

As discussed above, Equiano's narrative recounts his capture in Africa, his enslavement at the hands of cruel white men, the development of his agency as a hybrid Anglo-African subject, his fight against enslavement of Africans, and his sustained interest in the economic development of Africa. *Sankofa*'s opening scene, however, reverses the trajectory of Equiano's journey and focuses the viewer's gaze on Mona (played by Oyafunmike Ogunlano), the self-loathing, contemporary African American model, who has acquiesced to Western prejudices about blackness and disconnected herself from Africa. She misguidedly accepts to use one of Africa's old slave castles for a photoshoot and is seen completely controlled by a white photographer who objectifies and treats her like an excessive sexual commodity (as he commands her, "give me more sex"). This reminds viewers of how enslaved African women were treated by white men at the same castle and on the ships that took them across the ocean centuries ago (see Byrne 2014:36–48). In his patronizing and colonizing interaction with Mona, who sports a swimsuit and a blonde wig, the photographer interposes himself between her and the Devine Drummer, and through this positioning, Gerima effectively depicts the exclusive, territorializing structure of Western modernity. However, undaunted by the photographer's callous prohibition to Mona, Sankofa insistently urges her to reconnect with her African memory and reconstitute

Narrative of the life of Olaudah Equiano 21

herself as a postcolonial, diasporic subject: "Sankofa! Sankofa! Go! Go!" (Gerima). Sylvie Kandé and Joe Karaganis summarize Gerima's therapeutic project as depicted in his film this way:

> What Gerima proposes to that segment of the black liberal bourgeoisie indifferent or recalcitrant to Africa—a group symbolized by Mona in the film—is in substance a three-step plan: first, a return to the period of slavery, then to the deeper past and a more profound encounter with Africa, and finally a resurfacing in the present and a joining into a black community proudly conscious of its African origins. The therapy he envisions for all the Monas of the world [...] is a kind of re-education through work on the plantation-- a tropical gulag, so to speak.
> (Kandé and Karaganis 1999:132)

In addition to his call to Mona, the Devine Drummer also reminds white tourists who are leisurely and playfully shuffling around in the old castle to know that it is a sacred place that calls for a cool-headed reflection on a tragic episode of human history. He educates them that if they have to visit the place, they should remember that "blood has been spilled here!" (Gerima). Here, Gerima brings into the film the emotional debate that opposed the Ghanaian government of J. J. Rawlings, on the one hand, and an African American pressure group, on the other, about the uses of Elmina Castle in the 1990s. As reported by the *Washington Post* edition of April 17, 1995:

> African-Americans accuse Ghanaians of trampling on their past for profits. They say Ghanaians are handcuffed because 'white' institutions such as the U.S. Agency for International Development and the Smithsonian Institution have pledged major financial backing and technical aid for the 5.6 million [dollar] project. Ghanaians charge Black Americans with being overly sensitive and contend they should bear more of the financial burden for the project if they do not like the current donors.
> (qtd. in Kandé and Karaganis 1999:141)

As a griot, the Devine Drummer is articulating a nativist vision for the African diaspora, and his call agrees with the sentiments of the African American pressure group mentioned above. He believes that a reconnection with Africa and its history will benefit those like Mona who have been separated from their roots. At first, Mona reacts with fear at the sight of the Devine Drummer and his call for a profound meditation on history. However, as she detaches herself for a moment from the photographer's control, changes into a casual costume (long pants, a shirt, and a hat) as an American tourist, and enters the dungeons where slaves were held for months before being shipped to the New World, Mona unwittingly undertakes an introspective, self-discovery journey. In a trance-like moment, Mona comes face to face with an epiphanic scene of chained enslaved African women and men and becomes one of them under the gaze of white slavers. She screams "I'm not African [...] I'm an American," but from the white slavers' collective gaze, the only thing that defines her is the objectified black body. She is thus grabbed, stripped of her clothing, and burned with a hot iron like other African slaves. This is the lesson that Gerima teaches those that Langston Hughes calls "self-styled 'high-class' Negroes" in his essay entitled "The Negro Artist and the Racial Mountain" (Hughes 2004:1311). Mona's self-loathing detachment from African and African American folk memories stands in contrast to Hughes' articulation of the mission of the Harlem Renaissance cultural movement (1919–1930) that sought to assert black or African American agency within modernity. Gerima's cultural vision in *Sankofa* certainly reiterates Hughes' concern in this quotation:

> We younger Negro artists who create now intend to express our individual dark-skinned selves without fear or shame. If white people are pleased we are glad. If they are not, it doesn't matter. We know we are beautiful. And ugly too. The tom-tom cries and the tom-tom laughs. If colored people are pleased we are glad. If they not, their displeasure doesn't matter either. We build our temples for tomorrow, strong as we know how, and we stand on top of the mountain, free within ourselves.
> (1314)

The epiphanic scene of chained Africans in dungeons frightens Mona, but at the same time, it invites her to reassess her current positioning as a modern black subject in the world. In this reassessment, Mona revisits the beginning of Africans' entry into modernity through enslavement. Here, Gerima creates a frame story in which Mona becomes a slave woman named Shola, the agent narrator of life stories of the enslaved Africans on a Southern American or a Caribbean sugar plantation. As viewers follow the enslaved Africans' tortuous journey into the New World through the questing consciousness of Mona who has become Shola, Gerima sharply focuses their attention on the cultural translation that these Africans experienced as they negotiated a postcolonial diasporic identity in the intersection of Western modernity and African memory.

As the enslaved Africans are being taken to Lafayette plantation in the New World, the iconic Sankofa bird, a symbol of the Akan people's cultural resilience and authority (Kandé and Karaganis 1999:129) circles over them. And just as the Devine Drummer holds a staff crowned with the Sankofa bird signifying his authority as a griot at the castle, so are the maroon Shango (played by Mutabaruka) and Nunu (played by Alexandra Duah), respectively, associated with the Sankofa bird and the Ashanti people's iconic figure of porcupine. As Rhea Kumar (2017) has pointed out, "The porcupine is considered a symbol of the Ashanti people's strong defense mechanisms and prowess in war. But in today's peaceful times, it is perhaps best interpreted as a symbol of resilience and survival" (1). Both Shango and Nunu are therefore the carriers of the African memory that they try to inculcate in the minds of those born into enslavement on the Lafayette plantation like Shola and Nunu's son Joe (played by Nick Medley).

Being a synecdoche of every plantation in the New World, Lafayette plantation is depicted in the film as a space of torture, hard labor, rape, and death for the enslaved. It is a space that controls the body and the mind/soul of the enslaved through enforced spirituality (Christianity) and forced labor. Unlike Equiano whose exploration and acceptance of Christianity (under the influence of the Quakers) follows a personal and deliberate process, Shola and Joe do not have a choice under the Catholic religion regimen enforced by the intransigent Father Raphael (Reginald Carter). For Father Raphael, African beliefs, as invoked by Nunu and Shango, are devilish. Although Joe's own mother, Father Raphael calls Nunu a demon-possessed "Guinea woman" (Gerima) and works hard to separate him from her and other slaves who are still connected to the African memory. On the plantation, Christianity and enslavement function as two sides of the same coin. Both institutions of Western modernity conjoin as their agents violently dehumanize the enslaved. Gerima foregrounds the complicity of the Catholic Church in the enslavement and colonization of Africans in the graphic, memorable scene in which Shola is jointly tortured by Master James, the owner of Lafayette plantation, and Father Raphael for associating herself with Nunu, Shango, and other rebellious slaves they call "heathens." Shola is seen stripped naked with her hands tied up with a rope as Master James cuts her hair and father Raphael presses a cross on her chest while forcibly asking her to state: "I belong to God...I'm his slave" (Gerima). But as soon as the two leave Shola alone, emotionally and physically shattered in a slave house, Shango comes in to nurse her back to health. Shango soothes Shola's body with natural leaves that look like rhizomes and reconnects her with African memory through his prayer, saying to her, "run...run" and telling her the story of the dear ones (his sister and his friend Jack) he has lost in the struggle against enslavement and his determination to fight against it. Shango then culturally and spiritually empowers Shola by placing on her neck the hand-carved necklace of Sankofa bird, a symbol of the resilience of African memory, that his father passed on to him. From that time, as Shola herself confesses, she becomes a "rebel" against enslavement.

Led by Nunu and Shango, the enslaved move to the hills and cave which they transform into a site of freedom and cultural resistance. In this space, Nunu assumes the function of the traditional African griot. She speaks Akan, tells African folk stories about the importance of community and the environment (medicinal plants), braids women's hair as styled in Africa, and invokes the spirits of her ancestors as she initiates the enslaved into resistance. Under Nunu and Shango's rebellious, subjective direction, the enslaved plant "new seeds" (Gerima) and nurture a new diasporic memory. They worship their "own god," not the one prescribed to them by white slavers. In this interstitial space, the past and the present merge, and a free, hybrid diasporic identity takes root. As Simon Gikandi remarks:

> [W]hat was striking about spatial configurations in slave communities, especially in the Caribbean and the antebellum South, was the slaves' determination and capacity to create real and imaginary spaces of placement, to presuppose 'a space-analogue within which one finds one's way.
>
> (Gikandi 2011:239)

It is from such "Low ground and Inaudible Valleys" (Baker 1988:88) that African diasporic folk expressive culture—the spirituals, the blues, and the vernacular—and the "Black Church" emerged during the enslavement. Examining the origins and the modern positioning of the Black Church as a spiritual locus of subjectification for Black Americans, Larry Neal states:

> The Black Church ... represents and embodies the transplanted African memory. The Black Church is the Keeper ... [of the memory of the Motherland], the spiritual bank of our most forgotten visions of the Homeland. The Black Church was the institutionalized form that Black people used to protect themselves from the spiritual and psychological brutality of the slave master.
>
> (Neal 1972:152, see also Baker 1988:157)

Although Shola is initially torn between Father Raphael's and Nunu's binarily territorizing influences on her, she slowly heeds Shango's advice and is seen more and more drawn to the liminal, diasporic memory that the enslaved are shaping in the hills and cave. For her, Shango is not only a caring lover but also a healer. As a creolized subject, Shango knows that he, Shola, and the other enslaved can never totally recover and live according to their ancestors' pre-enslavement African memory transmitted to them by Nunu. But as Shango cleanses Shola at the river with rhizomic leaves and walks down with her in the water, he is teaching her that they are the makers of a new memory in the interstice between Western modernity and African memory, in the hills and the cave. Empowered that way, Shola reconstitutes herself into a subject and rises against Master James' attempt to rape her again. She pushes him away and then attacks him with her machete. By so doing, Shola turns a tool of oppression (machete) for the enslaved into an instrument of their liberation. As she kills Master James, Shola also resists and repulses a colonizing "white masculinity" (Magee 2012:39), something that Mona fails to do with the photographer in the opening scene of the film.

Like Shola, Joe is also subjected to the Catholic Church exclusive doctrinal regimen by Father Raphael. Joe is Nunu's son who was conceived on a slave ship when Nunu was cruelly raped by a white man at the age of fourteen. Perhaps because of his racial positioning as a mulatto, Master James appoints him a head slave on Lafayette plantation, and Father Raphael calls him "my son." As a head slave, Joe regards himself as different, disciplines other slaves, and distances himself from his own mother, Nunu, and Shango, who represent an opposing view of self to that he learns through white power structures (the Catholic Church and Western modernity). Nunu calls Joe a "rotten fruit" because he "mistreats his people" and tries hard to pull him away from the assimilationist influence of Father Raphael. As a result, Joe is often seen being torn between Nunu (African memory) and Father Raphael (Christianity). For example, when Joe goes to father Raphael's confessional in order to denounce Nunu's persistent influence on him, Father Raphael tells him that "the devil is trying to get to you through your mother" and encourages him to "fight back." However, Joe remains an "undecidable" figure (Bauman 1991:58) as he also asks Father Raphael, "Father, whose son am I?" (Gerima). Father Raphael reassures him that he belongs to God (the Son Jesus Christ and Mary), but as he does so, the sound of an African lullaby from Nunu who is caressing Kuta's baby (that she helped deliver after her brutal murder at the hands of the enslavers and who has become a symbol of the new diasporic memory) invades the church and certainly, Joe's consciousness. Lucy's sexual attraction to Joe can also be seen as therapeutic as she says to him "we can make a beautiful brown baby," a symbol of resistance against enslavement and colonial assimilation symbolized by the Christian Madonna. Indeed, Lucy, Shola, and Shango act in the film as transformative, carnivalesque agents who are determined to lure Joe to join them in the making of the new memory. At the request of Lucy and Shola, Shango prepares a curative concoction out of natural leaves that Lucy gives to Joe. Shortly after consuming the concoction, Joe becomes erratic, throws up, and rushes to the river for cure. It is here that Nunu comes to rescue him. But as Nunu rips off the Christian Madonna necklace from Joe's neck while invoking her African ancestors and nursing him back to health, Joe gets angry, rejects her attempt to totally locate him within the originary African memory, and kills her. Confused by his action, Joe turns to Shola who has arrived at the scene for self-knowledge. Joe then learns for the first time the story of Nunu's rape by an unknown white man and his conception on a slave ship crossing from Africa. With that knowledge, Joe reaches self-discovery and acknowledges Nunu's humanity as well as the validity of African memory, calling her a "porcupine woman" and "a Saint." No longer considering Nunu a devil, Joe carries her lifeless body to Father Raphael's church, places it on the Christian alter, kneels down, and prays to a translation of both her African beliefs and Father Raphael's Christianity—the foundation of the diasporic Black Church. Like Equiano, Joe's return to Christianity at this point is an act of agency rather than a passive acceptance of an ordered modern identity being forced on him. And when Father Raphael refuses to accept his newly found postcolonial agency (telling Joe that by bringing Nunu's body to a Christian alter, he is equating himself with other "Niggers"), Joe kills him as well. By killing Nunu and

Father Raphael, Joe refuses to be singularly defined by either of the memories they represent. Instead, he translates both memories into a hybrid, postcolonial diasporic memory articulated by Shango and others in the hills and cave. As he kills Father Raphael, Joe's new consciousness is punctuated in the film with a Southern gospel tune playing in the background rather than that of a traditional church organ. In terms of naming and identity, Joe dies bearing two names, Joseph (Joe) given to him by Father Raphael and Tumey, an Akan name, given to him by his mother Nunu.

The master's death, much like the deaths of Nunu and Father Raphael, occurs on grounds of rebirth and regeneration within the space of new identity. When Shola then returns to the present, she does not return as the Mona she once was; instead, she exits through the door of the dungeon of the slave castle, like a baby being born into the world, crying and shocked. She ignores the white photographer who asks her where she has been and instead joins a cast of African diasporic people as well as the drummer Sankofa, facing not to the interior of Africa, but outward to the Atlantic Ocean. Inspired by the Devine Drummer's call, these people sit facing the Americas as postcolonial diasporic subjects, conscious of their self-defined views of blackness. This group encapsulates African diaspora in its diversity: Afro-Brazilians, African Americans, Afro-Caribbeans, and Afro-Europeans clothed differently, hair styled uniquely, and bearing different hues to their black skin. As Assata Wright states in his review of the film, "Clearly, Gerima intends for *Sankofa* to expand the boundaries of Black representation in ways that include more diverse, realistic, and empowering images and, in turn, enable Black audiences to see themselves in new ways that are divorced from dominant images" (1994:26).

Belle

Like Equiano's narrative and Gerima's film *Sankofa*, the film *Belle* (2013), directed by British-born filmmaker Amma Asante, depicts the complicated, marginalized positioning of the modern Black subject in the Western world in the 18th century. Mona, previously ignorant of her African ancestry, recognizes and embraces it in the end, which allows her to connect with others who also choose to recognize and respect the past. Mona gains a great deal of character depth through this, going from a two-dimensional model who cowers behind the symbol of oppression and colonization to a powerful woman of depth who belongs to a culture distinctly her own. This is the kind of woman that Dido Elizabeth Belle Lindsay exemplifies in Asante's film *Belle*.

Belle is based on the actual story of the encounter between Captain John Lindsay, a noble navy officer who commanded the British navy ship *Trent* in Africa and the West Indies, and an enslaved woman Maria Belle he probably met on a captured Spanish ship in 1761. Perhaps, in the same year, Maria Belle gave birth to a mulatto girl whom Captain John Lindsay named Dido Elizabeth Belle Lindsay, the subject of the film (Byrne 2014:22–27). Unlike the cases of Joe in *Sankofa*, the abolitionist Frederick Douglass (1994) and the persona in Langston Hughes' poem "Mulatto" (1995:263), who were cruelly rejected by their racist biological white fathers, Dido was warmly embraced by her father.

At the beginning of the film, viewers are introduced to the humane character of Captain Sir John Lindsay (played by Matthew Goode) as he emotionally approaches his anxious six-year-old daughter Dido and reassuringly tells her: "I am your father" and further adds: "Do not be afraid sweet thing. I am to take you to a good life. The life you were born to" (Asante). Not seeking to disconnect Dido from her mother's memory and affirming the latter's humanity (though a dead slave), Captain Sir John Lindsay includes "Belle" in the full name he gives her—Dido Elizabeth Belle Lindsay. That way, he positions himself as a rebel or an unorthodox to the societal rules of his time and refuses to separate Dido from her mother's heritage. Dido's beautiful physical features remind Captain Lindsay of her mother and the genuine love he has for both of them. His next task is to convince his aristocratic uncle Lord Mansfield and his wife Lady Mansfield to put aside their positioning within the structure of the rigid English societal rules about class and race and accept Dido as a full member of the Murray family. So, as Captain Sir John Lindsay has to return to his duties as a naval officer, he decides to entrust the care of his mulatto daughter to his uncle Lord Mansfield (Chief Justice of the King's Bench) and his wife Lady Mansfield for an aristocratic upbringing alongside her cousin Elizabeth Murray at their countryside estate Kenwood House. Unlike what he has hoped, however, Captain Sir John Lindsay is confronted at Kenwood House by the conservative attitude of his uncle and his wife who find it embarrassing to accept Dido because, in the words of Lady Mansfield, "she is black." Despite the Mansfields' anger and protest at what they see as his dishonorable action, Captain Sir John Lindsay emotionally and determinedly appeals to them: "I beg you, uncle... love her—as I would, were I here. And ensure that she is in receipt of all that is due to her as a child of mine" (Asante). They eventually accept her under certain conditions (such as not dining with the rest of the family when hosting visitors) and decide to call her Dido rather than, in the words of her Aunt Lady Murray, "have another Elizabeth in the household" (Asante).

Before Captain John Lindsay leaves Kenwood, he fondly addresses what would turn out to be his last reassuring and empowering words to Dido. These words not only unsettle the Mansfields but they also surprise the guardian of the estate Lady Murray:

> Little Belle—sweet child ... My wish is to keep you ... keep you with me ... but a ship ... it is no place for one so precious as you. In these walls, yours will be a life equal to my blood ... You will not understand in this moment, but hold this in your heart ... you are loved ... Just as I loved your mother.
>
> (Asante)

In response, Dido strongly bonds with and shows her affection to her father by wiping his tears as he tenderly embraces her for the last time. Though viewers can question whether Maria Belle, a submissive slave, could freely reciprocate Captain Lindsay's love to her before her death, what is certain is that Dido, who now represents her mother, loves her father. Dido's attachment to Captain John Lindsay comes vividly through in this scene described by the screenwriter Misan Sagay:

> A tear spills and Dido's little fingers come up to wipe it from his cheek. He presses his lips to her hand, sobbing a moment, and then he is gone— to stay any longer would be too much to bear.
>
> (Sagay and Asante)

From now on, Dido will critically judge Lord Mansfield's interactions with her through the lens of her father's humanity.

As depicted in the film, at Kenwood House, Dido (Gugu Mbatha-Raw) faces similar challenges to those of Mona. She finds herself in a culture that does not reflect the past she identifies with in terms of race, class, and gender. That leads her to ask her great-uncle Lord Mansfield this question: "How can I be too high in rank to dine with the servants, but too low to dine with my family?" (Asante). Dido's question touches on the pillars of the early modern British society (race and class), and through it, Asante invites viewers to imagine her as a potential disruptor of the established, consensual order of that society. In spite of the paradoxical situation Dido finds herself in, she remains remarkably strong in who she is and negotiates a new subjective identity against all odds put in her way. Dido learns more and more about herself and the societal rules of the 18th-century Britain as she searchingly interacts with her aristocratic great-uncle Lord Mansfield (Tom Wilkinson) and his wife Lady Mansfield, her authoritative aunt and the estate maid Lady Murray (Penelope Wilton), her cousin Elizabeth Murray (Sarah Gadon), the Black family's servant Mabel (Bethan Mary-James), her cousin Elizabeth's racist and misogynistic suitor James Ashford (Tom Felton), her racially ambivalent first suitor Oliver Ashford (James Norton), and Lord Mansfield's progressive legal apprentice (the son of a low-class vicar) John Davinier (Sam Reid) who later becomes her abolitionist companion and fiancé.

Following their reluctant acceptance of Dido, the Mansfields decide to educate her on the values of the aristocratic Murray family of which she has become a bloodline member (polite courtesies, dressing manners, and leisure habits like reading and piano playing). Lord Mansfield is seen walking Dido through the house gallery hall and proudly showing her family portraits on the wall including that of her father which she readily recognizes. But while pointing out different members of Dido's aristocratic family, Lord Mansfield is silent on the presence of the submissive, melancholic figures of black servants on the paintings, which Dido equally and attentively gazes at. Her focused gaze on these black figures, together with the subservient position of the black servant Mabel, no doubt reminds her of her mother's and her own subaltern positioning in Western modernity. Even her six-year-old cousin Elizabeth Murray echoes the racialized attitude of British society when Dido is introduced to her on her arrival at Kenwood House. Elizabeth initiates the first conversation with Dido by asking her: "Are you...a nee-gro?" And when Dido innocently ignores the question, she further insists: "Are you what they call 'a negro?' I heard them talking" (Asante). By adding the last sentence, Elizabeth affirms her childhood innocence, and through her uncertain utterance, Asante foregrounds the entrenched extent of the marginalization and dehumanization of Black others (free or enslaved) in the early modern British society.

Although marginalized because of her race, Dido's position in the Murray family and society is uplifted after Captain Sir John Murray's death. She is saddened by the death of the father she has been looking forward to knowing more, but she is happy to learn from Lord Mansfield that he left a handsome inheritance of £2000/year for her. She now realizes that she is richer than her cousin Elizabeth who did not inherit anything from her father when he passed away. Despite her fortune, however, the Mansfields presume that Dido would not be able to find a suitor within the aristocratic class because of her marginalized racial positioning. They therefore can only imagine her future in the family as a replacement for her aunt Lady Murray, the family maid, when she retires. The Mansfields' observance of the racialized and class order of the British society means that Dido has to be deprived of the privilege of meeting with other visiting aristocratic families at dinner. The most puzzling thing for Dido at Kenwood House is, therefore, the fact that the Mansfields insist that she find a suitor within the upper-class club, while not allowing her to meet them at dinner. The fact that her materially poor cousin Elizabeth is allowed to dine with guests (and she is not because of her skin color) is a pauser that leads her to ponder her status in that family and society. That pauser also calls upon her to think about a possible existentialist, corrective course of action she should take in the face of that incongruity. It is this incongruity that also makes Dido anxious about the expected outcome of the painting of her and Elizabeth that the Lord Mansfield has commissioned Zoffany (David Gant) to produce. Her presumption, which does not materialize in the end, is that the portrait that will emerge will show her as a subaltern Black subject to her white cousin Elizabeth.

At the age of twenty, Dido has sufficiently become familiar with the structure of attitudes (Said 1993) that regulates social relationships and public policy in the early British modern society around race, class, and gender. And instead of naively accepting the subaltern status that her family and society have ordained for her and the enslaved Black people, she transitions to activism and steadily develops a rebellious, subversive agency comparable to what viewers can see in Shola and Joe toward the end of the film *Sankofa*.

When the Mansfields ask her to remain behind at Kenwood House while the family travels to London for the "London Season" that would provide Elizabeth Murray with an opportunity to meet "gentlemen," Dido angrily rejects their offer. For Lady Mansfield, "A gentleman of good breeding is unlikely to form any serious attachment to Dido, and a man without, will lower her position in society" (Asante). But Dido boldly tells Lord Mansfield that she will not be the house maid like Lady Murray: "No! I am not Lady Murray. I am not an unwanted maid" (Asante). She is supported by Elizabeth who refuses to go to London without her. Under that pressure, both girls are eventually taken to London, and there, they meet other aristocratic families at garden parties, including the bigoted Ashfords. The Ashfords had already been introduced to the girls at Kenwood House where Oliver started to show a romantic interest in Dido, despite his mother's warning: "You will refrain from any intercourse with the negress" (Asante). On that occasion, Oliver Ashford's brother James also expressed his racist disdain for Dido: "I find her repulsive...One does not make a wife of the rare and exotic, Oliver. One samples it on the cotton fields of the Indies" (Asante).

At the London garden parties, Dido faces racism as she discovers that despite her wealth, she can only be tolerably solicited for marriage because of her racial background. Oliver Ashford, who is not in line for a family inheritance, is interested in a relationship with Dido solely because of her wealth and "rare and exotic" look rather than genuine love. Inviting Dido for a romantic stroll, Oliver, who has just been chastised by his Brother James for flirting with Dido, tells her: "I am utterly taken with you, Miss Lindsay." But when the skeptical Dido reminds him of his brother's "pronounced protestations," Oliver ironically confirms his conformity to British society's negative construction of the image of the black people and can be said to agree with his brother on that point in his response: "He (James) cannot overlook your mother's origins, as I do. Foolish. Why should anyone even pay her regard when your better half has equipped you so well with loveliness and privilege" (Asante). Although shocked by Oliver's response, Dido does not rebuff his flirtatious bodily contact immediately and even accepts him as a suitor in defiance of Lord Mansfield's objection. Dido's action here is more a gesture of rebellion against her great-uncle's lower expectations for her because of his observance of British society's social strictures rather than a genuine love for the person who does not wholly accept her. In fact, at that moment, Dido's heart is somewhere else, especially after being physically assaulted by the unmannered, misogynist James Ashford, who also regards women as "men's property." In the end, Dido rejects Oliver's offer of marriage, boldly telling his condescendingly class-conscious mother Lady Ashford:

> My greatest misfortune would be to marry into a family who would carry me as their shame, as I have been required to carry my own mother—her apparent crime to be born negro, and mine to be the evidence. Since I wish to deny her no more than I wish to deny myself,

you will pardon me for wanting a husband who feels forgiveness of my bloodline is both unnecessary and without grace.

(Asante)

Dido is undoubtedly a member of the upper-class British society, and she is also proud of her African heritage, refusing to shirk away from it in order to please others. She does not want a man who loves her despite her being black—she wants to marry a man for whom her blackness is not something to get over, but rather to love as an integral part of her identity. She embraces her blackness and the history of her mother while also observing good mannerisms of British society.

Since her first encounter with John Davinier, son of the vicar Reverend Davinier, Dido seems to be surprised and attracted by his unconventional simple manners. Unlike the conformist, bigoted Ashfords, John Davinier and his father display a sense of humanity that reminds us of the Quakers in Equiano's narrative. In order to facilitate his son's entry into the British legal establishment, Reverend Davinier recommends John to Lord Mansfield's tutorage. Lord Mansfield interviews John in the presence of Dido and quickly realizes that he is in front of a brilliant and assertive young man, especially when he answers his question about "the purpose of the law." According to John, the purpose of the law is "to provide certainty where there might otherwise be none." And when Lord Mansfield asks him to give an example, John refers to the controversial case under his consideration: "The Zong ship and those drowned" (Asante). Lord Mansfield is embarrassed by John's response because of the presence of Dido, but John boldly states further as Dido attentively stares at him: "I am no member of the nobility—I have a little, but...where my father relies on the bible, I...I wish to rely on the law courts." And when the uncomfortable and now skeptical Lord Mansfield further asks John whether he is aspiring to the judiciary, again John assertively responds: "One day ...yes...m'lord. I wish to make the laws not only administer them—for that...that is how **I may truly change this world. I mean to say, make it...a better place**" (Asante, emphasis added).

At the end of the interview, Lord Mansfield appears morally subdued and disarmed by John Davinier's assertively articulated sense of social justice, on the one hand, and Dido's uncanny presence, on the other. And moving from certainty and rigidity to undecidability as he deliberates on the pending Zong case evoked by John Davinier, Lord Mansfield turns to Dido for advice on whether he should appoint the latter as his legal apprentice. At this point, Dido, who sees in John Davinier a potential ally and companion for a possible struggle for social justice in British society, readily supports his appointment. As soon as John Davinier settles down in his position as the first ever legal pupil to Lord Mansfield, Dido cannot wait to know more from him about the Zong ship and why is the case before his great-uncle's supreme court. Reluctantly, John tells Dido the story of how the crew of the Zong drowned 132 slaves during the crossing from Africa to the West Indies:

> The slaves were intentionally drowned, that is not the question. Chained! Thrown into the waters – chained together as one. They were diseased – worth more as dead insured merchandise, than as alive spoiled goods. The captain hoped it would pay to kill them.
>
> (Asante)

Dido's question is "Why?" and that question leads her to sift through piles of documents in Lord Mansfield's library in search of possible clues. Here, she finds a map detailing the ship's itinerary with at least eight stopover ports where the ship could replenish their food and water supplies but the captain heartlessly chose instead to massacre the slaves. Dido shares this information with John Davinier, and the latter uses it as part of his arsenal of evidence to convince Lord Mansfield who is under pressure from the traders and his aristocratic friends, like Lord Ashford and his wife Lady Ashford, to rule in their favor. For Lady Ashford, abolitionists' protest against the killing of the slaves is just "a lot of fuss over dead cargo"; but for Dido and John Davinier, it is a noble fight for humanity.

As Dido teams up with Davinier and increasingly puts moral pressure on Lord Mansfield to give a ruling that would lead to the abolition of slavery, she also enlists the support of the black house servant Mabel who has become a motherly figure for her, the Mansfield driver Harry who secretly takes her to meet John Davinier, and her cousin Elizabeth who has been jilted by her misogynist and racist suitor James Ashton. On his part, John Davinier also enlists the support of law student activists in London for protest activities (including pamphlets and papers). In a surprising turn of events, Lady Mansfield also sides with Dido and Davinier in persuading Lord Mansfield to do the right thing: "It is possible that even you cannot fight change, my darling…And sometimes you cannot fight it because you are a part of it." As the screen writer Misan Sagay comments on this scene, "Her words resonate, shifting him (Lord Mansfield) into thought" (Sagay and Asante). In the end, their joint effort bears fruit when Lord Mansfield defies the expectations of his aristocratic class and sides with the abolitionists and insurance companies in his landmark ruling:

> It is my opinion, that the state of slavery is so odious a position that nothing may support it. This case has displayed with searing clarity the depravity of any such nation whose choice is to practice it. You may be certain that I have laboured over my judgement and statements today and am in full understanding of all of the ramifications. Justice be done, though the heavens may fall. I find in favour of the insurers and overturn the decision of the lower court. I order a retrial.
>
> (Asante)

The real historical event happened on November 29, 1781, when the Zong captain Luke Collingwood decided to drown about 132 slaves out of his dangerously overcrowded cargo of 442 African slaves before reaching Jamaica so that the British shipowner William Gregson could claim insurance money (to the value of £30 per slave). According to Paula Byrne:

> When Gregson and his syndicate made their claim of £30 for each of the slaves who had been killed, they stated that the ship's water supply had run out, and the captain had taken the 'necessary' step of sacrificing a few for the many.
> (Byrne 2014:189)

The lower court ruled for Gregson and other slave traders, but the case was appealed by the insurers. The final judgement was rendered by Chief Justice Lord Mansfield against Gregson and his syndicate and in favor of the insurers who refused to pay. That judgement is believed to have sanctioned the official end of the enslavement of Africans in Britain.

As dramatized in the film, the joint role played by Dido and John Davinier was crucial in persuading Lord Mansfield's judgement in favor of the insurance companies and by implication the dead slaves. Through Dido and John Davinier, Asante effectively depicts how ex-slaves like Equiano, Ignatius Sancho, Mary Prince, and Ottobah Cugoano worked closely in the Abolitionist Movement with humanist white authors and activists like Granville Sharp, James Stanfield, Thomas Clarkson, Samuel Coleridge, William Cowper, William Wilberforce, James Ramsay, Lady Hardy, Lady Margaret Middleton, and Hannah More. These white abolitionists disrupted the racialized and class order of the early modern British society from within as they joined the marginalized black subjects in their struggle for its transformation by calling for the end of Africans' enslavement. Like Shola/Mona and Joe in *Sankofa*, Dido affirms her postcolonial agency by validating the humanity of her mother and identifying with her African heritage. The 1779 painting of Dido and her cousin Elizabeth illustrates her blended identity beautifully. As accurately captured by Zoffany, Dido is depicted as an aristocratic black woman. She is not depicted as a caricature, but as a lady of the time, smiling next to her cousin. The film ends with the jubilant romantic scene where Dido and John Davinier emotionally proclaim their mutual love for one another. Their engagement exemplarily breaks down societal racial, class, and gender barriers. And in accepting their engagement, Chief Justice Lord Mansfield also signals the possibility of an inclusive modern British society that is also envisioned by the likes of Equiano and other abolitionists mentioned above.

Note

1 As remarked by Paula Byrne, "One Powerful abolitionist metaphor was sugar tainted with blood. The Quaker William Fox wrote that 'for every pound of West Indian sugar we may be considered as consuming two ounces of human flesh'" (2014:216).

II
The Black American stranger and postcolonial agency in Africa
The Congo narrative

2 The anti-enslavement/-colonial activist
George Washington Williams (1849–1891)

George Washington Williams was born on October 16, 1849 in Bedford Springs, Pennsylvania. Although free blacks, his father Thomas Williams and mother Ellen Rouse struggled to garner enough resources to provide a good education for their children. George Williams, therefore, joined the Union Army in 1864 at the age of fourteen (with an assumed name and a falsified age statement). As John Hope Franklin remarks, at that time, "For a young black male with no education and few marketable skills, the army appeared to be one of the most attractive of the few options open to him" (1998:6). After the civil war (and following his brief adventurous stint with General Espinosa's republican forces that fought to dethrone Emperor Maximilian in Mexico), Williams reenlisted in the United States Army until September 1868. Thereafter, he enrolled at Howard University (a historically black university) before moving to the Newton Theological Institution in Massachusetts in 1870. For four years in Newton, Williams combined his studies with social activism and became well known in the circle of high-profile members of the black community in Boston. In November 1873, he spoke at a meeting organized by "the colored citizens of Boston" to denounce what they termed "the general mistreatment of blacks in the South" (Franklin 1998:12), and in December 1873, he sent a letter to the *New National Era*, a Washington newspaper edited by the social activist and abolitionist Frederick Douglass, urging black people in the whole country to support the then forthcoming Washington convention that was to advocate a speedy passage of the civil rights bill. Before the convention, Williams had already been in contact with prominent black activists and writers in many parts of the country, including J. Sella Martin of Washington and James M. Trotter of Boston. On June 2, 1874, he married Sarah A. Sterretts in Chicago and became the first black student to graduate from Newton Theological Institution on June 10, 1874. A day after his graduation, Williams was ordained as a Baptist minister in Watertown, Massachusetts.

Pastoring for racial and social justice in America

The excellent, foundational liberal education that Williams received at Newton, together with his personal experiences as a black soldier in the United

States Army and as a social activist, focused his interest on a profound exploration of black people's history and on a social vision of Christianity that could actively promote the common kinship of humanity. The mentors who played a great influence in shaping his critical thought at Newton include Galusha Anderson who publicly spoke against slavery and later became the president of the old University of Chicago, and Herman Lincoln who taught him church history.

Williams's first public articulation of his desire to see the spread of Christianity to Africa and the end of Africans' enslavement came out in the valedictory speech he gave to his classmates, faculty, and invited guests at the 1874 commencement. The title of his address was "Early Christianity in Africa." He started off his address by pointing out the painful travail that accompanied the rise and spread of Christianity in Africa with early leaders such as Athanasius, Origen, Cyprian, Tertullian, and Augustine. Then, he proceeded to indict the greedy Western world for hampering the march of Christianity through their inhumane and immoral preoccupation with the enslavement of Africans. Williams concluded his speech by asserting the validity of the theory of "manifest destiny" or "providential design" (Jacobs 1982:16) for African Americans in relation to the evangelization and modernization of Africa:

> For nearly three centuries Africa has been robbed of her sable sons. For nearly three centuries they have toiled in bondage, unrequited in this youthful republic of the west. They have grown from a small company to be an exceedingly great people—five millions in number no longer chattel, they are human beings; no longer bondsmen, they are free men, with almost every civil disability[...].With his Saxon brother, the African slakes his insatiable thirstings for knowledge at the same fountain[...].The Negro of this country can turn to his Saxon brothers, and say, as Joseph said to his brethren who wickedly sold him, "As for you, ye meant it unto evil, but God meant it unto good, that we, after learning your arts and sciences, might return to Egypt and deliver the rest of our brethren who are yet in the house of bondage." That day will come!
> (Williams, June 10, 1874)

Williams continued to uphold this vision when he was appointed the pastor of the Boston Twelfth Baptist Church, following the death of its famous pastor and his Christian mentor Leonard Grimes. In the introductory sermon he gave to church, he said about Africa:

> My heart loves that land, and my soul is proud of it. It has been the dream of my youth that that country would be saved by the colored people of this country. And my heart is more hopeful today than at any previous period.
> (Williams 1874:60–61)

The sense of activism for racial and social justice that Williams developed while in Newton no doubt guided his action in his versatile professional career as a Baptist clergyman, a journalist, a historian, and a politician in the United States and as an explorer in Africa. The passage of the civil rights bill in March 1875 brought a sense of hope for African Americans throughout the country, and Williams seized that opening to move his activism from the confines of the Baptist church to a more far-reaching public arena. He then decided to resign from his position as pastor of the Twelfth Baptist Church in Boston and move to Washington D.C. to found a journal that would educate Black Americans about their struggle, rights, and possibilities in the United States. Williams articulated the goals of his project in a letter he wrote to poet Henry Wadsworth Longfellow on July 24, 1875:

> The time has come when the Negro must do something. [...] This is a plastic period. The Negro will begin to make history. What manner of history will it be? That is the question. [...] To this end I go to Washington and edit a journal. It will be their teacher, their friend, their mirror. As a teacher it will discuss educational and social problems; as a friend it will lead them from the political arena to the firm foundations on enlightened citizenship and nobler manhood; as a mirror it will reflect the virtue, genius, and industry of the emancipated millions of this country.
> (Williams 1875, July 24)

With the endorsement and financial support of the Washington Black elite that included the abolitionist Frederick Douglass (whose newspaper the *New National Era* had just ended) and the poet Langston Hughes's uncle John Mercer Langston (dean of the Law School and vice president of Howard University), Williams founded a weekly journal *The Commoner* and thus filled in the vacuum left behind by the demise of the *New National Era*. He published a sample in September 1875, and it was well received. He then travelled throughout the country promoting the journal as the mouthpiece of the black people's cause. During his travels in Southern States (Alabama, Louisiana, and Mississippi), Williams saw firsthand racial violence perpetrated against Black Americans and deplored the unraveling failure of the American Reconstruction project in his lectures and subsequent journal editorials. In his public lectures, Williams emphasized the importance of what he called "the Agencies of Race Organization" in the development of a collective Black American subjectivity. The maiden issue of the journal appeared on November 6, 1875, but it folded after only seven other issues due to a lack of financial support from its subscribers (mostly working-class Black Americans).

Following the collapse of his journal, Williams accepted an invitation to pastor the Union Baptist Church of Cincinnati in Ohio and was inaugurated on March 2, 1876. As he did in Boston with Twelfth Baptist Church, here, he also successfully integrated the gospel mission of the church with social activism and expanded the church membership exponentially. He continued to give public lectures on his cherished themes of "The Agencies of Race Organization," the contributions and sacrifices of black soldiers in the Union Army, and the anti-colonial struggle of the 18th-century black leader of the Haitian revolution Toussaint L'Ouverture (1743–1803). He also used liberal-leaning newspapers like *The Cincinnati Commercial* to advocate better social conditions and civil rights for the black people in Ohio and the rest of the country. In August 1876, Williams became a member of the executive committee of the Colored Protective Association, an organization that fought for the civil rights of the black folks in Cincinnati. He remained an astute pastor and social activist until December 1, 1877, when he resigned from the Union Baptist Church in order to devote more time to his law studies and political activities as a member of the Republican Party. After two years of political campaign and social activism punctuated by public lectures that promoted the interests of black people and those of the Republican Party in Cincinnati, Williams was elected to represent Hamilton County of Cincinnati in the Ohio House of Representatives. He took his seat on January 5, 1880 and immediately went to work. During the first legislative session, Williams sponsored progressive bills such as the one on the regulation of the police power in Cincinnati and the other that sought to repeal the act against interracial marriage that the Ohio legislature had passed in 1861. Although the latter bill did not pass, the debate on it certainly refocused the attention of the Ohio legislators and the public on the inhumanity of that racist law.

Williams had already gained prominence as a champion of black people's rights and a staunch member of the then liberal Republican Party when he declined to seek reelection to the Ohio legislature. Between 1881 and 1885, Williams spent most of his time researching black people's history and giving public lectures on the retrogressive stance of Southern States to the projects of Emancipation and Reconstruction in America. His research project resulted in the publication of his two landmark books on Black American history, *History of the Negro Race in America from 1619 to 1880: Negroes as Slaves, as Soldiers, and as Citizens* (1885) and *A History of the Negro Troops in the War of the Rebellion, 1861–1865* (1887). From 1884 to 1889, Williams continued to crisscross the country giving lectures and worked hard to secure an appointment as the United States diplomatic representative to Haiti (after being nominated for the post by the outgoing Republican President Arthur and confirmed by United States Senate). When he finally lost his bid for that diplomatic post to Frederick Douglass, Williams turned his attention to the persistent, inhuman slave trade that continued to take place in Africa. He called on the United States government and the American people to fight against it, and on September 28, 1889, he sailed to Europe in order to attend an antislavery conference in Brussels as a reporter for S.S. McClure's *Associated Literary Press*.[1] The conference was held on November 18, 1889, and it brought together delegates from seventeen countries that sought to end the slave trade.

Crusading against black people's enslavement and colonial brutality

In Brussels, Williams made useful contacts with influential individuals who had interests in the Congo Free State, including King Leopold II with whom he had an interview, the American railroad tycoon Collis P. Huntington, and Henry S. Sanford, a former United States minister to Belgium, who (from a racist and segregationist stance) encouraged Black Americans to move to Africa and "civilize" the continent. At the end of their interview, both King Leopold and Williams came out with favorable opinions of each other. Williams, like Alexander Crummel and John J. Coles (see Walter Williams 1982:134–135) before him, bought into King Leopold's ostensibly proclaimed philanthropic mission in the Congo. According to him, during the interview, King Leopold proudly stated that the Belgian people had two motives in occupying the Congo: "One is trade and commerce, which is selfish...and the other is to bring the means and blessings of Christian civilization to Africa, which is noble" (quoted in Franklin: 1998:181). In turn, Williams succeeded in persuading the King to allow Black American low-level professionals to join in his administration in the Congo Free State as laborers and office workers.

Captain Albert Thys, the chief administrative officer of the Belgian Commercial Companies in the Congo Free State, also welcomed Williams' proposal and commissioned him (with a monthly salary of $150) to go ahead and recruit a number of Black American clerks, carpenters, engineers, and mechanics. Williams enthusiastically returned to the United States and arrived in New York on December 9, 1889 to carry out the mission. Shortly thereafter, he visited and addressed students and faculty at Hampton Institute (now Hampton University) but failed to persuade skeptical young Black Americans to join the Congo project. After only spending three weeks in the United States, Williams returned to Belgium. As he returned to Europe without the promised Black American recruits for the Belgian Commercial Companies, Williams' contract was terminated by Albert Thys. King Leopold, who had been in the meantime informed of Williams' political activism in the United States (probably by Henry Sanford), also became reluctant to support his trip to and stay in the Congo Free State. However, determined to fulfill what he and many other Black American activists of his time saw as a "Providential Design" mission for the development of Africa, he sought assistance from other sources. Franklin states:

> Even without a commission from King Leopold and the Belgian Commercial Companies, Williams had sufficient assignments to make a visit to the Congo worthwhile. He would visit as much of the country as possible in order to give President Harrison a detailed report on the state of affairs there, as he promised. He would write a series of letters to the Associated Literary Press to be distributed to its subscribing newspapers,

pursuant to his commission from S. S. McClure. He would also look at the route of the proposed Congo Railway and make a report, presumably to Collis P. Huntington, regarding its feasibility.

(Franklin 1998:188)

King Leopold's withdrawal of his support for Williams (he denied him access to any of the state vessels) turned out to be salutary for the latter in the end as it enabled him to carry out an independent investigation on the activities of the Congo Free State administration and its treatment of the Congolese natives. Upon receiving the financial assistance he had solicited from Collis Huntington (£100), who was keen to secure a railroad construction in the Congo, Williams wasted no time to get ready for his exploratory journey to Africa. In the letter that he enclosed with the check, Huntington wrote to Williams:

> I hope all will go well with you in your new field of work, and shall await with interest your first letter giving impressions of the Congo country. I think you are well qualified to enlighten Americans upon this subject – particularly as to the actual condition and extent of civilization of the native population, concerning which I believe much misapprehension exists.

(Huntington 1890, January 7)

On January 30, 1890, Williams sailed from Liverpool for the Congo aboard the *Gaboon*, the vessel owned by the British and African Steam Navigation Company. As the ship made stops at different African ports along the Atlantic coast, Williams frequently stepped out and talked with African natives, observing their cultural practices, visiting churches, and critically examining Europeans' interactions with African natives. He did this in Sierra Leone, Liberia, Gold Coast (Ghana), Ivory Coast, and Nigeria. After fifty-three days from Liverpool, the ship finally arrived in Boma, the capital city of the Congo Free State, and Williams immediately started his investigative mission that the Congo Free State saw as a threat to the interest of King Leopold II and Belgium. In his first correspondence to Huntington, Williams gave him a hint at the suffering of the Congolese people at the hands of a cruel colonial administration and underlined the importance of his mission not only for them but also for humanity at large. He talked about a "dozen excellent reasons why my coming is, in the Providence of God, the best thing that could happen for the poor native and the misguided Belgian." Williams called the Congo "the Siberia of the African Continent, a penal settlement" (Williams 1890, April 14) and decried the injustices meted out to the natives in terms of the fraudulent dispossession of their land, the brutal exploitation of their labor on railroad work and rubber extraction, poor health facilities and rampant mortality, the importation of liquor and firearms, the unethical system of justice and punishment, and the brutal military recruitment. He communicated these concerns not only to his main sponsor Collis Huntington but also to Republican Senator George Frisbie Hoar of Massachusetts and the prominent Washington Black American attorney Robert H. Terrell so that they could expose to the American public the atrocities committed by the brutal regime of King Leopold II in the Congo. These critical reports angered the King and Belgian authorities, and Williams became afraid for his life. In an earlier letter to Huntington, he voiced this concern but defiantly stated: "However, I shall take every precaution to preserve my life, and shall do my duty to history and humanity with unflagging zeal and dauntless courage" (Williams 1890, February 6).

On May 15, 1890, Williams assembled a caravan of eighty-five Congolese men and travelled to the interior of the Congo. Unlike Europeans, he treated his workers humanely to the best of his abilities. He followed the route travelled earlier by the American journalist and explorer Henry Morton Stanley from the lower to the upper Congo. Other notable explorers of Williams's time include the Irish Roger Casement and the Polish-English writer Joseph Conrad who also later on decried the colonial, inhumane brutality of the regime of King Leopold II in 1890. During his travels, he met hospitable missionaries like the Reverend George Grenfell of the Baptist Missionary Society of London in Bolobo, who gave him useful information about the conditions of the Congolese natives and their ill treatment by the Congo Free State administration (even though they were reluctant to criticize the Belgian King's administration for fear of reprisal). As he moved from the Congo River's Stanley Falls to the Kasai and Lomami rivers, Williams admired the landscape and noted Congolese people's ethnic diversity without judging them. He also admired and collected a sizable number of Congolese art objects. In the course of his journey, some villages welcomed him warmly while others misrecognized his mission and regarded him and his caravan as members of the oppressive colonial administration. In fact, in the Congo and in other parts of Africa he visited, Williams was regarded as a stranger and called "a white man."

After gathering a lot of information on the Congolese environment (the climate, soil, topography, flora, and fauna) and the people's miserable condition under King Leopold's rule, Williams returned to Stanley Falls (now Boyoma Falls) and spent a few days writing his controversial open letter to King Leopold II, as well as a report on the feasibility of a railroad project that he had promised Huntington. In a letter to Huntington from the Falls, he expressed his utter disappointment with "deceit, obtrusiveness, ignorance and cruelty of the State of the Congo" (Williams 1890, July 16).

Protest open letter and reports

On July 18, 1890, Williams sent out to the whole world a scathing open letter of protest addressed to King Leopold II: *An Open Letter to His Serene Majesty Leopold II, King of the Belgians and Sovereign of the Independent State* of Congo, By Colonel the Honorable Geo. W. Williams, of the United States of America. Like Toussaint L'Ouverture, his admired revolutionary leader of the Haitian anti-colonial revolt in the 18th century, Williams used the tenets of Western modernity (Truth, Liberty, Humanity, and Justice) as benchmarks in his evaluation of King Leopold's rule in the Congo in the 19th century. That way, his open letter could be read as a call to action against the dehumanizing, anti-modern regime of the King. Williams expressed his bitter disappointment with the King Leopold's heartless deceit reminding him and the general audience:

> My Friendship and service for the State of Congo were inspired by and based upon your publicly declared motives and aims, and your personal statement to your humble subscriber: —humane sentiments and work of Christian civilization for Africa. Thus I was led to regard your enterprise as the rising of the Star of Hope for the Dark Continent, so long the habitation of cruelties; and I journeyed in its light and laboured in its hope. All the praiseful things I have spoken and written of the Congo country, Sate and Sovereign were inspired by the firm belief that your Government was built upon the enduring foundation of *Truth, Liberty, Humanity* and *Justice*.
> (Williams 1998a: 243)

In the letter, Williams deploys the arsenal of rhetorical skills he first learned at Newton Institute and perfected throughout his career as a Baptist minister, a journalist, a lawyer, a politician, and a social activist. Starting from the title of the letter, Williams sarcastically localizes the power of the King, calling him the "King of the Belgians" and thereby implying that he is not the King of Africans or the world. It is a reminder to him that he should not regard his occupation of the Congo as unaccountable to the Congolese people and other Western powers. He also treats the King with irony in his salutation when he addresses him: "Good and Great Friend." In fact, the King regarded Williams as a threat and an enemy, not a friend, and Williams was constantly afraid for his life while in the Congo.

Speaking/writing like a traditional African griot, Williams introduces his letter with words that convincingly establish the validity (truthfulness) and objectivity of his account. He takes care of informing his readers that his letter is "based upon a careful study and inspection of the country and character of the personal Government you have established upon the African continent" (243). He further adds with an activist tone that the charges he brings indirectly and formally against the King are based on numerous horrible accounts by the Congolese natives and Christian missionaries as well as on his personal observations on the ship (*Gaboon*) that took him to the Congo and during his journeys in the interior of the country:

> Every charge which I am about to bring against your Majesty's personal Government in the Congo has been carefully investigated; a list of

competent and veracious witnesses, documents, letters, official records and data has been faithfully prepared, which will be deposited with Her Brittannic Majesty's Secretary of State for Foreign Affairs, until such time as an International Commission can be created with power to send for persons and papers, to administer oaths, and attest the truth or falsity of these charges.

(243–244)

Williams also foregrounds the universal importance of his intention and the noble duty (in contrast with King Leopold's self-serving deceits) that history has called upon him to perform for humanity when he states in the second paragraph of the letter:

In order that you may know the truth, the whole truth, and nothing but the truth, I implore your most gracious permission to address you without restraint, and with frankness of a man who feels that he has a duty to perform to History, Humanity, Civilization and to the Supreme Being, who is himself the "King of Kings".

(243)

Thus, with a stern, anti-colonial tone, Williams levels the first indirect charge against the King: his illegal occupation of the Congo land by means of fraudulent treaties that the natives could not understand and were deceived into signing. Most of these treaties were conceived by Henry Morton Stanley who would deceptively present himself and the white man, in general, to warring local chiefs as a powerful peacemaker. Boxes of gin and technological tricks like electrical batteries, fire-generating glass lenses, and guns were used by Stanley and his company in order to impress the natives about the superior technological and supernatural powers of the white man and entice local chiefs to sign the treaties. Williams states in the letter:

Your Majesty's title to the territory of the State of the Congo is badly clouded, while many of the treaties made with the natives by the "Association Internationale du Congo," of which you were Director and Banker, were tainted by frauds of the grossest character. The world may not be surprised to learn that your flag floats over territory to which your Majesty has no legal or just claim, since other European Powers have doubtful claims to the territory which they occupy upon the African Continent; but all honest people will be shocked to know by what groveling means this fraud was consummated.

(244)

The second indirect charge that Williams levels against the King is his deception to the United States and the international community about the proclaimed benevolence of his administration for the natives of the Congo

46   *The Congo narrative*

Free State and their purported ready acceptance of his rule. The program that King Leopold II advertised to the world and won him the support of the United States included "'*fostering care*', '*benevolent enterprise*', an '*honest and practical effort*' to increase the knowledge of the natives and '*secure their welfare*'" (245). However, Williams states that since his arrival in the country, he has only seen misery, dejection, and lack of trust for the government. Everywhere, the natives complain that "Your Majesty's Government has sequestered their land, burned their towns, stolen their property, enslaved their women and children, and committed other crimes too numerous to mention in detail" (246). Williams also emphatically affirms in the letter that "There has been, to my absolute knowledge, no '*honest and practical effort made to increase their knowledge and secure their welfare.*' Your Majesty's Government has never spent one franc for educational purposes, nor institu[t]ed any practical system of industrialism" (246). He mentions that unlike their white counterparts, African workers and soldiers (mostly imported from Zanzibar, Sierra Leone, Liberia, Ghana, and Nigeria) do not have adequate housing and health facilities and are poorly remunerated. According to Williams:

> These recruits are transported under circumstances more cruel than cattle in European countries. They eat their rice twice a day by the use of their fingers; they often thirst for water when the season is dry; they are exposed to the heat and rain, and sleep upon the damp and filthy decks of the vessels often so closely crowded as to lie in human ordure. And, of course, many die.
> (247)

The third indirect charge that Williams brings against the King is what he sees as the illegal recruitment of inexperienced and ignorant young Belgians to serve in a personal project, the Free State army. Williams states that these young officers

> are ignorant of native character, lack wisdom, justice, fortitude and patience. They have estranged the natives from your Majesty's Government, have sown the seed of discord between tribes and villages, and some of them have stained the uniform of the Belgian officer with murder, arson and robbery.
> (247)

He also notes that government officials are equally inexperienced and lack creativity in their handling of tasks. In fact, the boring character of the accountant in Joseph Conrad's novella *Heart of Darkness* first published in 1899 confirms Williams's observation here.

In the letter, Williams considers the accusations (that I call indirect charges) mentioned above as "general observations," and in the next section lays out in detail his twelve formal charges against King Leopold and his administration. In the first charge, he accuses the King's government of being "deficient in the moral, military, and financial strength, necessary to govern a territory of 1,508,000 square miles, 7,251 miles of navigation, and 31,694 square miles of lake surface" (248). As a result, the government cannot control violence, enslavement, and cruel inhuman ritualistic practices amongst the natives. The second formal charge accuses the King's government of failing to supervise "mercenary slave-soldiers from the East Coast" who are brought in to be in charge of "the Black Zanzibar soldiers." These soldiers are left free to fend for themselves and garner food stuffs for white officers by raiding villages and compelling the natives to provide them with

> fish, goats, fowls, and vegetables at the mouths of their muskets; and whenever the natives refuse to feed these vampires, they report to the main station and white officers come with an expeditionary force and burn away the homes of the natives.
> (248)

The third charge accuses the government of violating the terms of contract of foreign workers brought in the country to work as "soldiers, mechanics and workmen [...]. Their letters never reach home" (248). The fourth charge accuses the government of running a corrupt justice system that is biased against the natives:

> The Courts of your Majesty's Government are abortive, unjust, partial and delinquent. I have personally witnessed and examined their clumsy operations. The laws printed and circulated in Europe 'for the protection of the blacks' in the Congo, are a dead letter and a fraud.
> (249)

The fifth charge concerns the horrible treatments of prisoners (black soldiers and civilians). Here, Williams gives in graphic details how cruelly they are punished:

> Your Majesty's Government is excessively cruel to its prisoners, condemning them, for the slightest offences, to the chain gang, the like of which cannot be seen in any other Government in the civilised or uncivilised world. Often these ox-chains eat into the necks of the prisoners and produce sores about which the flies circle, aggravating the running wound; so the prisoner is constantly worried. These poor creatures are frequently beaten with a dried piece of hippopotamous skin, called a 'chicote,' and usually the blood flows at every stroke when well laid on. But the cruelties visited upon soldiers and workmen are not to be compared with the sufferings of the poor natives who, upon the slightest pretext, are thrust into the wretched prisons here in the Upper River.
> (249)

48 The Congo narrative

The sixth charge outlines the ill treatment of African women and children by King Leopold's administration. These women are often captured, objectified, and reduced to sex objects for the satisfaction of government officials' colonial, sexual desires. On this charge, Williams says:

> Women are imported into your Majesty's Government for immoral purposes. They are introduced by two methods, viz, black men are dispatched to the Portuguese coast where they engage these women as mistresses of white men, who pay to the procurer a monthly sum. The other method is by capturing native women and condemning them to seven years' servitude for some imaginary crime against the Sate with which the villages of these women are charged. The State then hires these women out to the highest bidder, the officers having the first choice and then the men. Whenever children are born of such relations, the State maintains that the woman being its property, the child belongs to it also.
>
> (249–250)

Atrocities committed against native women by government officials and soldiers are also elaborated on in the ninth formal charge.

In the seventh and eighth charges, Williams accuses the government of systematic violations of the Berlin Treaty about trade and commerce with natives and foreign companies, especially with regard to taxation and the trade of ivory and rubber. Natives are often expropriated of their goods at the slightest excuse. In the tenth charge, Williams accuses the King's government of engaging "in the slave-trade, wholesale and retail. It buys and sells and steals slaves. Your Majesty's Government gives £3 per head for able-bodied slaves for military service" (251). In the eleventh charge, Williams accuses the King's government of illegal sale of arms to Arabs. In the final charge, he accuses Henry Morton Stanley (the person commissioned by the King to acquire the Congo land and subsequently celebrated in Europe and the United States) of dishonesty and cruelty in his dealings with the natives:

> HENRY M. STANLEY'S name produces a shudder among this simple folk when mentioned; they remember his broken promises, his copious profanity, his hot temper, his heavy blows, his severe and rigorous measures, by which they were mulcted of their lands.
>
> (252)

According to Williams, Stanley created an unbridgeable gulf between Europeans and Africans in the Congo. He is therefore very skeptical about the railway project, as he thinks that "Emigration cannot be invited to this country for many years" (252).

Williams concludes his letter by first extolling the virtues and humanity of the natives (the so-called African savages) while outlining the spectacular savagery of the King Leopold's regime:

> Against the deceit, fraud, robberies, arson, murder, slave-raiding, and general policy of cruelty of your Majesty's Government to the natives, stands their record of unexampled patience, long suffering and forgiving spirit, which put the boasted civilisation and professed religion of your Majesty's Government to the blush. During thirteen years only one white man has lost his life by the hands of the natives, and only two white men have been killed in the Congo. Major BARTTELOT was shot by a Zanzibar soldier, and the captain of a Belgian trading –boat was the victim of his own rash and unjust treatment of a native chief.
> (253)

In the second paragraph of the conclusion, Williams casts aside the irony, sarcasm, and courtesy of respect to nobility seen in the introductory section of the letter and deploys a combative, anti-colonial tone toward King Leopold. He boldly puts the responsibility of the crimes against humanity committed by Congo Free State officials squarely upon the King's shoulders and emphatically warns that he has to answer for them. Here is how he aggressively and engagingly addresses him:

> All the crimes perpetrated in the Congo have been done in *your* name, and *you* must answer at the bar of Public Sentiment for the misgovernment of a people, whose lives and fortunes were entrusted to you by the august Conference of Berlin, 1884–1885.
> (253)

And turning to the responsibility of the international powers that in the first place gave legitimacy to King Leopold's occupation of the Congo land in Berlin, Williams calls upon them to open an investigation into his brutal and inhumane rule in the Congo:

> I now appeal to the Powers, which committed this infant State to your Majesty's charge, and to the great States which gave it international being; and whose majestic law you have scorned and trampled upon, to call and create an International Commission to investigate the charges herein preferred in the name of Humanity, Commerce, Constitutional Government and Christian Civilisation.
> (253)

In the rest of the concluding section, Williams also appeals to the Belgian people and government, anti-slavery societies, philanthropists, Christians, statesmen, "and to great mass of people everywhere, to call upon the Governments of Europe, to hasten the close of the tragedy Your Majesty's unlimited Monarchy is enacting in the Congo." He then ends his letter on an evangelical tone, pointing out the purity of his motives in leveling the above charges against King Leopold II:

> I appeal to our Heavenly Father, whose service is perfect love, in witness of the purity of my motives and the integrity of my aims; and to history and mankind I appeal for the demonstration and vindication of the truthfulness of the charges I have herein briefly outlined.
> (253–254)

In addition to the *Open Letter*, Williams also completed "*A Report on the Proposed Congo Railway*" (that he promised Huntington) on July 16, 1890. Like Olaudah Equiano, Williams advocates in this report the industrialization of Africa that should benefit the whole humanity and that places education of natives at the center. In his recommendation, he writes:

> The Congo Railway ought to be built, and from the bottom of my heart I hope it will. But capitalists and philanthropists must remember what I have declared, that it cannot be built for less than 40, 000, 000 francs, nor in less than eight years. By skillful and practical management, and with all the machinery employed in the construction of European and American railroads, the time could be reduced by two or three years. Meanwhile Africa needs the blessing of a practical labor system which, while it addresses itself to the soul, will not ignore the body, its early temple; and, while inculcating spiritual truths, will not fail to teach the native the primal lesson of human history: For in the sweat of thy face shalt thou eat thy bread.
> (Williams 1890b: 255)

With the completion of the open letter and the railway report, Williams believed that he had achieved his investigative mission and service to humanity in the Congo and that it was time to move on and carry out his investigations about African natives' conditions as they faced European colonial occupation in other parts of the continent. So, on July 18, 1890, he left Stanley Falls for the Lower Congo via the French Congo (now Congo Republic or Congo Brazzaville). In the port city of Loango in the French Congo, Williams was warmly received by the French, Portuguese, Dutch, Americans, and English, who saw in him an ally and champion of the Berlin accords on commerce, trade, and freedom of navigation in the Congo basin. After visiting a number of villages there, he left for Banana, a port city in the Congo Free State, where he spent a few days shipping his "five large boxes of curiosities, such as arrows and bows, spears, swords, knives, paddles, grass mats, shields, etc." (Franklin 1998:196).

After spending a little over a month in Banana, Williams sailed for Loanda, Angola, aboard the Dutch ship *Andrea*, and arrived there on September 17, 1890. While he decried the enslavement of Africans in Angola, Williams was relatively pleased with the conditions of freed African slaves and other natives under Portuguese rule there. In a letter to his friend Robert Terrell, Williams pleasantly wrote (against the background of his bitterly disappointing experiences in the Congo Free State):

> Every black man in Loanda has a vote at the municipal elections. There are mixed schools. There are no separate churches—a great thing for the Catholic religion—Wherever you find a black man here with education and means, a man who displays ability of the most ordinary kind, he is appreciated and treated with consideration.
> (qtd. in Franklin 1998:196)

While resting and investigating Portuguese "Penal Servitude and Labor Systems" during a month-long stay in Loanda, Williams made time to write a report on the atrocities of the Congo Free State administration for the President of the United States of America. He completed the report on October 14, 1890 and entitled it: *A Report upon the Congo-State and Country to the President of the Republic of the United States of America, by Colonel the Honorable Geo. W. Williams.* In the report, Williams reminds the president of the support that the United States and individuals like Henry Sanford and himself gave to what they thought was a noble, philanthropic intention of King Leopold II in forming the "Association Internationale du Congo," which he later transformed into a sovereign "État Indépendant du Congo" (August 1, 1885). He then reiterates the accusations he leveled against the King in the open letter and urges the United States to redeem its good will and its influential international standing by disavowing his regime and working toward the formation of a local postcolonial African State. Here is how Williams describes the responsibility of the United States in the Congo carnage and the possibility of its redemption in his wide-ranging report quoted here at length:

> Although America has no commercial interests in the Congo it was the Government of the Republic of the United States which introduced this African Government into the sisterhood of States. It was the American Republic which stood sponsor to this young State, which has disappointed the most glowing hopes of its most ardent friends and most zealous promoters. Whatever the Government of the Republic of the United States did for the Independent State of Congo, was inspired and guided by noble and unselfish motives. And whatever it refrains from doing, will be on account of its elevated sentiments of humanity, and its sense of sacredness of agreements and compacts, in their letter and spirit. The people of the United States of America have a just right to

know *the truth, the whole truth* and *nothing but the* truth, respecting the Independent State of Congo, an absolute monarchy, an oppressive and cruel Government, an exclusive Belgian colony, now tottering to its fall. **I indulge the hope that when a new Government shall rise upon the ruins of the old, it will be simple, not complicated; local, not European; international, not national; just, not cruel; and casting its shield alike over black and white, trader and missionary, endure for centuries.**

(Williams 1998c: 279-279, emphasis added)

Despite the meager resources at his disposal, Williams left Loanda on October 14, 1890 in order to pursue his investigations on routes of slave traffic and African natives' living conditions in European colonies. He visited the Cape Colony, Natal, and the Orange Free State (all in present Republic of South Africa), where he met a number of government officials; Mozambique, a Portuguese colony, and a very important commercial maritime hub in South West Africa; and arrived in Zanzibar (present Tanzania) on November 25, 1890. In Zanzibar, Williams was warmly welcomed by two anti-slavery officials, Sir Charles Euan Smith, the British consul general, and E.D. Ropes, the United States consul. Both readily assisted him in his investigations of African natives' enslavement and slave trade. He was also able to secure a private audience with the Sultan of Zanzibar, Sayyid Ali, who had promulgated an emancipation edict in August 1890. The Sultan was impressed by Williams's investigations and gave him a number of gifts. Williams was also enthusiastically received by another prominent anti-slavery figure in Zanzibar, Charles Alan Smythies, bishop of Zanzibar and missionary bishop of East Africa. He also met with Baron Major Weissmann, the Commander of the German forces in East Africa, in order to seek clarification about German policy on slavery and slave trade in German East African territory.

After gathering a lot of information about slave trade in Zanzibar as well as in Mombasa and Lamu port cities (both in present Kenya), Williams left for Cairo via Aden, an Asian city. At Aden, he got useful information about the massive, horrible slave trade that was taking place between Arabia and Egypt. He arrived in Cairo on January 21, 1891 and continued his investigations with the support of the British Minister, Sir Evelyn Baring, the acting American consul general, and local Egyptian officials. Unfortunately, his stay in Cairo was cut short when he took ill and had to leave for Britain at the end of April 1891.

By the time Williams arrived in Britain, his health was steadily declining, but he was certainly pleased to learn that his open letter had been extensively featured and debated in media and in the political arenas in Belgium, France, Britain, and the United States. Almost all the newspapers (conservative and liberal) in Belgium debated its content, some supporting the King while others asking for investigations, and the newspaper *Le Temps* featured it in Paris. On November 4, 1890, R. Cobden Phillips of the Manchester

Chamber of Commerce read the *Open Letter* to a public forum in London. The New York *Herald* carried the story in mid-April 1891.

Williams died and was buried in Blackpool, England, on August 2, 1891. His revolutionary, anti-colonial call to action against King Leopold's brutal rule in the Congo echoed later on vigorously in the international crusade launched by E.D. Morel's *Congo Reform Association* formed in 1904. It is surprising that Roger Casement and Joseph Conrad, who visited the Congo during the same year that Williams did and saw the atrocities documented in his open letter, made no mention of him in their critical writings that appeared later in the beginning of the 20th century. Certainly with his protest open letter, Williams boldly planted the revolutionary, anti-/postcolonial seed that germinated and blossomed with a variety of nuances into Joseph Conrad's novella *Heart of Darkness* (1899), Roger Casement's Report (1904), E.D. Morel's Congo Reform Association (1904), Mark Twain's *King Leopold's Soliloquy* (1905), William Sheppard's report on the Belgian Kasai Rubber Company (1908), and Simon Kimbangu's anti-colonial religious syncretism "Ngunzism" (1921). As Williams' biographer John Hope Franklin has stated:

> Thus, of all the 1890 observers and critics of Leopold's rule in the Congo—Grenfell the missionary, Casement the diplomat, Conrad the novelist, Williams the reporter, and doubtless others [like William Henry Sheppard]—only Williams saw fit to make his unfavorable views widely known immediately. The others had their own reasons for remaining silent at the time; and in due course they would all express their disapproval with varying degrees of fervor. When they did speak out, not one mentioned Williams's Open Letter or his other reports.
> (Franklin 1998:220)

Note

1 Contributors to S.S. McClure's magazine *Associated Literary Press* include famous American and British writers like Robert Louis Stevenson, Rudyard Kipling, Arthur Conan Doyle, Mark Twain, Henry James, and Randolph Churchill (Franklin 1998).

3 The postcolonial pragmatist
William Henry Sheppard (1865–1927)

One month after George Washington Williams's departure for the Congo, another Black American, William Henry Sheppard, also left for the country on a Christian mission motivated by the same theory of "Providential Design." William Henry Sheppard was born in Waynesboro, Virginia, in March 1865. His father, William Sheppard Sr., was the Saxon of the local First Presbyterian Church and a barber whose barbershop (unusually at the time) was frequented by both blacks and whites. Sheppard's mother, Sarah Frances Martin (a mulatto), was born free in 1837. She managed a Ladies' Health Bath and, like her husband, was a devout Christian known in her community for her acts of generosity to the needy of all races. Sheppard says of her mother in his autobiography, *Presbyterian Pioneers in the Congo*: "Mother never turned anyone from her door who came begging, whether white or colored, without offering them such as she had" (1917:15). Thus, Sheppard's early childhood was immersed in Christian ethics that includes brotherly and sisterly love, justice, humility, and service. It was during this period that, as he recalls:

> A beautiful Christian lady, Mrs. Ann Bruce, said to me one day, 'William, I pray for you, and hope some day you may go to Africa as a missionary.' I had never had heard of Africa, and those words made a lasting impression.
>
> (1917:15–16)

At about the age of ten, Sheppard's parents allowed him to go to Staunton and live with Dr. S.H. Henkel, a prominent white member of the local First Presbyterian Church, and his wife. There, the Henkels informally homeschooled Sheppard, who, in return, performed household chores for them, including cleaning and taking care of the horse. From there, Sheppard worked as a McCurdy House waiter in other towns outside Staunton and became a headwaiter at Covington. Having saved enough money from the jobs, he enrolled at Hampton Normal and Industrial Institute (now Hampton University) in 1880 at the age of fifteen. There, he was well received by General Samuel Armstrong who (after Emancipation Proclamation by

DOI: 10.4324/9780429322426-6

President Lincoln) founded the institution of higher learning in 1868. Its mission was to "educate the whole black race by creating the people who would be its teachers and leaders" (qtd. in Phipps 2002:5). Here is how Sheppard recounts his first experience at the Hampton Institute in his autobiography:

> General Armstrong, President of the institute, received me kindly. The first year I worked on the farm, and later worked in the bakery, going to school at night. [...] General Armstrong was my ideal of manhood: his erect carriage, deep, penetrating eyes, pleasant smiles and kindly disposition drew all students to him. He was a great, tender-hearted father to us all, and the teachers were also deeply interested in the welfare of the students.
>
> (1917:16–17)

Sheppard's interest in the evangelization of Africa that Ann Bruce first planted in his mind was rekindled at Hampton by Dr. H.B. Frissel, a Presbyterian minister, who was the Institute Chaplain (he later replaced Armstrong as president in 1893). It was under his influential zeal for home mission evangelism amongst "poor colored people" around Hampton that Sheppard realized "that my future work was to carry the gospel to the poor, destitute, and forgotten people" (1917:17). He must have also been influenced by Dr. Edward Wilmot Blyden's appeal to the student body there in 1882, urging them to think of returning to their forefathers' land (Africa) in order to plant churches and schools, as he himself had been tirelessly doing in Liberia.

Following his graduation from Hampton, Sheppard enrolled at Tuscaloosa Theological Institute in Alabama (now Stillman College), where he studied theology, homiletics, moral and mental philosophy, literature, physiology, and mathematics. He also devoted time for community home mission, and African evangelization was always on his thoughts. He says in his autobiography:

> A question asked me in my examination by both the Presbytery in Waynesboro, Va., and by the faculty of Tuscaloosa Institute was: 'If you are called upon to go to Africa as missionary, would you be willing to go?' I promptly answered, I would go, and with pleasure.
>
> (1917:18)

In 1886, Sheppard graduated from the Institute and was ordained by Atlanta Presbytery to pastor Zion Church in 1888. However, as Walter Williams states, "He did not adapt well to the strict segregation of the urban South, and in 1887 he petitioned the mission board to send him to Africa" (1982:23). His petition was delayed for almost three years as the unwritten racial ordering of the Southern Presbyterian Church allowed no black missionary to go abroad without a white superior. So, Sheppard had to wait until Samuel Lapsley, a twenty-three-year-old son of a former slaveholder (one year younger than him), was identified as a suitable white Presbyterian minister to go with him to Africa in 1889.

Subverting the racialized order of the southern Presbyterian Church

As soon as Sheppard and Lapsley were commissioned at a service held at the First Presbyterian Church in Nashville, Tennessee, in January 1890, both started bonding together as they went about garnering resources and visiting churches in several states. From that time, their two lives became so intertwined that in their letters and autobiographical writings, they mostly shed light on each other. As S.H. Chester notes in his introduction to Sheppard's autobiography, *Presbyterian Pioneers in the Congo*, "The reader will be struck with the way in which, in telling his story up to the time of Mr. Lapsley's death, he always keeps Mr. Lapsley to the front and himself in the background" (1917:1). In fact, Sheppard speaks very little of himself in the book— his history, his origin, his thoughts, or his feelings—as he focuses primarily on his calling into the ministry. In that respect, other facets of Sheppard's life as a family man, educator, linguist, cultural analyst, art collector, explorer, and anti/postcolonial activist are only known through his letters, lectures, Presbyterian Church reports, and other people's observations and comments. Sheppard's discourse can, therefore, be said to be a construct of double entendre: the "consensual" (his autobiography which reflects the expectations of the Church) and the "dissensual" (anti-colonial letters, lectures, and investigative reports), to use Jacques Rancière's terms (2015). William Sheppard and the Irish American Samuel Norvell Lapsley left the shores of New York on Wednesday, February 26, 1890 aboard the steamship *Adriatic*, and headed to the Congo via London and Brussels. As Christian missionaries, they were a part of the larger 19th-century Western colonizing and "civilizing mission" of non-Western others. As Sylvester Johnston has argued, "The role of missionary religion [...] is inseparable from the efforts to expand secular Western rule over indigenous polities throughout North America and in Asia and Africa" (2015:5). However, because of their marginalized positionality within the so-called postcolonial or post-reconstruction America based on race (blackness) and cultural origin (Irishness), Sheppard and Lapsley moved to the Congo as ambivalent or "undecidable" colonial subjects. There is therefore little wonder that upon their arrival in the Congo and following their deep interaction with the natives as they sought to convert them into Christianity, Sheppard and Lapsley came to a different understanding of the natives and themselves as human beings. Both enthusiastically learned local languages, familiarized themselves with natives' cultural practices (including the rituals they perceived as "primitive") and foodstuffs, as well as their environment, and developed a positive socio-political vision for their Christian mission. This vision carried a double entendre as it simultaneously subverted the racial, hierarchical ordering of the American Southern Church (which subordinated the older and pastorally more experienced Sheppard to the younger Lapsley on the grounds of racial difference) while recognizing the humanity of the Congolese natives. In the Congo site, Sheppard and Lapsley became equal coworkers, and their relationship sharply brought to light the kind of humanity that the Southern Church and the entire American society of the time lacked. As Walter Williams observes, "Lapsley and Sheppard worked well as a team [...]. Racial proscriptions broke down, and they worked together as equals" (1982:24). In fact, Sara Pratt Lapsley, Sam's mother, sowed the seed of that vision when, consciously undermining the racist and absurd arrangement of the Southern Presbyterian Church, she entrusted her twenty-three-year-old son to Sheppard's care as she bade them farewell in New York, saying: "Sheppard, take care of Sam!" (Sheppard 1917:15). Apart from her knowledge of her own marginalization as a woman and Irish American in American society, Sara's intervention here could have been also inspired by the anticolonial radical ideological developments that were taking place during that time in Britain and its empire and spreading to America. Commenting on this rise of anti-imperial radicalism, Elleke Boehmer notes:

> During the same 1890–1920 period the metropolis witnessed a rising social and political radicalism, galvanized at crucial points by the campaigns for Irish Home Rule, by women's struggle for self-representation, and by the international spread of socialist and Marxist ideas, formalized within the (Euro-centered) Second International (1889–1914). The time therefore marked the beginning of the development of a more global dimension to radical networking and organization.
> (2005b:4)

Sarah Lapsley's sense of social justice and Christian ethics can be compared to that of two Irish veterans of the Congo Christian mission, Dr. Henry Guinness (the founder of the Livingstone Inland Mission in the Congo and the Director of the Bolobo Baptist Mission) and his wife Fanny, who warmly welcomed Sam Lapsley and Sheppard as coequal Christian brothers at the foreign missionary training East London Institute called "Harley House." Acknowledging their hospitality, Sheppard writes in his autobiography:

> We received the greatest hospitality possible at 'Harley House' from Dr. Henry Grattan Guinness and family. They spared no pains in helping us in every way they could. We hadn't words to express our gratitude to them. This whole family was imbued with the missionary spirit.
> (1917:20)

Their humanistic dispositions contrast sharply with the racially biased attitude of the American diplomat Henry Sanford who, disregarding Sheppard, only recommended Sam Lapsley to his European friends for assistance and for a visit with King Leopold II in Belgium. As William Phipps remarks, "Like Morgan in Washington, Sanford gave no attention to Sheppard; both white politicians shared the usual secular [racist] outlook on blacks" (2002:17). Thanks to Sanford's introduction, Sam Lapsley was received by King Leopold II who, being apprehensive about Black Americans' empathetic, investigative interactions with natives in the Congo, insisted "that if American negroes came, they must not hope to remain a separate colony, distinct from the State, but become citizens of the country and obey its laws" (Lapsley 1893:44). Like George Washington Williams before him, Lapsley ironically came out of his audience with the King with a positive idea of the latter's deceptive, proclaimed philanthropic intention for the Congo: "I treated him just as I would any man I thought good and great. I asked nothing of him but his protection" (45). However, Lapsley ignored all Sanford's and the King's attempts to racially privilege him over his coworker and companion Sheppard. Sheppard confirmed this in his letter to Sara Lapsley upon his son's return from Brussels to London: "We spent a month in England, being together always" (1917:85).

Unlearning western invention of Africa

After a month of preparation in London in the company of the Guinnesses and other Christian well-wishers, Sheppard and Lapsley left for the Dutch port city of Rotterdam. From there, they sailed to the Congo aboard a Dutch vessel the *Afrikaan* and arrived at the port city of Banana in the Congo Free State, on May 9, 1890, after three weeks. As Phipps states: "Any homesickness Sheppard might have felt on leaving the United States was quickly dispelled after he set foot on the continent of his ancestors" (19). In Banana, they had their first encounter with a dignified Congolese royalty, King Domgolia, who received them well. Sheppard reports this visit in a somewhat condescending tone in the Christian magazine *The Missionary*:

> We were escorted by a native brother to visit his majesty King Domgolia [...]. The King has not learned to wear pants, hat, or shoes yet. He had a piece of cloth around his shoulders and waist, and a staff in his hand.
> (Sheppard 1890:355)

Sheppard's tone here surprisingly contrasts with Lapsley's positive impression of the King, and it reflects his early Western-inculcated idea of Africans as savages:

> We went on beyond the mission station to the native village, where we saw our first live African king, his royal highness, Domgele, imposing, deliberate, wrapped in a toga like Roman senator, and walking with a royal reed studded with brass nail heads.
> (Lapsley 1893:54)

Before moving hinterland toward the Kasai River where they had been planning to establish a Presbyterian mission station, Sheppard and Lapsley spent about a month in the Lower Congo (present Bas-Congo) and learned a lot about the natives' varied attitudes toward Western strangers (white government officials, settlers, explorers, and missionaries). On this, Lapsley reports:

> Since Stanley, the State officials, and even the white settlement here, is called *Bula Matari*. (Stanley's native name; it means breaker-of-rocks, from his road-making achievements! [in fact torture of natives]) White man is *mundila*; the missionary is *mundila –nzambi*, "God's white man"; or, sometimes, *nganga-nzambi*, "God's medicine man." If a party of white men approaches a lower Congo village the cry goes round: "Who is coming?" Answer, "*Mundila*." "What *Mundila*?" Answer, "*Mundila-nzambi*," then out they all come to talk to and welcome the traveller. But if "*Weh! Bula Matari*" then "*Sh-sh!*" and whiz they all go to hide in the long grass!
> (Lapsley 1893:55)

Earlier than Lapsley's observation, another open-minded English missionary, Mr. Richard, of the Banza Manteke Mission Station, had explained the genesis of the natives' mistrust of white people in the manner that reminds us of Equiano's experiences. Richard advised:

> Remember that they knew white men before they knew missionaries! It is not long since slavery was done away with. Traders and officers are not always so kind as they should be. Anyway, the African idea of a white man is that he is a devil; and it takes a good deal of intimate association with one who obeys the law of love, and treats him as a brother and an equal, before he begins to feel that a white man can be a human brother!
> (Guinness 1890:94–95)

This knowledge of the natives' deep mistrust of brutal white colonial officials and settlers (which started with the brutal regimen of hard labor, torture, and killing designed and implemented on behalf of King Leopold II by his agent Henry Morton Stanley) led Sheppard and Lapsley to reassess the validity of King Leopold's proclaimed humanitarian intention of his regime in the Congo. It also motivated them to learn more about local cultures, life-worlds, and languages by directly engaging the Congolese natives in dialogue rather than listening to white officials and settlers. This became their guiding vision as Sheppard and Lapsley moved up the Congo River with a caravan of two dozen African porters. On their way, they passed native villages (some welcoming, others hostile because of their bitter experiences with government officials) and stopped over at different protestant mission stations (at Boma, Matadi, Palabala, Banza Manteke, and Lukunga). They reached Stanley Pool or Leopoldville (present Kinshasa) after a two-week exhausting trek during which they witnessed the untold suffering of the Congolese natives at the hands of government officials and traders. Sheppard was particularly abhorred over coming across the "sun-bleached skeletons of native carriers here and there who by sickness, hunger or fatigue, had laid themselves down to die, without fellow or friend" (Sheppard 1917:28–29). These are the same colonial atrocities witnessed and criticized also by the Anglo-Polish writer Joseph Conrad (as depicted in his novella *Heart of Darkness*), whom Lapsley met and dubbed "gentlemanly fellow" at Doctor Aaron Sims's hospital in Kinshasa (Lapsley 1893:83).

While in Stanley Pool, Lapsley took a trip to Bolobo Baptist Mission to visit with and seek advice from George Grenfell, whom George Williams also had spent time with earlier, on a possible mission site in the Kasai region. Meanwhile, Sheppard went back to Lukunga to recruit porters for the next travel and took that opportunity to bond with the natives; he endeared himself to native Bateke and shared a sense of conviviality with them. He hunted hippopotami with his Martini Henry Rifle under their guidance and supplied them with the much-needed meat ration. However, during one of his hunting expeditions, Sheppard went against the natives' wise counsel, swam in a crocodile-infested river to retrieve a hippopotamus that he had just shot, and almost paid the price with his life. Here is how he narrates this episode in his autobiography:

> Taking the rope and putting the loop on my arm, I jumped in and swam to the hippo. As I began to tie the rope around her nose, up came a monster crocodile and made a terrible lunge at her neck. Not a moment did I tarry to see what effect his sharp teeth had on the hippo, but turned the rope loose and under the water I went, and was half way to the shore when I came up. The natives were very much excited and assisted me in landing. I begged their pardon and was ashamed of my bravery. Many times in Central Africa foreigners get into serious difficulties from which they cannot extricate themselves, by disregarding the advice of the natives.
>
> (1917:39)

From that point on, Sheppard decided to no longer disregard local knowledge and could even accommodate some of their "superstitious" beliefs. For example, at the request of the natives, he refrained from killing "a very large bull hippo [that] bowed his neck, grunted in a deep, and came rushing towards the bank" (37). The natives believed that that hippo was their chief's totem, and that if killed, chief Banqua would also die. In a letter to his home headquarters published in the Christian magazine *The Missionary*, Lapsley commented admiringly on the bond that Sheppard had developed with Congolese natives:

> Brother Sheppard has, in every way, justified the predictions of his friends. He has won the esteem of missionaries as a true man and a

gentleman, while with natives he is, according to Dr. Sims, the most popular man that ever came to this station [Kinshasa]. He has the constitution needed, and the gift of getting on in Africa. While I was away he devoted much time to hunting on the river, and has actually brought home twelve "hippos," to the great delight of the blacks and admiration of Europeans.

(*The Missionary*, 1/1891:34)

In December 1890, Sheppard, Lapsley, and their company boarded the Baptist steamer *Henry Reed* on the Congo River and headed toward the mouth of the Kasai River in search of a new and easily accessible mission site for their Presbyterian mission station. Disembarking at the mouth of the Kasai River, they canoed and hitchhiked rides on it. During their journey, Sheppard interacted and worked equally with native boatmen and porters while continuing to hunt along the way. When they reached the Musye village, where they decided to rest so that Lapsley could recover from a bout of malaria, Sheppard came across another dignified, hospitable royalty in the person of Queen N'Gankabe. Sheppard describes her in his autobiography as "tall, broad-shouldered, bronze colored, well-featured woman [...]" (44). The fearless and self-assured Queen, whose houses were adorned with human skulls, had also previously impressed Henry Stanley who described her a number of years before Sheppard in these vivid words:

Without the slightest sign of timidity she steered her fort-five foot canoe alongside [....] She brought her paddle inboard, and with her right arm to her waist, she examined us keenly [....] Her attentive survey of 'Bula Matadi' was with interest reciprocated.

(Stanley 1885:424)

Queen N'Gankabe is believed to be the African woman, often called Kurtz's African mistress, in Joseph Conrad's novella *Heart of Darkness*.

Politely declining the Queen's invitation to establish their church in her village, Sheppard, Lapsley, and their native assistants continued their journey up the Kasai River through hostile villages and environment until they reached the village of Boleke near the junction of the Kwango and Kasai Rivers. Thanks to Sheppard's convivial interactions with local natives there (including sharing hippo meat with them), they were welcomed and invited to establish their mission station amongst them. Lapsley described their encounter with the Boleke natives and Sheppard's humane, reassuring approach in one of his letters:

They were a little timid, but not ill disposed, afraid to invite us ashore, yet not at all desirous that we should leave. So we landed quietly and stood about, as unconcerned as could be. They crowded around us in a few minutes, but if we happened to look straight at any fellow, he would dodge behind somebody like a flash. Finally Sheppard, born a trader, started buying wood and fish, and the ice was broken. Women crowded around with enough wood to build a small shanty, and fish for two meals, fresh, sweet and large, for a trifle.

(Lapsley 1893:108)

Sheppard also describes in his autobiography how his party won the Boleke natives' friendship by "smiles" and pleasantry, the attitude that sharply contrasted with the callous, colonial behaviors of government officials and greedy foreign traders (Sheppard 1917:36).

Sheppard, Lapsley, and their party continued their exploration up the River Kwango, reaching and exploring a part of one of its tributaries the Kwilu River. However, as Sheppard recounts, they decided to return to Boleke because "The country was too low and swampy, the villages small and far apart. They had no king, but were governed by small chiefs" (Sheppard 1917:47–48). Upon their return to Boleke on January 24, 1891, Sheppard and Lapsley were shocked and angrily appalled to find out that the large welcoming village and others that they had left only a few days before were devastated and burned down by Captain Guillaume Van Kerckhoven who commanded 14 Belgian officers and 500 native soldiers armed with rifles into the hunt for ivory along the River Kasai. The Captain's expedition known as the "Van Kerckhoven Expedition" was commissioned by King Leopold II toward the end of 1890 to hunt for ivory in Congo Free State. As a result of their brutal atrocities, the natives in Boleke and other riverine villages became hostile to all whites and could no longer accommodate the Americans. Since Lapsley was the one mostly treated with suspicion by the angry natives, he decided to strongly disassociate Sheppard and himself from Belgian officials while pledging loyalty to the Boleke villagers' cause:

> I took this chance to explain that our business was not to trade, but to teach the will of their King and ours, the God who made us both; and that we teach that God forbids men to kill, steal, and commit adultery; and that our teaching is the best pledge that we will be good neighbors.
>
> (Lapsley 1893:126)

However, facing a distraught people (especially upon hearing the news that Queen N'Gankabe's two sons had been captured and taken into servitude to the Lower Congo), Sheppard and Lapsley decided to go back to Leopoldville (Kinshasa). On March 17, 1991, they took another exploratory trip on board the steamer the *Florida* (formerly owned by Henry Sanford's defunct ivory and rubber trading company and for a short time commanded by Joseph Conrad) in search of a mission site in the Upper Kasai, where the Belgian Trading Company had just established several stations accessible to steamers.

As the *Florida* cruised during its month-long journey up the Congo River toward the mouth of the Kasai River and on its tributary the Lulua River,

Sheppard took the opportunity to appreciate the very rich Congolese fauna and flora as well as the African life-world and lived experiences during the colonial encroachment. He was appalled upon coming across villages devastated by Captain Van Kerckhoven's raiders and hunters of ivory, but he often found a relief in the bustling Congolese trading activities along the river and their rich environment. Of the Congolese fauna and flora, Sheppard writes:

> We saw scores of large black monkeys leaping from tree to tree, and droves of parrots flying in the air as thick as blackbirds [...]. On both banks of the river there is a dense forest of mahogany, ebony, iron wood, evergreens and palms [...]. The streams all abound with splendid fish [...]. There are plenty of elephant, buffalo, and antelopes; their tracks and trails are all along the river bank. In this dense and impenetrable forest there must be everything imaginable.
> (1917:58–59)

The realistic, picturesque portrait of the Congolese environment given by Sheppard here is a far cry from Joseph Conrad's conditioned imagining of it through Marlow's gaze, as depicted in *Heart of Darkness*: "Going up the river was like travelling back to the earliest beginnings of the world, when vegetation rioted on the earth and the big trees were kings. An empty stream, a great silence, an impenetrable forest" (Conrad 1946:92–93).

On the ship, Sheppard and Lapsley also empathized and shared whatever little food rations and medicines they had with starving and sick African workers and defended them against the cruel Belgian Captain's physical abuse (the whipping with Chicote). On one occasion, Sheppard was called upon by the Captain to help steer the vessel into the right course as they entered the "strong current of the Kasai River" and he "did so with pleasure." Sheppard's remarkable bonding with Africans and his readiness to assist people in need wherever they travelled since touching the Congo soil gradually transformed and humanized Lapsley. As noted by Pagan Kennedy:

> After two months of floating through the Kwango with Sheppard, Lapsley had changed; he 'd watched how Sheppard coaxed the Africans, charmed them, fed them, flirted with them. [...] Lapsley seemed not to know which tribe he belonged to anymore.
> (Kennedy 2002:57–58)

Turning Luebo into a postcolonial outpost

The *Florida* finally reached the town of Luebo, the main ivory and rubber trading center for the State-owned Belgian Trading Company in the Upper Kasai. Lapsley described the strategic town as "the center of influence from which the trade radiates" (1893:163). Following the advice of Mr. Engeringh, the Belgian Commissioner of the Kasai district, who happened to be in Luebo at the time of their arrival, Sheppard and Lapsley went to a nearby Kete village of Bena Kasenga to negotiate with the elders for permission to establish a Presbyterian mission amongst them. As reported in *The Missionary* (2/1905:60), the cordial and respectful negotiation for a piece of land went this way with the help of an interpreter: "They [the Kete elders], 'Will you trade in ivory or rubber?' We said, 'No, we do not wish to trade; our work is to teach about God.' They laughed and thought that was a strange business." This dialogue contrasts the arrogant and colonial attitude of the Belgian Commissioner toward the natives and their land with that of the American missionaries who recognized the Kete people as the true owners of the land. While the Commissioner gave them permission to go and start their evangelization of the Congolese natives at the Village of Bena Kasenga without any regard to its elders' opinion, Sheppard and Lapsley respectfully decided to seek the true land owners' approval. By so doing, they positioned themselves as postcolonial allies of the natives in their resistance against colonial occupation of their land.

With the approval of the Kete elders, Sheppard, Lapsley, and their Congolese assistants pitched their tent near Bena Kasenga on the hill overlooking the Lulua River. There they sowed the seed of what later on became the most flourishing and influential Presbyterian mission station in the Upper Kasai. Its proximity to the then unexplored Kuba land, its attraction to local traders from other neighboring regions, and its accessibility to steamers from the Lower Congo ports delighted the American missionaries, even though they were on the first day overcome by feelings of forlornness and nostalgia on being far away from their land of birth, America.

With their "broadest and best smiles," Sheppard and Lapsley quickly engaged in a deep exploration of the Congolese natives' life-world and lived experiences. Through their open-minded, sustained cultural dialogue with the Congolese natives, the American missionaries put their drive for evangelism in the back seat. On the one hand, Sheppard and Lapsley learned the local languages (Tshikete and Tshiluba), carefully observed local belief systems and social practices, admired local architecture and arts, familiarized themselves with the Congolese rich environmental diversity, learned to eat local foodstuffs (cassava, game meat, crickets, birds, and other delicacies), and mostly understood natives' hostility and resistance to white government officials and traders as well as their African soldiers; and on the other, they gradually introduced the natives to aspects of Western modernity like literacy (books), modern medicine, Western clothing, Western technology (matches, watch, mirror, and rifle), and Christianity. Rather than impose Western modernity on the natives or manipulate their conception of the white people by means of technological trickery, as Henry Stanley had done before them, Sheppard and Lapsley encouraged the natives to freely encounter its positive and empowering aspects through the process of education and observation as autonomous subjects. In the style reminiscent of Olaudah Equiano's description of the Ibo society that he got captured and enslaved from in the 18th century, Sheppard positively describes their cordial interactions with the local Kete people and their socio-economic activities this way:

> We made daily visits to the village, mingling with the people, learning their language and curious customs. They all wore their native cloth ranging from the waist to their knees. They were given to hearty laughter, joking, playing games, and running races. Many of them cultivated the ground, raising manioc, peas, beans and tobacco, and others spent their time hunting and fishing. Every night there was a dance held in the big square in the center of the town. The noise from their toms-toms, ivory horns, and singing filled the air until midnight.
>
> (1917:67)

Like Equiano, Sheppard also dispels the Western-imagined notion of African savagery in his description of the Kete people's spiritual beliefs and judicial system:

> Every fourth day no one on account of the spirits went a long journey, hunted, fished or worked his fields. The day was spent sweeping around their houses, mending their nets, making mats, weaving cloth, and holding court. Court was held in the square of the town under a large shed. The people had their judges, jurors, lawyers and officers of the town, but no written laws, and all evildoers were punished by fines. A man that was found guilty of murder was forced to hang himself.
>
> (72)

Lapsley who grew fond of the Kete people also debunked the Western constructed image of black people as lazy, dishonest, barbarous, lacking in ingenuity, and frozen in time. He said of them:

> They are very genial and good humored, as you know, and lying, stealing, and impurity are considered disgraceful [...]. They have an idea of God, the Creator and preserver of all things, and a tradition that a closer acquaintance with him existed.
>
> (1893:228)

Lapsley further stated in two of his letters quoted at length here because of their standing as a part of the counter-discursive corpus enunciated by the enslaved and colonized black subjects like Toussaint L'Ouverture and Olaudah Equiano in the 18th-century modern world:

> Busy folks. Very few without something to do. But the principle business outside of bread-making [...] is the manufacture of plain grass

cloth. It is not made of grass at all, but of the inner strips of the leaves of a small, dark palm [...]. I saw the manufacture in all its stages—boys stripping off outside of the leaf blade, and leaving the delicate green ribbons within, and tying them into hands like yarn. Men were separating it, threading the loom with the warp; and then came the clack of the simple, but complete weaving machine, the simple, silent passage of the long polished stick which does duty as shuttle, and thus the usual everyday waist or loin cloth is finished. But the women pound a few choice pieces in a mortar with flour of maize or manioc till it is soft and satiny to the feel. These are dyed and worn on special occasions.

(1893:167)

Having settled down and being accepted by the people of Luebo as good friends, reliable neighbors, and respectful strangers, Sheppard and Lapsley decided to move out of the tent and build an environmentally suitable dwelling. For that, they respectfully approached a property owner who was willing to sell them his side-by-side houses for a bargaining session. Both parties amicably agreed on the price, and they bought the houses.

After many months of fruitful and mutually empowering interactions with the Bakete and the Baluba, Sheppard and Lapsley started preaching Christianity to the Congolese natives while allowing them to ask probing questions about the new faith. Sheppard was particularly enthusiastic in encouraging African music and dancing in the church. As Kennedy states:

when it came to dressing Africans in cheap calico cloth and forcing them down on their knees to pray, Sheppard was profoundly ambivalent. He had too much respect for Africans to strip them of their culture and teach them to imitate Americans.

(Kennedy 2002:82)

In addition to preaching the gospel, they ransomed slaves like the orphan girl Malemba, who later became a leading Christian figure in Luebo, and treated the sick (Lapsley was especially regarded as the village doctor). They also started thinking of exploring other areas of the Kasai region. In June 1891, Sheppard and a number of native assistants took a two-month exploratory trip toward Weismann Falls, south of Luebo, and came across other hospitable Kasai villages. They also discovered a lake, which he named "Lake Sheppard" and other tributary streams.

As soon as Sheppard returned to Luebo, Lapsley, who had remained behind to take care of business at the mission station, also left for an exploration of the southeastern Kasai in November 1891. The main purpose of his trip was to recruit construction workers from other ethnic groups for the development of the Luebo mission station. During his trip that took him to Luluaburg (now Kananga), the headquarters of the Kasai District, Lapsley came across other ethnic groups (the Lulua, the Luba, and the slave traders

Zappo Zaps) who were very receptive to his Christian message and wanted him to remain amongst them. As Phipps states, there "Inhabitants of two villages were surprised to see a different kind of white man, one who was not threatening and who was accompanied by well-behaved men" (Phipps 2002:63). And on Lapsley's return journey to the mission station, Sheppard reports that "All along the route natives who had fallen in love with him joined the caravan. In many cases men with their wives, children, goats, sheep, and all their belongings followed him to Luebo" (1917:79–80). Most of the people who followed him were members of the large Luba ethnic group looked down upon by other ethnic groupings in Kasai. Lapsley arrived in Luebo with tattered clothes and in a declining state of health, but he received a hero's welcome by his concerned coworker Sheppard and enthusiastic native friends. Sheppard reports: "How happy we were when a runner announced Mr. Lapsley's arrival. With the big ivory horn blowing and the drums beating, we ran down the banana walk to greet and welcome him home" (1917:80).

While Lapsley was gone, Sheppard and his native assistants worked hard on the property, clearing the ground, and planting pineapple and banana trees. On this, Lapsley delightfully wrote: "I found Sheppard had improved the place greatly, cleaning and clearing up the ground and planting us a banana avenue up to our door" (217). Soon after their arrival in Luebo, the workers that Lapsley brought with him further cleared the mission ground felling trees, uprooting stumps, and putting up additional buildings.

Thus, thanks to Sheppard and Lapsley's progressive Christian vision, informed by a strong sense of social justice and racial equality, Luebo was transformed into an empowering postcolonial space, a haven for Congolese natives (like the Baluba) who sought refuge from colonial brutality, interethnic oppression, and enslavement. It became an exemplary space of a progressive encounter (or locus of cultural translation) between the English and African languages, Christian songs and African dancing styles, and Western modernity and African cultures. The encounter was appropriately marked by two symbolic acts: on the one hand, Sheppard and Lapsley named two streets after the French capital Paris and the White House Street Pennsylvania Avenue, and on the other hand, the natives renamed the two missionaries: Mundele Ndombe (Sheppard) and N'tomenjila (Lapsley). Because of its postcolonial standing, the Government of the Congo Free State saw the station as a danger to their exploitative and inhuman interests. It was therefore not surprising that the Governor-General of the Free State in Boma wrote the missionaries a letter that the land on which the mission station was standing had been given to another company. The letter went against the advice they had received from the Kasai District Commissioner and the Bena Kasenga village elders' approval, and Lapsley decided to go down to Boma in order to personally appeal to the Governor-General.

In January 1892, despite his vulnerable health condition, Lapsley boarded the *Florida* on its return journey to the Lower Congo. Here again, on boarding the ship, he shared in the suffering of the ill-treated African crew members and tried to alleviate it. As Kennedy notes:

> But now, perhaps because he himself suffered, he spent time among the African crew. He noticed the lines of worry that wrinkled their faces; the scabs on their legs; the glances they traded among each other; the ways that they, Nigerians, were different from the Kete he'd come to know.

From his postcolonial gaze at that stage of his self-transformation, Lapsley saw them as "fellow-sufferers: disease-ridden, lonely for their families, haunted by what they'd seen in war camps and burned villages" (Kennedy 2002:76).

The *Florida* reached Kinshasa in January 1892, and Lapsley went to see Dr. Aaron Sims for a medical checkup. Because of his poor state of health, Dr. Sims advised him to return to the United States, but he declined his advice, preferring to continue his work amongst the Congolese people. In fact, Lapsley and Sheppard were already planning to venture into the hostile Kuba land and establish another Presbyterian mission station as well as schools there.

Lapsley eventually made it to Boma and on March 17, 1892, had a dinner with the Governor-General who, in his own words, "was very obliging— only heard my case at four p.m., put it through, and handed me the letter when we came to dinner. Thanked God and took courage. I go back to Matadi tomorrow" (1893:225–226). So, thanks to his courage and sacrifice, the land on which the mission stood (10 hectares) in Luebo was finally registered as American Presbyterian Congo Mission (APCM) property. A few days after his fruitful meeting with the Governor-General, Lapsley became seriously ill with a prolonged, severe fever at the American Baptist Mission station at Tunduwa. He was cared for by Baptist missionaries, including Grenfell of the Bolobo American Baptist station, who happened to be at Tunduwa at the time. To the great grief and consternation of the missionaries, Sheppard and the natives he had endeared himself to, Lapsley succumbed to "bilious hematuric fever" on March 26, 1892. He was laid to rest at Tunduwa cemetery alongside earlier missionaries, only two years into his eventful Christian and humanistic labor in the Congo.

The postcolonial Samuel Lapsley

Indeed, during the two years that Lapsley spent in the Congo, he exemplarily transformed himself from an agent of the rigid Western modernity to a pragmatic postcolonial worker. Pagan Kennedy has cogently described Lapsley's remarkable transformation (which stood against his own initial expectations, and those of his home public and Church) in this full-length quotation:

> Lapsley had sailed to Africa believing that a missionary's job was to convert as many people as possible. He would preach to the half-clad

heathen, and they—weeping with joy to hear Truth—would dress in three-piece suits or billowing skirts and file into the makeshift churches he built for them. Every year, he would send a figure back to the Presbyterians at home, and it would be published in Foreign Missions annual report under the heading "Converts to Christianity." Lapsley, the dreamy young man, must have imagined that his number of converts would someday be very high indeed. [...] But things had not gone as he hoped. After a year and a half in Africa, he hadn't managed to make a single convert. Instead, he kneeled before the Nigerian boatmen, swabbing pus from the cankers on their legs. And as he did so, something quite unexpected happened. Without the permission of the Presbyterian elders or their Foreign Missions board, Lapsley humbled himself before the men he once called savages. He emulated Christ.

(Kennedy 2002:76–77)

Because the cultural translation process that led to Lapsley's remarkable transformation was unique during that time (and is still relevant today), it would be pertinent to elaborate a bit on it in the following section of the chapter. Before Samuel Lapsley traveled to Africa as a missionary, he had sent a letter to the Southern Presbyterian Church Secretary of Foreign Missions, Reverend M.H. Houston, stating:

I hereby ask to be sent by Your Committee as your missionary to the Congo Valley, in Africa. I do so because it is my desire and conviction that I should preach Christ to the heathen, and for several reasons I want to go to Africa, if God and the church permit me.

(Lapsley 1893:21)

So, like his Black American companion Sheppard, Lapsley imagined himself as a kind of savior the African people needed in order to emerge from what the Western mind had misrepresented as their pre-historic darkness (see, e.g., Conrad 1899). However, as he began his long journey to the Congo, Lapsley had first to reconcile himself with his mother's progressive vision of racial equality by first undermining the grammar of White Americans' racism toward their black compatriots and considering Sheppard as his coworker. Both the ship that took him from New York to England (*Adriatic*) and England itself surprisingly provided him with opportunities to revise his American society's negative attitudes toward blacks. In a reassuring letter to his mother, Lapsley indicated that on the ship "Sheppard is very politely treated" (Lapsley 1893:27) and that in England "the English don't notice at all what seems very odd to us" (34), the skin color of his black fellow. He also described Sheppard as "very modest, and easy to get along with; also quite an aid in sight-seeing, and in anything else where I need help" (34). In return to Sheppard's assistance and guidance to him, Lapsley also blurred the racial division between them by showing concern for his wellbeing and praising him. However, when they arrived in the Congo, both Sheppard and Lapsley showed ambivalent attitudes toward Congolese people's humanity as they still maintained their civilizing mission. Even as Lapsley was being transformed by his encounter with the Congolese people, his inconsistent representations of them in his public diaries and private letters betrayed a sense of ambivalence in his attitude toward their cultural values. It is this ambivalence that they displayed at the initial point of their encounter with Africans that made Lapsley and Sheppard appear as undecidable colonial subjects amenable to change.

Lapsley first documented his encounter with Africans as he and Sheppard approached the Congo shore in his diary on May 9, 1890:

> Then came the first boat alongside, with its crew of half-clad Africans, just like our own darkies; it made me feel quite at home to see them, muscular, active, rather slight than big, and with faces I liked to watch. It was pleasant to hear them sing, as a boat crew rowed Sully, Sheppard and myself to the shore. The "stroke," a fine-looking fellow, took the verse and the rest joined heartily in the refrain. The words were simple sounding and musical; the syllables are so many and quick that the rhythm is marked and carries you along with it. The tones are weird and strange. I liked it.
>
> (Lapsley 1893:52)

In this first encounter with Africans, Lapsley ambivalently imagined them against the framework of the then American society's constructed grammar of the black people, the "darkies," which he had been trying to dissociate himself from in his attitude to Sheppard. When Lapsley first interacted with West African "Kruboys," he condescendingly called their creolized English a "queer feature of West coast life," and "a perverted English, seasoned with bad French, with no inflection, and very limited vocabulary, one word being made to do duty for ten kindred shades of meaning" (Lapsley 1893:54). That way, he initially constructed the native African as the negative other of the Western modernity. As Bill Ashcroft has rightly argued, this "concern for 'proper' speech [is] a classic demonstration of cultural hegemony" (2001:58).

However, although he stereotypically described the first Africans he came across as other Western observers of the time would do (half-clad Africans, the tones of their music weird and strange), Lapsley felt a certain common kinship with them and their music. Unlike his negative description of the Kruboys' English, he showed a keen interest in and admiration for a native Congolese language, *Ki-fiote*, which he later learned and constantly interpolated when describing his interactions with the natives in his diaries and letters. Lapsley's quick mastery of the language bridged the gulf between him and the natives. In a letter to his mother describing how he learned *Ki-fiote*, he mentioned that part of the process was listening to how his workers spoke and writing down the new words he heard. Throughout the process, Lapsley was humbled by his

The postcolonial pragmatist 71

hosts who encouragingly and proudly "patted me on the back very patronizingly" when he responded to their questions "in good grammar" (1893:130). Very soon, he became more comfortable talking with the natives in what he called "white man's *fiote*" rather than English. For example:

> At Lutete, or N'Gombe's, I preached in English, and one of the missionaries interpreted; but it was very unsatisfactory, hard to 'keep up steam.' I like it much better to speak in 'white man's *fiote*,' though it was little I could say, and that in perfect innocence of grammar and of the language. Still I could tell for myself the story of Jesus, and they understood me. We were in touch.
>
> (1893:71)

Here, Lapsley made the English language subservient to the native idiom and was able to enjoy a sense of conviviality with the natives. By encouraging Lapsley to use their language, the natives also resisted the force of the foreign language that sought to shape them as antithetical "others" and induced him to undergo the process of cultural hybridity. As maintained by Deborah Kapchan and Pauline Strong, this blending of languages, or creolization, as articulated by Lapsley in the Congo context, "facilitates a two-way uncontrolled transfer of goods, or knowledges" (1990:241). Like Said's notion of calculated disruption of the colonial order, this process of cultural translation, exchange, and interpolation emphasized "the ambivalent, fluid, chaotic relationships within the colonial exchanges and indeed of social reality itself" by turning to "the concept of the *rhizome*, first coined by Deleuze and Guattari" (Ashcroft 2001:50, see also Losambe 2005).

This rhizomic system (see also DeLoughrey 2007) challenges the binary system of colonizer and colonized, self and other, and more accurately portrays Lapsley's mutually transformative interactions with the natives. As Ashcroft has noted, the "rhizomic structure of imperialist discourse leaves many spaces or discursive fractures in which ambivalence and intention meet. These fractures are the spaces opened up for counter-discourse" (Ashcroft 2001:52, see also Bhabha 1994:129–131, and Bauman 1991:179). This transformation occurs at all points of contact, especially through language appropriation. Even as Lapsley introduced Christianity to the natives and traded goods with them, he had to do so in "white man's *fiote*" or creolized *Ki-fiote* that connected him with the natives and turned his ambivalent positioning into postcolonial agency. In the "Prefatory Note" *to Lapsley's Life and Letters*, James Lapsley indirectly acknowledged his son's cultural transformation in the Congo when commenting on Lapsley's unusual use of the English language in his diary:

> In his daily intercourse with people of divers tongues, he acquired polyglot capacities and habits which naturally show themselves in his familiar writings, in editing which an effort was at first made to translate or substitute the strange words that occur with others.

James Lapsley further noted: "there are no established rules of spelling, and hence we must not think it strange to find the same word written by him in different ways at different times" (Lapsley 1893:iii) in his diary. Sam Lapsley's father's reaction to his son's unusual English should be noted as a tacit acknowledgement that he was initiating a disruptive counter-discourse to Western modernity's colonial "structure of attitudes" (Said 1993). Although Lapsley and Sheppard's initial motivation in learning local languages was instrumental (they needed the languages in order to spread Christianity), it inevitably became integrative as their interaction with the Congolese natives deepened and transcended the confines of their missionary limits. It is in acknowledgement of this integrative motivation that Sheppard was able to confess in one of his letters: "I am certainly happy in the country of my forefathers" (qtd. in Williams 1982:23–24). As a result of this affinity that Sheppard developed with the Congolese natives, he was ready to fight for their human rights as well, and Walter Williams is right when he states that "The missionary who made the most significant protest against imperialism was William Sheppard. He exerted a major influence in exposing atrocities in the Belgian 'Congo Free State'" (1982:138).

Through trade, Lapsley and Sheppard also engaged in mutually transformative interactions with the natives. Describing the importance of trade for the natives, Lapsley wrote that "The ruling passion [for them] is trade. What they make they keep, and many of them are very 'nigh'—I might say all. There is none of the thriftlessness and wastefulness characteristic of many negroes at home" (Lapsley 1893:69). Here, he simultaneously praised the natives (although he still called them "unsophisticated busmen" and "heathens" in his letters and diary), while criticizing the Black Americans back home and thus inviting the reader to decouple race and culture. In praising Sheppard's sense of commitment to duty, he positively compared him to the natives and debunked the Western constructed myth of the laziness of the black people. In the Congo, every time Lapsley and Sheppard went to a village, Sheppard was always the first to create a connection with the villagers by dialoguing and exchanging goods with them. When they first got to the Kwango River, for example, Lapsley reported that Sheppard "born trader, started buying wood and fish, and the ice was broken" (Lapsley 1893:108). As they interacted with Sheppard and Lapsley, the natives also started to revise their construction of the whiteness and its association with colonial brutality. So, as much as they trusted Sheppard more than Lapsley, a white man who reminded them too much of the colonial State officials in some instances, they still related to him convivially. It is in acknowledgement of what natives saw as Lapsley's cultural open-mindedness that they named him "Mutomba Ndjila," meaning "Pathfinder" (Lapsley 1893:207 and Sheppard 1917:87). The natives' positive attitudes toward Sheppard also encouraged further Lapsley's deep sense of respect toward him as a fellow Christian and American coworker. Thus, even though Sheppard was appointed under his command because of his race, in the Congo, Lapsley ironically treated him as his superior guide because of the way that he interacted directly with the natives, especially in trade and hunting activities. Because of Sheppard's respect for the natives, they also named him "Mundele Ndombe," the "black white man." In a letter to his mother, Lapsley noted that Sheppard was

> a most handy fellow, and is now a thorough river-man. I don't feel quite green myself now. His temper is bright and even—really a man of unusual graces and strong points of character. So I am thankful to God for Sheppard.
>
> (Lapsley 1893:94)

Thus, by logging his multifaceted, daily interactions with the Congolese natives in diverse ethnic locations, Lapsley produced a document that encouraged anticolonial action and postcolonial thought. Yet, at the same time, that document contains letters with contradictory statements, such as "I have got quite often used to black faces, or rather bodies bare down to the waist, and half way up the leg" (Lapsley 1893:82), sent to his Aunt Elsie, as well as the following statement sent to his mother: "You don't know how satisfying it is to see a white lady after so many months of savagery" (223–224). Although Lapsley's overall representation of the natives in his diary and letters is ambiguous, it, nevertheless, pushes at the dominant modernist discursive order, blurring the binary of us and them into a rhizomic web of interactions. An instance of his critical attitude toward the inhumane treatment of the natives by the colonial regime of King Leopold II, with the complicity of Christian missions and trading companies, can be seen in the following extract from his letter to "The Fowler Hall Clan:"

> Every ten minutes, I really believe, I met a little party of these carriers trotting nimbly through the pretty avenues in the upland woods, a line of shining blacks, surmounted by boxes or bales, and always in Indian file, though the State has had the various chiefs clear a road twenty feet wide all the way. Though very familiar now, it seems to me like a dream, that this should be done in thirteen years after the discovery of the Congo. The traders certainly see reason to believe there is money in it; but what does God mean by it?
>
> (85)

The Kongo native chief and his subjects who wept upon hearing the news of Lapsley's death certainly endorsed his humanistic work amongst them. Sheppard describes Lapsley's mutually endearing relationship with the natives as he was about to embark on his last and fateful journey to the Atlantic coast from Luebo this way: "The beach was crowded with natives to wave him good-bye. The stranger who had come to their land on a strange errand was now known and loved" (1917:85).

Expanding postcolonial cultural hybridity to Kuba land

After Lapsley's death, Sheppard carried on with the same engaged vision but with a strong sense of political activism directed toward the brutal, colonial rule of King Leopold II in the Congo Free State. While Lapsley was away in Boma, Sheppard started preparations for their jointly planned expedition to the anti-colonial, "forbidden" Kuba land. The first crucial thing he did was to learn the Kuba language (the Bushong) and social manners. In order to do this, he developed a convivial relationship with Kuba traders and tax collectors, who frequently visited Luebo, by inviting them to share meals and wine. Through their conversations, Sheppard not only acquired a working knowledge of the Bushong language but also learned the names of the most important market towns and their chiefs between Luebo and the Kuba capital Mushenge. Once he had achieved basic fluency in Bushong, he gathered an expedition party of nine willing native assistants and started the exploratory trip into the dreaded Kuba land. Using the trading skill he had developed since his arrival in the Congo, Sheppard tactically led his caravan through market towns. He posed as a harmless explorer and trader and was hospitably welcomed along the way by villagers and their chiefs who sold him and his party eggs and other needed food rations. Their first stop was at a very large Kete village of Bena Kapunga where Sheppard, his party, and the locals joined in a festive evening of dancing, singing, and eating (1917:88–89).

After spending three days in this town, Sheppard and his assistants decided to move on, but had to find a guide to the next town. Although all the chiefs of the towns neighboring the Kuba land had been warned by the Kuba king, the Lukengu, to not give directions to his land to foreigners, the chief of Bena Kapunga very reluctantly gave in to Sheppard's pleading and gave them a man to show one of his assistants the trail to the town of Ngallicoco. As Sheppard states, the two men

> together journeyed to Ngallicoco and returned, bringing many dozens eggs and other food.[...] so the following day we packed up and were off. We passed through a number of small villages, slept in one, and in due time came to Ngallicoco.
>
> (89)

Here again, Sheppard came across a people living their lives peacefully, hunting, growing crops, singing, and dancing to the rhythm of their drum beats and horns, and surrounding themselves by their protective "idols" or physical representations of deities and ancestors. On this subject, Sheppard says: "I don't know of a place where I saw more idols than here at Ngallicoco." As for the inhabitants of the town, Sheppard observes:

> These people seemed to spend most their time in hunting, from the numerous animals brought in—wild hogs, antelope, hyenas, wild cats,

The postcolonial pragmatist 75

monkeys, bush rats, field rats, etc. The women busied themselves bringing in from the fields roots of cassava, bananas and greens.

(90)

Here, Sheppard and his party were welcomed by a skeptical chief and puzzled inhabitants who wanted to know more about their real intention. So, in the night of their arrival, a suspicious town crier called on all the villagers not to give directions to strangers, but Sheppard was lucky to meet and quickly befriend a Kuba traveler, Bope Ng'ola Minge, who invited him to go along with him to the Kuba town of M'boma. About this man, Sheppard says: "I was delighted, knowing that this man had full knowledge of King Lukenga's (sic.) edict and yet cordially invited me to his town" (90).

At M'boma, Sheppard and his assistants were warmly welcomed by Chief Hong N'joka and the locals, but none of them was willing to give them directions to the next town. They remained there for a month during which Sheppard says in his autobiography: "I had the pleasure of preaching, praying and singing for them [the locals] in their tongue daily" (94). They finally found a way out when they came across Lukengu's ivory traders who emerged from the forest and were on their way back to the capital Mushenge. Sheppard asked N'goma, his headman from the Lower Congo, who (like the locals) wore a loincloth and carried a spear, to follow them at a distance and make a cross mark at cross trails so that he and others could follow him. Led that way by N'goma for two days, they reached the Kuba town of Bishibing (Sheppard calls it Bixibing). Here is how Sheppard describes their dramatic arrival in that town: "As we marched in the people were frightened and ran to the bush, but I called to them in a loud voice in their tongue, 'Ko-cinaka! Ko-cinaka! (Be not afraid! Be not afraid!). They returned and settled down" (95). Sheppard and his caravan were eventually warmly welcomed by the town chief, Kueta, and other town dignitaries:

> In the afternoon Chief Kueta came, accompanied by some of the first men of the town, the judge, a lawyer, a witch doctor, and the town's blacksmith, and presented me with about twenty bushels of corn, five chickens, a very large goat, a ham of a wild boar, a basket of sweet potatoes, a big basket of blackeyed peas, dried fish, bananas, plantains, pineapples, a small basket of field mushrooms, and five jugs of water.
>
> (96)

Chief Kueta also offered them a shelter for the night, but insisted that the next day they had to leave the town and go back by the same way they came to his town.

In return, Sheppard thanked the King. However, instead of leaving the town (as requested by the chief), Sheppard spent the next two days convivially greeting and socializing with the villagers: he observed their social and farming activities, admired their iron work, visited a local blacksmith, bought carved ebony drinking cups, suggested, and took part in the widening of the road to the stream where people brought their drinking water from, shot guinea fowls, and sang English songs in the Bushong translation to the crowd.

In spite of his demonstrated interest in the local community and their life-world, however, on the third day, the anxious chief Kueta came to give Sheppard and his assistants another warning:

> Chief Kueta came to me early the third morning and said in gestures which bespoke earnestness and uneasiness, 'Foreigner, you can't stop here.' So I said to Kueta, 'Well, why?' 'it is against the word of our king,' he said. 'You must return the way you came,' and he continued: Not only will we be killed, but you and all your people'.
>
> (99)

Soon after the warning, Lukengu's fighting men, led by his fearless warrior son N'Toinzide, approached the town, and their arrival caused all the townsfolks, including Sheppard's assistants, to run helter-skelter. Here is how Sheppard describes the pandemonium that engulfed the town upon the arrival of the anti-colonial King's army:

> In less than two hours from the time of my warning the town was in an uproar. The King's trading men, who had threatened my man N'goma, had reached the capital and reported to the King Lukenga (sic.) having seen a foreigner on the road moving in his direction, and the King had sent down his specially picked fighting men to intercept, fight, and drive me back. I sat quietly in my seat in front of the tent and watched the people in their flight for the forest. My people began to gather around my chair, and the youngest of the caravan, N'susu, nestled on his knees very close to me. The King's people were now in full sight standing at attention near to the big shed. The leading man with his big spear called in a voice that rang through the village, "Now hear the words of King Lukenga: Because you have entertained a foreigner in your village, we have come to take you to the capital for trial."
>
> (99)

But instead of adopting a selfish cut and run approach that would have exposed Chief Kueta and his people to certain deaths, Sheppard humbly approached the intimidating headman of the group, N'Toinzide, and took responsibility for his presence in the town. Speaking in Bushong, Sheppard pleaded with him in this dialogue:

> 'I understand you are sent by your king to arrest these people.' 'It is the word of the king,' said he. I continued, 'The chief of this village is not

guilty; he gave me warning and told me to go away, to return the way I had come, and I did not. It is my fault and not Kueta's'.

(99–100)

Perplexed and almost disarmed by the fact that Sheppard spoke the Bushong language, N'Toinzide retreated with his fighters for a moment in order to ponder the situation. They then resolved to leave the town, return to Mushenge, and report what they saw as a mystery (the stranger's knowledge of the Bushong language and his possible connection to the Kuba people) to the King. He told Sheppard: "I will return to the capital and report these things to the king" (100). And, in response, Sheppard reassured N'Toinzide: "Tell your king I am not a bad man; I do not steal nor kill; I have a message for him." Sheppard also handed him a large cowrie shell, saying "This we call the father of cowries; present it to the king as a token of friendship" (100).

When back in the capital Mushenge, N'Toinzide and his men went straight to Lukengu, King Kot aMbweeky, and reported: "We saw the foreigner, he speaks our language, he knows all the trails to the country" (101). The puzzled King then summoned his council, shared N'toinzide's report with them, and after deliberation, they concluded that they knew who Sheppard was. They thus advised the King:

> The foreigner who is at Bixibing, [...] who has come these long trails and who speaks our language is a Makuba, one of the early settlers who died, and whose spirit went to a foreign country and now he has returned.
>
> (101)

The King accepted the narrative of Sheppard's existence and presence in his land as subjectively and authoritatively shaped by his councilors and asked his son N'Toinzide to go back and bring him along to the capital. When he returned to Bishibing, "N'Toinzide stood in the center of the town and called with his loud voice saying who I was and giving briefly my history." And "The villagers were indeed happy. They flocked around as the king's son drew near and extended their hands to me" (101). At first, Sheppard tried to resist the new narrative about his identity, saying in his autobiography: "I arose from my chair and made these remarks: 'I have heard distinctly all that you have said, but I am not a Makuba; I have never been here before'" (101). But the anti-colonial N'Toinzide prevailed. He

> insisted that they were right, and said that his father, the king, wanted me to come on at once to the capital. The people were mighty happy, Kueta, our host, the townspeople and my people, too. Their appetites came back, and so did mine [...]. With a hasty good-bye, 'Gala hola,' to Kueta, we were off.
>
> (102)

78 The Congo narrative

On their way to the capital, Sheppard admired the beautiful Kuba country's landscape, describing it poetically in his autobiography:

> The forest everywhere was ever green. Trees blossomed and bloomed, sending out upon the gentle breeze their fragrance so acceptable to the traveler. Festoons of moss and running vines made the forest look like a beautifully painted theatre or an enormous swinging garden.
>
> (102)

After journeying for two days, through a number of villages (full of protective charms) and crossing a big river that almost took away the life of one of his assistants Muxihu, Sheppard and his caravan approached one of the capital's fortified four entrances. From here, a man was dispatched to inform the King of their arrival, and as Sheppard writes, "In a short while the people came out of the town to meet and greet us, hundreds of them, and many little children, too" (104). Led by N'Toinzide with a spear in hand, Sheppard and his caravan were warmly welcomed into Lukengu's capital by an enthusiastic crowd:

> We marched down a broad, clean street, lined on both sides by interested spectators jostling, gesticulating, talking loud and laughing. The young boys and girls struck a song which sounded to me like a band of sweet music and we all kept step by it.
>
> (105)

Here, Sheppard did not have to pitch his tent as he and his caravan were provided with a well-equipped house:

> The house was made like all others of bamboo and had two rooms. There were a number of clay pots of various sizes for cooking and six large gourds for water. My caravan was comfortably housed. I did not put up my tent, but took my seat in a reclining chair under a large palm tree in front of my door.
>
> (105)

The self-assured and revered King, whose movements usually involved elaborate rituals and pageantry, could not see Sheppard on the day of his arrival. He nevertheless sent his Prime Minister, N'Dola, to deliver his greetings and gifts to him. The welcoming gifts that the King sent Sheppard and his assistants include "fourteen goats, six sheep, a number of chickens, corn, pumpkins, large dried fish, bushels of peanuts, bunches of bananas and plantains and a calabash of palm oil and other food" (105).

Early in the morning the following day, ivory horns were blasted in the capital, alerting people to put on their most beautiful attires and get ready for the King's parade. Soon, Sheppard was escorted by two of the King's guards to the town square. Here is how the subdued stranger, William Henry Sheppard, was received by the great Lukengu, King Kot aMbweeky, seating in full royal regalia on his throne made of carved ivory tusks with his feet resting on lion skins:

> I was dressed in what once had been white linen. Coat, trousers, white canvas shoes and pith helmet. The officials on either side took me by the arm; we walked a block up the broad street, turned to the right and walked three blocks till we came to the big town square. Thousands of the villagers had already taken their position and were seated on the green grass. King Lukenga (*sic.*), his high officials and about 300 of his wives occupied the eastern section of the square. The players of stringed instruments and drummers were in the center, and as we appeared a great shout went up from the people. The king's servants ran and spread leopard skins along the ground leading to his majesty. I approached with some timidity. The king arose from his throne of ivory, stretched forth his hand and greeted me with these words, "Wyni" (you have come). I bowed low, clapped my hands in front of me, and answered, "Ndini, Nyimi" (I have come, king).
>
> (106–107)

As Sheppard sat next to the King delightfully watching his sons with "their brandishing big knives" dance to the harmonious tune of drum beats and harp sounds during the big reception, he leaned toward the King and vainly tried once again to correct the mythic narrative constructed around his identity by the King's councilors. Sheppard recounts:

> I leaned from my seat toward King Lukenga (*sic.*) and getting his attention said briefly, "I understand, king, that your people believe me to be a Makuba who once lived here." The king replied with a smile, "N'Gaxa Mi" (It is true). "I want to acknowledge to you [...] that I am not a Makuba and I have never been here before." The king leaned over the arm of his great chair and said with satisfaction, "You don't know it, but you are 'Muana Mi' (one of the family).
>
> (107–108)

Commenting on the end of the memorable ceremony at the close of the day, Sheppard recounts with a sense of admiration: "It was the most brilliant affair I had seen in Africa, but my! I was so glad when it was all over" (108).

Following Lukengu's total rejection of Sheppard's account of his Western originary identity, he accepted the new narrative of his identity while in the Kuba territory. He won the friendship of Prince N'Toizinde through gifts like shells, beads, and Western cloth, and the latter became his valuable guide around the town. The day after the ceremony, N'Toinzide took Sheppard to visit the King's palace, and he had the much-anticipated first interview with Lukengu. Here is how Sheppard describes the decorum that accompanied the interview:

> The king in ordinary costume was seated on a low stool and we were seated on a large exquisitely woven mat. The king greeted us with "Wyni" (You have come). We both leaned forward and clapping our hands twice repeated together, "Ndini" (We have come). During all the interview we clapped our hands after every sentence. If the king coughed we coughed, if he sneezed we sneezed. N'Toizinde's wife, Mbiwata, came in and sat with us, and so did the king's principal wife. Two slaves on their knees supported the king's back.
>
> (110)

Sheppard started the interview by modestly telling the King more about the late Lapsley, "a splendid young white man whom the Bakete named N'Tomanjela—'a path finder,'" than himself. This was perhaps Sheppard's diplomatic way of preparing the King for the arrival of friendly white people, the missionaries, in his territory. He talked about how, before his death, Lapsley introduced Bakete children to literacy and taught them "[...] about the Great Spirit, a great King. This King made everything—the trees, the rivers, the elephants, the ants, the sun, the moon and stars" (111). Sheppard then concluded the interview by revealing his evangelical mission to Lukengu, saying "So I have come alone, and my real purpose here is to tell you of the Great King and have your full permission to tell about Him everywhere" (111). Though he appeared skeptical and amused as he listened to Sheppard, Lukengu, nevertheless, accommodated his request: "It is right; you can tell it everywhere, but you can't leave the capital; you must stay here" (111). He even gave Sheppard a piece of land where he could build a mission and a school for Kuba children.

With that permission from the King, Sheppard had a large shed built in front of his house and settled down in Mushenge. As he reports: "Many nights the Bakuba gathered around my house and with harps and voices made sweet music" (116). In addition to occasional gospel preaching to the inquisitive crowd that constantly came to his shed, Sheppard used most of his time learning about the Kuba people's oral history, legends, arts, beliefs, social practices or customs, gender roles, healing methods, judicial system, sporting activities, indigenous knowledge of the cosmos and ecology, homestead education for children, iron technology, garment technology, hunting techniques, fishing skills, and farming activities. He also traded with the natives, who brought him local items like "hoes, knives, rugs, mats, cloth, leopard teeth, wild boar teeth, live monkeys, parrots and other birds, eagle and aigrette feathers and things innumerable" (113). In return, Sheppard sold them modern Western items they had never seen before like looking glasses and buttons.

As he leisurely toured and gazed at the capital Mushenge, Sheppard became more and more impressed by its architectural layout as well as its

The postcolonial pragmatist 81

inhabitants' social cohesion, cleanliness, and reverence for the King. Here again, Sheppard's representation of this 19th-century African town and its people contrasts sharply with the negative Western, colonial imagining of Africa and its peoples during the same period:

> The town [Mushenge] was laid off east and west. The broad streets ran at right angles, and there were blocks just as in any town. Those in a block were always related in some way. Around each house is a court and a high fence made of heavy matting of palm leaves, and around each block there is also a high fence, so you enter these homes by the many gates. Each block has a chief called Mbambi, and he is responsible to King Lukenga (*sic*.) for his block. When the king will deliver a message to the whole village or part of it, these chiefs are sent for and during the early evenings they ring their iron hand bells and call out in a loud voice the message in five minutes. The king desired of his own heart to give me peanuts for my people. I heard the messengers delivering the word and the next morning we had more peanuts than we could manage. In some of the yards there were trees with blooming flowers.
>
> (117)

Besides N'Toinzide, Sheppard became a close friend to another prince, Maxamalinge, who invited him to dinner after a short visit to his house. The dinner turned out to be a convivial space of cultural encounter and learning for both Sheppard and his hosts:

> Dinner was prepared for six, and we all sat down on mats and used our fingers eating from the various pots fresh fish, buffalo, greens and corn bread. The visitors as well as my host and hostess [Maxamalinge's wife Bulengunga] asked question after question, but it did not prevent me from enjoying a good, hot meal.
>
> (116)

As a mark of his affection for the royal family that renamed him after the late King Bope Mekabe and his personal friendship with Prince Maxamalinge, Sheppard later named his son after the latter.

While Sheppard was mostly full of admiration for the Kuba people and their way of life, he was also appalled by some of their cruel practices such as "the poison cup" and "the burying of the dead with the living." So, although he obeyed Lukengu's order that he desist from using soap to wash clothes and his gun to shoot birds because of his people's metaphysical complaints, in one instance, Sheppard confronted the King fearlessly in his attempt to lead him and his people to jettison a cruel custom:

> My interference with the men who were dragging the woman to her death had been reported to Lukenga. He mentioned it to me, saying,

> "The burying of the living with the dead was far beyond the Bateke, who only bury goats with their dead, and that is why we bury slaves; they serve us here and then go with us on the journey to wait on us there". I told the king in the strongest language I could command that it was wrong without the least shadow of justification. I tried to prove to him that the poisonous cup was a very cruel and unjust practice and there were no witches. And if they gave the poison to anyone whose stomach was not easily moved, they would die. The King thought me very foolish, saying, "if a person is innocent they can never die."
>
> (131)

Despite the King's resistance to Sheppard's opposition to this practice, however, he did not despair as he believed that "Only by preaching God's word, having faith, patience, and love will we eradicate the deep-rooted evil" (132).

After sojourning in Mushenge for a period of almost two months, Sheppard politely approached King Kot aMbweeky and expressed his desire to return to Luebo. At first, the King refused to grant him permission to do so, but later on yielded with the caveat that Sheppard return to Mushenge in the near future. The King also provided him with two men to guide him and his caravan back to Luebo through a labyrinth of trails. Here is how Sheppard respectfully presented his request to the King:

> I told the king Lukenga(*sic*.) that I loved him and his people, and that it was a real pleasure to live in his town, but that his subjects at Luebo were looking for my return, and we had started a school and other good work down there, and I desired to continue it. The King replied to my request that he wanted me to remain with him and not to return again to Luebo. After a number of appeals in succession my request was granted with the provision that I return to him in the near future.
>
> (138)

With the help of the two guides, the saddened Sheppard and his men received a rousing farewell ovation by the crowd as they left the capital town with loads of collected art objects, curios, and gifts. They went back by a different route and passed many hospitable villages along the way and came across another lake, which he named after Mary Baldwin, a prominent educator and supporter of PCUS foreign missions, at Staunton, Virginia. Whenever they spent a night at a village or town, Sheppard and his company made a campfire and that attracted a crowd of inquisitive, knowledge-thirsty villagers who bombarded Sheppard with questions about the foreign country he came from, the language he spoke, and the food he ate. One such a welcoming town was Ibanche or Ibanj, "a great market center" that brought together traders from neighboring villages, and where Sheppard and his wife Lucy Gantt established the first Presbyterian mission station and a school in the Kuba land a few years later. After visiting a few nearby villages there,

Sheppard and his caravan resumed their journey back to Luebo through Bakete towns like Bena Kabau, Bena Nsangala, Bena Kabash, Bena Kapunga, Bena Kalamba, Bena Chitala, and Bena Kasenga. All these Bakete towns were under the authority of the Kuba King, Lukengu, who boastfully told Sheppard so during his first interview with him in Mushenge. At Bena Kabau, Sheppard, who had just enjoyed the company of the hardworking Kuba people in their secured country, was appalled to come across a group of the inhumane slave traders and the Congo Free State government collaborators Zappo Zaps. As Sheppard reports, "They were from the Baluba country far south and traveling north with a caravan of slaves to sell in exchange for ivory, rubber, cam wood and goats" (145).

When they were four miles from Luebo, Sheppard dispatched N'Goma to go ahead of the caravan and announce their arrival. Sheppard and his company then received a rousing, emotional welcome by the friends they had left behind as they approached Luebo: "The caravan was soon relieved of their loads, for our friends—men, women, and children, bore them away. [...] **No Place Like Home**—In a little while I was seated in a reclining chair on my broad, cool veranda" (148).

The following day, as Sheppard says: "I called a meeting of all the people, Bakete and Baluba, together and briefly made a report of our wanderings in the 'Forbidden Land' of King Lukenga" (148). Thus, welcomed by the Bakuba people and their King, Lukengu, who adopted him as a native son,[1] Sheppard came to appreciate the richness and beauty of their language, arts, folksongs, architecture, technological innovations (iron work), foodstuffs, and many cultural practices. As he describes them in his autobiography:

> I grew very fond of the Bakuba and it was reciprocated. They were the finest looking race I had seen in Africa, dignified, graceful, courageous, honest, with an open, smiling countenance and really hospitable. Their knowledge of weaving, embroidering, wood carving and smelting was the highest in equatorial Africa.
>
> (137)

So, rather than condescendingly treat them as "noble savages" that needed to be civilized, Sheppard came to regard the Bakuba people as dignified, civilized subjects who needed to be empowered in their struggle against the then threatening inhumane colonial rule of the Belgian king. This is the message that he decided he would enlighten the Western world with while on furlough in Britain and the United States between 1893 and 1894.

Counteracting negative western representations of Africa

Before embarking on his well-deserved year-long furlough, Sheppard left the Luebo mission station under the care of the ship machinist George Adamson and his wife Margaret, members of the Free Church of Scotland, recruited by Sheppard and Lapsley. They were also joined by four newly appointed members of the APCM that Sheppard met in Matadi, on his way to the United States: the English couple Reverend Arthur and Mrs. Margaret Rowbotham, and the American couple Dr. DeWitt and Mrs. Margaret Snyder. Dr. Snyder, a pharmacist, was later renamed *Ngangabuka* (Witchdoctor) by the natives in Luebo because of the medical care he gave them (Benedetto 1996:99).

Sheppard arrived in London in the spring of 1893 and immediately delivered a number of lectures on his expedition to the Kuba land. Backing the lectures with the culturally rich and complex Kuba artifacts he took along with him and exhibited in London's Exeter Hall, Sheppard awed his inquisitive audiences as he talked in detail about the Kuba people's humanity as well as their life-world and lived experiences. In recognition of his exploration of the hitherto unknown part of the world—the Kuba land (especially his discovery of two previously unknown Kuba and Kasai lakes)—on June 23, 1893, Sheppard was elected as a Fellow of the prestigious Royal Geographical Society (F.R.G.S). By this election, the twenty-eight-year-old Sheppard joined the rank of previous high-profile honorees, including David Livingstone, Henry Morton Stanley, George Grenfell, and Charles Darwin. He was also received by Queen Victoria. As Kennedy states, the corrective narrative that Sheppard delivered debunked Western constructed negative imaginings of Africa that were ubiquitous during his time: "The story he told was a reverse *Heart of Darkness*, a tale of a man who travels deep into the jungle and stumbles into a city of checkered order" (Kennedy 2002:109). Jan Vansina has also pointed out the decolonial efficacy of Kuba material and art objects like the ones exhibited by Sheppard in Europe and the United States, maintaining that Europeans

> seem to have been convinced that, unlike any other Congolese society, the Kuba were the heirs of a true ancient civilization. Already in 1885 Ludwig Wolf had deduced this from their industriousness, their technical know-how, the beauty of all the objects they made, and the art of their dancing exhibitions, combined with the considerable authority of their kings. Kuba art was greatly appreciated in Europe from the very beginning, especially by the avant-garde artists who launched art nouveau. As early as 1897 they had organized the first exhibition in Belgium about Congo, decorated the hall of honor with embroidered Kuba textiles, and celebrated Kuba sculpture elsewhere in their exhibition. By then it had become commonplace among well-informed colonials to believe that the Kuba were somehow heirs to the old civilization of pharaonic Egypt.
>
> (Vansina 2010:182)

As soon as Sheppard arrived in London, he sent a cablegram to his unsuspecting fiancée Lucy Gantt announcing that he was on his way to the

United States in a few weeks' time. They then started planning their wedding which they wanted to take place on her birthday on February 21, 1894. Returning to the United States in summer 1893, Sheppard visited President Grover Cleveland at the White House and "presented him with a cleverly woven rug, proof that African creations rivaled the maddest of New York fashions" (Kennedy 2002:110). In presenting the rug to the president, Sheppard took care of explaining the complex technology used in its making and underscored the Kuba people's sense of aesthetics. From the White House, he went to his alma mater, Hampton Institute, to give a public lecture on the arts and life-world of the Kuba people and his experiences amongst them. During the lecture entitled "Intro to the Heart of Africa," Sheppard illustrated the points he made about the ingenuity, bravery, and subjective agency of the Kuba people by brandishing Kuba knives and battle axes as well as by featuring their local foodstuffs, textiles, and other art objects. He donated a substantial part of his Congolese art collection to Hampton, and it is now lodged in the special collection section of the Hampton University Museum.

Before embarking on an extensive and enlightening lecture tour of many Northern and Southern Churches and colleges, Sheppard was enthusiastically received by a meeting of the PCUS Synod of Virginia and a number of crowded churches in Virginia. From there, he spoke to very receptive audiences at the McCormick Seminary in Chicago, in many predominantly white Churches in Kentucky, and in North Carolina. Indeed, Sheppard's inspiring lectures aroused his black and white audiences' interest in Africa. However, Sheppard's lectures about Africa did not carry the same ideological tenor. Whenever he addressed conservative Church audiences from whom he needed funding, he brought about the necessity to save Africans from evil rituals (such as the Kuba people's practice of the "poison cup," witch hunts, and the burying of the living with the dead). But when addressing liberal college faculty and students, his discourse extolled the humanity of the African people and the validity of their life-world and became postcolonial in its resonance.

Sheppard arrived in Jacksonville, Florida, where his fiancée Lucy Gantt lived with her mother Eliza Gantt, a day before the wedding. However, instead of focusing his attention on the wedding preparations, Sheppard, who was eager to connect Black American children with Africa (their roots), visited a nearby "school for Negro children" and gave the children an entertaining talk about Africa and his experiences amongst the Kuba people. The children were so much captivated by Sheppard's paralinguistic performance and the thrilling story he told them about Africa that they crowded the church at the wedding ceremony that took place on February 21, 1894. As Julia Kellersberger reports: "When 'that man' [Sheppard] walked down the aisle with his sweet-faced bride-to-be in white by his side, and they [the black children] discovered their friend of the previous day, audible exclamations swept over the congregation" (n.d.:10).

Soon after the wedding, the couple started thinking about the survival and expansion of the Luebo mission station and the planting of other stations in the Kuba land. At the center of their thoughts featured prominently the empowerment of Congolese boys and girls through education as well as the upliftment of Congolese women. With these ideas in mind, they toured Southern churches and seminaries to raise funds and also recruit qualified Black volunteers for the Congo mission. Sheppard's talks in Southern States about African beautiful landscape (its fauna, flora, rivers, and lakes) and the African people as hard working, dignified human beings with different values and beliefs (but who needed modern amenities and assistance against King Leopold's cruel regime) awakened the interest of Black Americans in Africa. At the end of their tour, the Sheppards successfully recruited three enthusiastic Black American volunteers: Rev. Henry Hawkins, a preacher trained at the Stillman Institute in Tuscaloosa, Sheppard's alma mater, and Lillian Thomas and Maria Fearing, both alumni of Talladega College in Alabama, Lucy's alma mater.

On May 26, 1894, the five missionaries assembled in New York and sailed to London. Rev. Henry Hawkins wanted to be joined by his wife for the Congo mission, but the Southern Presbyterian Church denied his request. After nine days of a tumultuous sea voyage that made Lucy terribly seasick, they arrived in London. Just as Sheppard and Lapsley did four years before them, while in London, the group spent their time mainly buying and packing the provisions (food, clothing, folding chairs, camp cots, and enameled dishes) that they needed for the Congo mission. Meanwhile, Mr. Sheppard was very busy with speaking engagements that attracted crowds of people at Y.M.C.A., Bishopgate, Exeter Hall, Congregational Church, St. John's Wood, East London Tabernacle, and Presbyterian Church, Regents Square.

After spending one month in London, the five missionaries embarked on their journey to the Congo aboard a Dutch vessel. Here again, they faced rough seas and endured seasickness for three weeks before they reached Boma, the capital city of the Congo Free State. The first sight of the Congo River by the Black missionaries filled them with a sense of awe that made them forget about their seasickness for a moment. For Lucy, the mouth of the Congo River stood like the door of the final exit for the enslaved Africans whose history she was a part of. The river brought to her mind not only the painful separation of Africans from their land but also their suffering and struggles for freedom in the New World. At the same time, the river awakened in her a sense of personal responsibility (as a black person and as a woman) for the future development of Africa as it negotiated a new subjective identity in the intersection of the encroaching colonial, Western modernity and local traditions. Julia Kellersberger recounts with Lucy's own words her deep sense of contemplation as she affectionately gazed at the majestic Congo River:

> Mrs. Sheppard will never forget her first sight of the mighty Congo River flowing by. Its coffee-colored waters were, to her, "a symbol of

the people whose bodies reflected its deep, dark sheen; whose souls had been as unfathomable as its depths; whose struggles for centuries had been as varied and as consuming as its rush to the sea; and whose future still remained as unknown as the depths of the river's bed in its whirlpool regions."

(n.d.:11)

In Boma, Lucy and the other three missionaries, who were setting foot on the Congo soil for the first time, came face to face with the deterioration of the native life under the brutal and morally corrupt regime of the Congo Free State which claimed to represent Western modernity. They must have realized the validity of the facts pointed out by George Washington Williams in his protest *Open Letter* to Belgian King Leopold (lack of hospitals and security for natives, physical abuse of native women and children, brutal exploitation of the natives' labor, and the destruction of the natives' moral compass by imported liquor). Soon after their arrival, Mr. Sheppard fell sick with fever, and they had to delay the next leg of their journey up the Congo River.

As soon as Mr. Sheppard recovered, the missionaries took a steamer and headed to the port city of Matadi, where they had to repack their loads and recruit porters for their journey to Kinshasa (Leopoldville). At the end of three weeks in Matadi, Mr. Sheppard and his party were able to assemble a caravan of eighty-five men, and they set out for Kinshasa. As they proceeded on their journey, the missionaries came across a horrible scene of the atrocities perpetrated by white traders who burnt down a village. This angered the porters whose families lived in the village, and they turned their anger toward all foreigners including the American missionaries. But for Sheppard's skillful dialogue with them in their language (explaining that all foreigners should not be blamed for the cruel action of Belgian traders), the angered porters would have deserted the Black Americans in the middle of the journey. Sheppard and his company were also overwhelmingly appalled by the untold suffering of the Congolese natives as they came across abandoned bodies of dead Belgian traders' porters and gazed desperately at women and children dying of hunger and disease on the way. Sheppard tried to treat some of them during their journey, but the task was enormous. They were relieved when they stopped and spent a night at the American Baptist mission station at Banza Mankete. Here, Mrs. Sheppard was pleasantly surprised to be awakened in the morning by two young Black American missionaries, graduates of Spelman Seminary in Atlanta, Georgia, who came to serve them breakfast of "freshly baked hot buttered biscuits."

After twelve days of physically and emotionally exhausting trek, the missionaries and their caravan arrived in Kinshasa. Soon after, Sheppard and his company boarded a small, shaky steamer and embarked on a dangerous sail upriver. Just after leaving the port for about an hour, the boat almost capsized. This was not the only danger they faced, for soon, the boat came under arrow attacks as it passed through hostile, anti-colonial villagers retaliating against the savage attacks of government officials. Though shaken, here again, the American missionaries were lucky to escape with their lives and without injuries.

Seeing the devastation of the villages by European rubber and ivory traders on their way, the Black American missionaries must have empathized with the natives in their struggles against the Free State government officials and European traders. The treatment they themselves received at the hands of the greedy European captain of the steamer, who demanded a one-week food supply from the passengers and then starved them in return, must have given them an insight into the anti-colonial struggle they might have to be involved in while in the Congo. True to himself, Mr. Sheppard relieved the boat passengers and the crew of hunger by killing a hippopotamus.

Since the lack of rains made it difficult for the steamer to venture into the shallow waters of the Lulua River, Sheppard secured a large canoe and four Bakuba oarsmen to take them and their loads to Luebo. Mr. Sheppard and the new Black American missionaries finally reached their destination, the Luebo station, at night, and they were welcomed by Dr. and Mrs. Snyder, who served them "hot coffee and a good supper." The following day, the missionaries received an enthusiastic African welcome by an excited crowd of Luebo natives, as described by Kellesberger:

> The next morning the five were royally welcomed in true African fashion and laden with gifts of chickens and eggs, topped by peanuts, dried rats, and caterpillars. The church bells rang loud and joyfully and the mud chapel was soon filled with worshippers in just proper mood to give heartfelt praise for the safe arrival of their new helpers. The little boys were wearing white loincloths and white slip-over shirts, and the little girls were dressed in loose calico print dresses belted in at waist, all the work of the hands of Mrs. Snyder. This especially appealed to the newcomers, as did the whole service, which seemed like happy Sunday School. The children sang heartily.
>
> (Kellersberger n.d.:16)

Returning after just one-year-long absence, Mr. Sheppard found the Luebo mission station in shambles. The white missionaries he left behind to run the station failed to connect with the local people. They miserably lacked the kind of pragmatism and entrepreneurial spirit that characterized Mr. Sheppard's missionary vision. They hated the natives' style of worship accompanied by drums and dancing, which had been encouraged by Mr. Sheppard. As a result, the Rowbotham left the mission just after four months, and following his wife's death, Mr. Adamson was demoted and redeployed to the lower Congo to take care of the transport. Only the disgruntled Dr. and Mrs. Snyder remained behind to take care of the eighty adult laborers and forty-three children that were in the station at the time of the arrival of Mr. Sheppard and the new missionaries in Luebo. Dr. Snyder was so disgruntled that in one of his homeward bound letters, he stated that he was "entirely outside the limits of civilization...among the...degraded savages of Africa" (qtd in Phipps 2002:103). The Sheppards and the new Black American missionaries, therefore, faced the task of quickly amending missionaries' relationship with the natives, rebuilding the station's physical infrastructure, schooling Congolese boys and girls, rehabilitating rescued slaves (mainly the Baluba) integrated into the mission's labor force, resisting racial division amongst the missionaries, and resisting King Leopold's brutal regime. Mr. Sheppard was also keen to reconnect with the Kuba king, Lukengu, in order to establish another mission station and school in Mushenge, as promised.

When they arrived in Luebo, Sheppard and Lucy occupied a small, porous mud hut with a leaky roof. Snakes easily found their way into the hut, as was the case with the python that Mr. Sheppard skillfully killed without alarming the unsuspecting Lucy. It was there that Lucy prematurely gave birth to a baby girl, Miriam. As described by Kellersberger: "The wee daughter lived only a few weeks, and was buried beneath a tall palm on the mission compound, in a little bamboo coffin covered and lined with her mother's white wedding dress" (16). Despite the sad loss of their first child, however, the Sheppards decided to press on with their vision to empower their brothers and sisters of race by leading them to a postcolonial cultural translation of their positive African values with Western modernity. In order to realize this vision, the Sheppards had to count more on the energetic and culturally forward-looking Black American missionaries (Miss Fearing, Miss Thomas, and Reverend Hawkins) than on the culturally conservative Dr. and Mrs. Snyder. In fact, Dr. Snyder stood in the way of Mr. Sheppard's idea of establishing a mission station in Kuba land and disapproved of his convivial interactions with the natives. Expressing his disappointment and impatience with the Bakete people's skepticism about Christianity, Dr. Snyder wrote in a letter to Joseph Hawley of Rochester, Michigan, on September 5, 1894:

> We have been here on our station [Luebo] for the past fifteen months; during this time we have had to unlearn much and learn more. Missionary work is not all we thought it was, and it is much more. We had hoped to find a people glad to receive our message; and that we would have only to learn the language and tell them the wonderful story, and then see them coming into the church. We were not prepared for the utter *indifference*.
>
> (Snyder 1996a:101)

Dr. Snyder also undermined Mr. Sheppard's Kuba project and experiences that validated the humanity of the Kuba people and won him recognition in Britain and the United States. In a letter to Mr. Phillips of Tampa, Florida, on January 13, 1894, Dr. Snyder, who had just been disappointed by the report of King Kot aMbweeky's cold welcome to Mr. and Mrs. Adamson, wrote:

> My wife and I must go and see that wonderful country of which Sheppard has so much to say. From what I hear and see here I cannot endorse all Mr. S[Sheppard's] talk[since] he is given to draw on his imagination and in the end will, I am afraid, do more harm than good.
>
> (Snyder 1996b:97)

Still in another letter to his former colleague at Luebo, Arthur Rowbotham, Dr. Snyder wrote:

> A short while ago Mr. and Mrs. A[damson] went into the Bakuba country [and] were gone about three weeks. Their report differs very much from Mr. S[heppard's] and I am afraid Mr. S[heppard]is drawing much on his imagination. I am going into the Bakuba country in a little while and shall let you know. But from what I have seen of the Bakuba back on the station I am not impressed with them.
>
> (Snyder 1996c:98)

Unlike his wife, who appreciated Mr. Sheppard's work and regarded him as "a brother in every sense of the word," Dr. Snyder treated him and the other Black missionaries as subaltern American Negroes. As Phipps remarks, "For DeWitt [Snyder), racial consciousness was so dominant that even blacks whom he acknowledged as sharing similar religious orientation, educational attainment, and social graces were not fully acceptable as friends" (Phipps 2002:103). He even went as far as to suggest that Black American missionaries did not have the capacity and the necessary skills to carry out missionary work in Africa by themselves.

Black American women missionaries' contributions

The first task that William Sheppard had to undertake was to build a spacious house for Lucy and himself. Thanks to the mission station labor force, they soon became the owners of a five-room house, which Lucy proudly called "The Ladies' Home Journal House." However, because of its proximity to the bushes, this house also attracted unwanted visitors—leopards, bugs, birds, frogs, insects, driver ants, and spiders. Here is how Lucy herself described the new house as she settled down and started her work for the empowerment of Congolese girls and boys, women, and men in Luebo:

> The making of a Christian home was part of my missionary task and I was glad that my house could be used as a demonstration and practice center. I called it *'The Ladies' Home Journal House'*, because so many of the ideas for making furniture and for simple colorful decorations came from that magazine. All of the furniture that I had was made from

packing boxes of various shapes and sizes. These I draped with bright cretonne and the results were both practical and attractive. I never possessed a cooking stove. For years my cooking was done out of doors. The kettle or saucepan resting on three stones, or upon several hard anthills. I managed to bake by putting live coals above and beneath a clay pot. Constant vigilance was required to keep the bread from burning. A small brick oven, later, made baking a less precarious adventure. Lights were another problem. Candles were a luxury. These were supplemented by a tin can filled with palm oil, with a rag serving as a wick. When I was finally able to obtain a glass lamp in which I could burn palm oil, I was so overjoyed that I felt certain no light in the homeland was any brighter.
(Kellersberger n.d.:18–19)

Here, through the practical tasks that she assigned Congolese girls and boys, Lucy, an accomplished teacher, didactically introduced them to the postcolonial notions of gender equity, self-sustainability, and creative living:

Congo girls took their turns, by twos, working in my house learning new methods of more abundant living. The laundry work was especially difficult for them, since their own washing was always done by beating their loincloths on boulders by the river's brink. Boys were trained in my kitchen to cook, for I had ever in mind the future homemaking of young Christian men and women.
(Kellersberger n.d.:19)

Another house was built for Miss Maria Fearing and Miss Lilian Thomas. And while awaiting its completion, Miss Fearing humbly joined the native women who engaged in various chores. She particularly "found pleasure in helping the other missionaries with their cooking, sewing, washing, ironing, and mending, thereby teaching the natives by example how to do these things" (Edmiston 1937:300). Soon this house became a home for orphan girls and babies that Miss Fearing invited and tenderly took care of. Just like Mrs. Sheppard, Miss Fearing started convivially mixing with the natives, visiting nearby villages, and inviting them to their home. That way, both women quickly learned the Tshiluba language and could communicate with them. They thus learned a lot about the Congolese people's life-world from the villagers, as much as the latter too learned a great deal about the encroaching Western modernity from them. Like Mr. Sheppard, these Black American women missionaries adopted a postcolonial pragmatic approach in their interactions with the natives. Here is how Fearing's coworker, Althea Edmiston, narrates her warm encounter with the Congolese women whom she daily welcomed to her house where they freely talked, sang, played, and told stories:

During the week she [Miss Fearing] made frequent visits to the villages nearby, and gathered together small groups, teaching them the same lesson that she had taught the Sunday before. As time went on she began to win their friendship, especially that of little children, who often followed her home where she would show them pictures and other things of interest. Soon the yard of the "foreign mother" [*mamu wa Mputu*], as they called her, became a regular rendezvous for native people, young and old. There was always a place for them on the long, front verandah, which was covered with nice, smooth slatting, on which they sat. There they could talk, sing, play, and tell stories, while the "foreign mother" went about her other duties. They came and went at will without disturbing anyone.

(Edmiston 1937:301)

As the number of the children brought to Miss Fearing increased year by year (reaching between forty and fifty), it became difficult for her to accommodate all of them in the house she shared with Miss Thomas. She therefore decided to sacrifice herself and use most of the money she received from time to time from the benefactors in the United States, who supported her good work, for the upkeep of the children. That source of support, together with her own raised salary as a full-time missionary, enabled Miss Fearing to put up "small houses of native style" for the children. With the exception of the babies for whom milk and sugar were reserved, all the girls were fed with affordable local foodstuffs: Indian corn, peas, manioc, peanuts, bananas, plantains, pumpkins, sweet potatoes, greens, goat meat, fish, and palm oil.

Miss Fearing gradually introduced the girls to Western, modern ways of living by applying John Dewey's educational philosophy of learning by doing. That way, she taught them sanitation (how to wash themselves and their clothes with soap), dressing manners, sewing, and ironing. Using her house as a didactic cultural site, Miss Fearing also taught the girls how to make the bed, cook, set the table, wash the dishes, and sweep the floors. When she assembled them every morning after breakfast for a devotional service, "She would talk to them about how to conduct themselves and how to be quiet, polite, and lady-like." Apart from this morning family gathering, the girls also attended the day school run by Mrs. Lucy Sheppard as well as "catechumen class, and all the religious services of the Mission." From time to time, Miss Fearing took the girls for a walk to the village for a visit, or to the river for a swim, or to the bushes to pick up mushrooms and grasshoppers. As Edmiston reports:

Miss Fearing loved her girls dearly. She lived with them and for them. When any of them became seriously ill, she nursed them as tenderly and as anxiously as if she were the one who gave them birth; and the girls gratefully returned her love, for she was indeed their only mother.

(307–308)

Miss Fearing's girls' home was later named "Pantops Home for Girls," in honor of a similar home with that name in Virginia. In addition to running the Home, she also taught a class at the Sunday school and another one at the day school.

Being the oldest member of the APCM, Miss Fearing treated other missionaries and their family members tenderly like her own family, though she was not given the same consideration by the racially biased Dr. Snyder. She cared for them whenever anyone of them was sick, grieved with them and made burial arrangements whenever there was a loss in a family (as in the case of the Sheppards who lost two children in Luebo), and celebrated with them whenever there was a birth or a wedding. Commenting on her generosity to other missionaries, irrespective of their racial affiliations, Edmiston remarks:

> She not only helped her fellow-missionaries in their times of sorrow and distress, but also in the time of their greatest joys. When the first missionary wedding took place at Luebo, she prepared for all the missionaries and visitors a most delicious wedding feast, including a beautiful bridal cake.
>
> (309)

By behaving to others this way, Miss Fearing taught her girls how to be one another's keeper, regardless of gender, race, and social status. In Miss Fearing's thoughts, Congolese girls and boys needed that lesson as they were being trained by the Black American missionaries to develop a new subjective agency in the interstitial space between their African tradition and the encroaching Western modernity.

Because of her formal training and experience as a teacher in America, Mrs. Lucy Sheppard was given the heavy task of starting a day school for boys and girls at the Luebo mission station. However, although she had some experience studying and working in poorly equipped black schools in America, in Luebo, she had nothing to start with—no desks, books, or writing materials of any kind. The only thing she had was an unfathomable determination to educate Congolese boys and girls and Miss Fearing's support. Here is how Kellersberger describes Lucy's classroom:

> Mrs Sheppard's classroom knew no dimensions. The sky was the roof and the four corners of the earth were the boundaries. There was not a textbook, not a slate nor a pencil, not a desk, and not a pupil who knew one letter of the alphabet from another. Most of the prospective pupils were slave children redeemed by the missionaries for salt, sea shells, or cloth. The educational methods which the new teacher had employed under similar difficult conditions in America were used again to advantage. She found the leaf from an old storybook, which had the alphabet upon it. This was pinned to a rude board and the assorted class recited their letters loudly in concert. Practice in forming these letters was obtained by using sharpened sticks on deep white sand. Later,

blackboards were made by covering shipping boxes with dark clothes. Letters were cut from books and papers, made into simple native words, and pasted on blank paper for spelling lessons. It was difficult to obtain them all of one size, so the effect was hard on the eyes, but quite satisfactory to the mind. Later, lessons were written by hand in blank books. Not until 1900 was money given for a small printing press. After this, first and second readers, Biblical parables, and song sheets evolved in rapid succession.

(Kellersberger n.d.:30)

That way, the children were taught reading, writing, and arithmetic. In 1897, Lucy Sheppard reported that forty-five native children enrolled at the school and that they were as talented as American children. In reporting that way, Lucy joined her husband's discursive effort at debunking the Western colonial narrative that misrepresented Africans as genetically less endowed than the Europeans.

While busy with the demanding schoolwork, Lucy gave birth to her second child, Lucille, in September 1896. Lucille only lived for eight months as she succumbed to high fever. Again, despite that loss, the Sheppards pressed on with their work to uplift the Congolese people as they faced the colonial onslaught. In September 1897, Lucy Sheppard gave birth to their third daughter, Wilhelmina. Given her exhaustion with frequent bouts of fever, her past losses, and the anxiety that the missionaries experienced under the threat of the native soldiers' mutiny (also known as Batetela rebellion or revolt) at that time, Lucy Sheppard was advised to return with her daughter to America. In 1898, Mr. Sheppard took Lucy and their daughter down the river to Kinshasa, from where they boarded a newly inaugurated freight train to the port city of Matadi. Lucy and Wilhelmina Sheppard were the first passengers to ride on the new rail line. Mr. Sheppard then bid his family farewell in Kinshasa (Leopoldville).

In June 1895, three years before returning to America with her daughter, Lucy had accompanied Mr. Sheppard on his trip to visit the Lukengu, King Kot aMbweeky, in Mushenge. During the trip, Lucy had an opportunity to gaze at the rich Congolese flora and fauna with a sense of awe. She also enjoyed listening to the singing and music of the natives when they stopped at very hospitable villages on their way and conducted worship services. At each service, Lucy sang a hymn in Bushong before Mr. Sheppard preached. When they entered Mushenge, the Sheppards were given a royal welcome by an enthusiastic crowd like the one Mr. Sheppard experienced during his first visit to the capital. The King was very delighted to see Mr. Sheppard again after a long time. In a letter from Mushenge, Mr. Sheppard recounted how the king, who had previously given a cold shoulder to Mr. Adamson, embraced him, saying: "My son! My son! Do you still love me, and have you come at last! I sent message after message for you, but no word came" (The Missionary 6/1896:271–273). The day after the Sheppards' arrival, a big reception was organized at the town square where Sheppard was received the first time. Lucy greeted the King, and she enjoyed the dancing and the music that took place at the reception. Mr. Sheppard then presented the King with gifts from America, including medicine, a silver cup, an album of modern buildings, and a pocketknife, and he was delighted.

While the Sheppards were in Mushenge, a ritual killing took place, and Sheppard expressed his disapproval of it to the King. Unlike the first time, however, this time the Lukengu yielded to Sheppard's request and promised to stop the ritual. Unfortunately, King Kot aMbweeky II died shortly after the Sheppards' visit, and the next King continued the cruel tradition.

Back in Luebo, Mr. Sheppard's evangelical mission started to have some success. In April 1895, five young men confessed their Christian faith and were trained as missionaries. One of the five who distinguished himself, Kachunga, was selected for translation work in America. Because of his evangelical success and his good rapport with the Congolese people, Mr. Sheppard was made the APCM Senior missionary at Luebo in 1897. This promotion no doubt vindicated Mr. Sheppard's postcolonial pragmatist approach to evangelism in Africa, which contrasted with the colonial, purist vision of white missionaries like Dr. Snyder and Mr. Adamson. The Sheppards' visit to Kuba land gave Lucy Sheppard a useful insight into the Kuba people's life-world and the validity of the postcolonial pragmatic approach adopted by Mr. Sheppard. During her stay in America, she further educated the American people about the African people's humanity and pointed out the importance of this pragmatic approach in evangelizing the Congo land, in particular, and the continent of Africa, in general.

While in America, Lucy Sheppard spent most of the time with her in-laws in Staunton, Virginia. Mr. Sheppard's parents had become staunch members of the First Presbyterian Church, and its congregation gave a significant financial support to the Sheppards' mission in the Congo. In October 1898, Lucy spoke to the Women's Society of the First Presbyterian Church. She enthusiastically described with concrete illustrations the very taxing work she had been doing for the empowerment of the Congolese girls and boys, and her audience was impressed by the talk.

In addition to giving talks and taking care of her baby, Lucy Sheppard also spent a considerable amount of time compiling and translating forty-six hymns into Tshiluba for the Luebo mission station. The translated songs were put together into a collection entitled *Musambu wa Nzambi* (Songs of God) and published by Curtiss Press in Richmond, Virginia, in 1898. For Lucy Sheppard and Maria Fearing, translation became a space of cultural encounter and a means of mutual self-subjectification. Through the act of translating, the Black American missionaries gave a sense of dignity to African languages and the people who spoke them; they also debunked the notion that those languages were just animalistic "mumbo jumbo" and encouraged a productive postcolonial engagement with Africans.

After dispatching his Pianga massacre bombshell report to Morrison in September 1899, Mr. Sheppard returned to Ibanche and remained the only missionary there until his wife, Lucy Sheppard, joined him in 1990. Lucy left their daughter in the care of Mr. Sheppard's sister in Staunton, VA, and devotedly returned to the Congo to care for native children and their parents. In Ibanche, Lucy faced new challenges: she had to learn the Bushong language, cultivate a convivial relationship with Kuba women, support her husband's missionary work, and start a school for boys and girls without adequate learning materials. As she did in Luebo, here also, Lucy opened her house to native women and their girls.

When she started the new school in Ibanche in 1900, Lucy only had fifteen students. However, the number exponentially increased year after year, as parents gradually realized the empowering value of the new education system introduced by Lucy. In addition to the school, Lucy also formed the first Woman's Society that she named "Sunshine Band" at the mission. She weekly brought together native mothers and daughters at her house, where they learned sewing, sang Christian songs in their language, prayed, and shared meals. Lucy also taught them Negro spirituals and how to take care of the sick amongst them. In fact, amongst the Kuba women and girls, Lucy distinguished herself as a teacher, a learner, a healer, a patient host, an open-minded missionary, and an excellent social worker.

While Lucy was busy expanding the school and the women's organization association, Mr. Sheppard was overseeing the overall development of the Ibanche missionary station. He also kept close contact with the Lukengu, King Mishaape, and tried to extend his missionary activities and an educational opportunity for the Kuba children in Mushenge. However, he faced a serious setback in 1900, when Free State soldiers raided Mushenge for the second time, and killed King Mishaape. This time the Kuba warriors bravely fought the invading colonial forces with their arrows, bows, and spears, but their resistance proved inadequate in the face of the government soldiers' guns. As the villagers deserted Mushenge, some sought refuge with the Sheppards at the Ibanche Station. Knowing well the anti-colonial stance of Mr. Sheppard, the Free State officials and soldiers spared the town of Ibanche and the mission station. Following this raid and the killing of King Mishaape, Mushenge went through a period of instability marked also by fratricidal killings amongst members of the royal family who contested for the Lukengu throne.

In 1902, Mbop Kyeen was installed as the new Lukengu. Unlike his predecessor King Mishaape, the new Lukengu was open-minded to the missionaries. As soon as he settled down, Mbop Kyeen recognized Mr. Sheppard as a vital anti-colonial ally and invited him to establish a station in Mushenge and build a school there. Unfortunately, King Mbop Kyeen succumbed to an epidemic that broke up in his land during his reign and passed away after one year in the throne. The next Lukengu, King Kot a Pe, was less friendly to the Sheppards. He did not like the fact that the Sheppards harbored Prince

Maxamalinge, whom he believed had bewitched the past two Kuba kings with a powerful medicine he purportedly buried in the ground in Ibanche and, as such, was a big threat to him. At one point, King Kot a Pe succeeded in persuading Prince Maxamalinge to visit him in Mushenge only to ask the Free State authorities to arrest him for the murders he did not commit. Maxamalingue was arrested, tortured, and taken to court, before Mr. Sheppard came to his rescue. Upon receiving the news of Maxamalinge's arrest on the murder charge based on the King's superstitious belief, Mr. Sheppard traveled a long distance to the district court, denounced his unjust arrest, and succeeded in liberating him. Mr. Sheppard also sent a strong message to the King to liberate immediately other innocent villagers he had intended to execute. In acknowledgement of Mr. Sheppard's influence upon both the Kuba people and the State government, King Kot a Pe liberated all his victims and invited him to visit the capital Mushenge, as his predecessors had done. In his conversation with the King, Sheppard expressed his disapproval of the ritual killings of the slaves at royal funerals, the poison ordeal practice, and the King's determination to do away with potential rivals to the throne. At the conclusion of their meeting, King Kot a Pe granted Mr. Sheppard permission to evangelize his people and build a school for boys and girls in the capital Mushenge. He promised to give them land and to put up a school building. He also promised to ban the poison ordeal practice and other human sacrifice practice. Thus, as he returned with his party to Ibanche, Mr. Sheppard was pleased and convinced that the pragmatic postcolonial vision of his mission amongst the Congolese people was progressing well. His main threat, however, remained the brutal Congo Free State government.

Meanwhile, Lucy and Mr. Sheppard welcomed their baby boy. He was named William Lapsley Sheppard and was dedicated to Christ by their Christian coworker W.W. Morrison. Conforming also to the Kuba tradition, the Sheppards brought the boy outdoors after two months, and the villagers officially welcomed him with gifts. They named him Maxamilange after Prince Maxamalinge. As he grew up alongside other children in the Ibanche community, the boy became more fluent in the Bushong language than English. The culturally conjunctive naming of this child posits him as a symbol of the postcolonial pragmatist vision that the Sheppards were inculcating in the Congolese people as they encountered Western modernity.

With the acquisition and installation of a printing machine at the Luebo station in 1900, the industrial education of the natives that the Sheppards had started was expanded by Morrison. The printing press provided a big job opportunity for the natives who were soon trained to typeset and produce the APCM quarterly magazine *Kasai Herald*, learning materials for schools (mathematics, science, and elementary reading textbooks) as well as hymnals, and other related materials for the Church. The *Kasai Herald* also became a valuable medium of communication between the APCM and the Southern Presbyterian Church in America, and the Sheppards were frequent contributors to the magazine. Thanks to the printing press, Morrison compiled and published the first Tshiluba language dictionary with the assistance of the Sheppards. In 1902, the press published the first book of English hymns translated by the Sheppards into Tshiluba, and compiled by Lucy. Lucy's "Bushong reader" became the first book to be printed in the Kuba language.

Encouraged by the production of school materials at Luebo, Lucy established a home for the Kuba girls at Ibanche, named "Maria Carey Home." Apart from the day school, another home was also established for the Kuba boys. The Sheppards' heavy workload and family responsibilities at the Ibanche station were only alleviated when another Black American female missionary, Miss Althea Brown, joined them by the end of 1902.

Althea Brown was born in Russellville, DeKalb County, Alabama, on December 17, 1874. When she was just one and a half years old, her parents Robert and Mary Suggs Brown, both devout Christians, moved Althea and her nine siblings to Mississippi. There, Robert bought one hundred acres of land and raised the children with a strict Christian discipline. Denied educational opportunities during the American Reconstruction and the Jim Crow periods of American history, the self-educated parents worked hard tilling the land in order to afford an education for their children. Althea started her education at home, where Robert taught his children the alphabet, using "a crude chart and blackboard" until a benefactor, "The wife of a German farmer whose land adjoined the Brown farm became interested in Althea and taught her to read. Later an elder brother became her teacher for fifteen months" (Bedinger 1937:264). Althea later entered and successfully graduated from Fisk University and soon after embarked on her mission to serve others. She stated later: "I still wanted to become a graduate of Fisk University, not that I might use my life to selfish advantage, but that I might spend it unreservedly in service for others" (Bedinger 1937:265). As she took up domestic works and part-time teaching jobs here and there during the vacations in order to garner financial resources for studies at Fisk, Althea gained valuable experiences that she later on drew from on her arrival in the Congo. Bedinger reports that in Mississippi "The majority of her pupils lived in one-room log cabins, and were almost as destitute and needy as later she discovered the native Africans to be. It was a valuable training for her life work" (265). It was, therefore, with this idea of serving others, especially the African people whom she considered as her kin that she left her loved ones for Africa on August 20, 1902.

Althea arrived in Matadi after sailing for two months and soon took a freight train to Kinshasa (Leopoldville). From Kinshasa, Althea boarded the Presbyterian Mission steamer *SS Lapsley* for a twenty-six-day sail up Congo River and the Kasai tributary. Despite the uncomfortable journey on the small, shaky steamer, Althea (like other Black American missionaries who travelled the same route before her) was fascinated and delighted by the rich Congolese flora and fauna that she admiringly gazed at. Recalling her experience later, she wrote: "The scenery along the way was grand; great broad plains, dense forests, high rocky cliffs, green hills, beautiful palm tree, and luxuriant vegetation. Occasionally elephants and antelopes were seen on the plain" (Bedinger 1937:267). Althea arrived in the progressive town of Luebo in November 1902 and was warmly welcomed by Morrison and eight other missionaries, six of whom were Black Americans. She spent six weeks at the Luebo station in the company of Morrison who was, at that time, studying the grammatical structure of the Tshiluba language and compiling a Tshiluba dictionary. According to her, it was Morrison who encouraged her to undertake a similar project with the Bushong language. Since there were nine missionaries at the already flourishing Luebo station, Althea was asked to join the Sheppards at the Ibanche mission station, and Morrison took her there. They arrived in Ibanche in December 1902, and Althea was warmly welcomed by the Sheppards and a crowd of native men, women, and children. She was pleasantly surprised to see the development of the station under the leadership of the Sheppards. Althea describes her journey to and arrival at Ibanche in this full-length quotation of her interview with Robert Bedinger:

> Late in the afternoon we reached Ibanche where were located our pioneer missionaries, Doctor and Mrs. William H. Sheppard. We were most warmly received and welcomed by them. The natives came around in great numbers and showered upon us their salutations. A prince, the son of a king of the Bakuba people, gave me another name, as is always their custom. Then and there I lost my American name, and have been known ever since by the Bakuba as **Mbawota**. The beautiful station, Ibanche, at the time one of the most charming and picturesque spots in all central Africa, proved to be the goal towards which I had been working for so many years. **I entered into the work with wholehearted enthusiasm, and was very happy—never homesick or lonesome.**
> (Bedinger 1937:268–269, all the emphases added)

Just a day after her arrival at Ibanche, Althea devotedly started her labor of love geared toward the empowerment of the Congolese people, especially women and girls, at the intersection of their African tradition and the encroaching Western modernity. Here is how she later described her duties during the years she spent at Ibanche:

> I began work the day after my arrival, and had five and a half years in the blessed work of my heart's desire. My special work was that of making a dictionary and grammar in the unwritten language of the Bakuba tribe, teaching in the day schools and Sunday schools, helping to organize the native women into Christian bands, being matron of a girls' home, making charts and textbooks for the school, and working among the women and children in general.
> (Bedinger 1937:270)

100   *The Congo narrative*

Althea performed those duties alongside Lucy Sheppard. Mr. Sheppard was busy overseeing the physical development of the station and organizing the Young People's Society of Christian Endeavor that he had started at the Station. In 1903, Sheppard proudly reported that more and more Kuba people were opening up to his postcolonial vision of their society, and that native evangelists and teachers were being trained at Ibanche.

However, in 1904, the Sheppards decided to return to the United States on a long furlough, and Althea was left behind alone to take care of the responsibilities that she had until then shared with Lucy Sheppard. In fact, as she herself stated later, she was the only foreign woman at the Ibanche Station for almost three years. Unfortunately, as soon as the Sheppards left, a conflict broke out between King Kot aPe and a callous state official, Captain DeCocke. The latter summoned the Lukengu to Luebo and ordered him to pay 100,000 cowrie shells as a fine for his overdue State taxes. As the king was unable to pay the exorbitant fine, DeCocke humiliated and arrested him. Because of the friendship that he had cultivated with Mr. Sheppard and the APCM missionaries, the King turned to them for assistance, and the mission quickly loaned him the 100,000 cowries. He was thereafter unchained and released to return to his capital Mushenge. However, upon his arrival home, the angered Lukengu issued a decree to his people to kill the State officers and foreign traders responsible for his arrest and humiliation. But instead of limiting their anger towards the Belgian officials and traders at the State-owned rubber trading station near the Ibanche mission station, the king's warriors also burned down the church and other buildings at the mission station. Fortunately, Althea Brown and other missionaries realizing the rioters' anger to all the foreigners, decided to flee to Luebo the night before the mission station was burned down. Certainly, had Mr. Sheppard been in Ibanche, the king's men could not have carried out their destruction of the beautiful station. It was therefore left to the government soldiers to quell the riots. The latter invaded Mushenge and other Kuba villages, chained the king, and subjected the hitherto forbidden Kuba land to the free state colonial rule. After the government intervention, things eventually calmed down, the previously cordial relationship between the Lukengu and the missionaries resumed, and the mission station was gradually rebuilt.

In 1905, Althea Brown married the Black American missionary she had met in Luebo the previous year, Mr. Alonzo L. Edmiston, another graduate of Stillman College. Soon after, they had a son whom they named Kuete, after the name of the then reigning friendly Lukengu, King Kwete Mabintshi. In the absence of the Sheppards, the Edmistons became the leading missionaries at Ibanche. Althea continued to take care of the Maria Carey Home and day school while devoting a great deal of her time to the linguistic study of the Kuba language, the Bushong. Her pioneering study resulted many years later to a 600-page volume entitled *Grammar and Dictionary of the Bushonga or Bakuba Language.* The book was published by the Luebo press in 1932. Like the Sheppards, Althea also compiled and translated folk tales, songs, proverbs, and textbooks. While Althea was busy with her duties mentioned above, Alonzo introduced young natives to an agricultural education.

In his agricultural education classes and field practicals, Alonzo Edmiston also adopted a postcolonial pedagogy that privileges local knowledges. He integrated modern techniques and implements in the local experiences. That way, he learnt a lot from the Congolese peasants as much as he shared his American farming knowledge with them. Jan Vansina has commented on the efficacy of Alonzo Edmiston's empowering, postcolonial pedagogy:

> At Ibanc[Ibanche], Alonzo Edmiston, eager to promote development, used his earlier experience as a schoolboy on a farm in Tuscaloosa, Alabama, and as a farmhand on the plantation of the Alabama State Hospital to organize an industrial school focused on agriculture. He set out to teach the selection of seed, the rotation of crops, the preservation of the soil, and up-to-date methods of cultivation. As with so many development projects, however, the local Bushong and the Kete knew better than he did how to farm in this region. Yet he also introduced new varieties of corn, garden vegetables, mangos, citrus fruit trees, and domestic pigeons [...]. Some of the corn varieties, cabbages, tomatoes, and mango and lemon trees are still planted today, while one giant dove cote survived in Ibanc until 1932.
>
> (Vansina 2010:300)

Following the passing of King Kot aPe, who fell victim to the then spreading Spanish influenza, Kwete Mabintshi was installed as the new Lukengu. In his picturesque, inaugural speech at a ceremony attended by a number of invited missionaries, the Lukengu tacitly acknowledged the diminished power of the Kuba royalty under the colonial regime and painstakingly admonished his people to respect the State government and collaborate with missionaries. Seizing on the openness pledged by the new Lukengu, the APCM requested Althea and Alonzo Edmiston to move to the town of Bulape, near the capital Mushenge, and start a new mission station there. They joyfully accepted the new appointment and quickly set out to develop the new station. As the Sheppards did at Luebo and Ibanche, the Edmistons started Day schools and catechumen classes and attracted many Kuba children, including members of the royal family. They spent several years at that station, providing modern industrial and Christian education to the Kuba boys and girls before they were again transferred to the town of Mutoto. There, Alonzo oversaw the development of a large farm and a Theological School, whilst Althea devoted her time to school work for the Lulua, Baluba, Zappo Zap, and Bakete boys and girls. In addition to taking charge of the Mutoto Girls' Home, Althea also took a special interest in the upliftment of the Kasai women whose condition she described with concern to potential sympathizers this way: "I need not tell you that no condition in Africa is more pitiable, more pathetic than that of the women who are the beasts of burden, slaves for service and victims of vice." Acknowledging Althea's emancipatory work for the Congolese women, one of her coworkers at Mutoto station wrote:

> Many are the Christians women scattered over this land who were taught by Mrs. Edmiston in school and Girls' Homes. Many have heard their courting days on her front porch, had their wedding garments made in her home, and all their wedding arrangements provided by her. Then as these girls left the shelter of the Girls' Home and began Christian homes of their own, the Christian ideals and training which they received from her have been passed on to their children, who in their turn will pass them on to others. Who can measure the results of a life given to teaching boys and girls?
> (qtd. in Bedinger 1937:284)

Only taking a couple of furloughs to take their two children back to the United States, Althea devoted thirty-eight years of service (1903–1941) empowering the Congolese people as they negotiated a new identity through the cultural translation of Western modernity and their African values.

During their long furlough in the United States (1904–1906), the Sheppards spent most of their time with their children (Wilhelmina and Maxamalinge) and Mr. Sheppard's parents in Staunton, VA. They also crisscrossed the country, visiting churches, schools, and colleges. At those sites, Lucy sang songs in the Bushong and Tshiluba languages, and Mr. Sheppard talked about the Congolese people's life-world and Black American missionaries' development work amongst them. Wherever they gave talks, the venues were usually overflowed with enthusiastic crowds. Such venues included Presbyterian and Methodist churches in Lynchburg, Virginia; the Warm Springs ballroom, Virginia; Hampton Institute, Virginia; the Monteagle Chautauqua in the Cumberland Mountains of Tennessee; Fisk University in Nashville, Tennessee; Talladega College in Alabama; First Presbyterian Church in Charleston, West Virginia; the Central Presbyterian Church in Atlanta, Georgia; Tuskegee Institute in Alabama; Stillman College, Tuscaloosa, Alabama; and Princeton University in New Jersey, where he was called "The black Livingstone of Africa." Mr. Sheppard was also received by President Roosevelt at the White House in 1905.

Through their lectures and songs in Congolese languages, the Sheppards extolled the humanity of the African people which was at the time contested and assaulted in Western discursive formations. While Morrison mainly campaigned for the political and human rights of the Congolese people who were then being exploited and killed by King Leopold's Free State government, the Sheppards also focused the world's attention on their sophisticated artifacts, songs, dances, economic activities, and sociopolitical organizations. Their representation of the Bakuba people, for example, no doubt led their audiences, especially Black Americans, to revise their negative preconceptions about Africa and to be proud of their roots.

In the spring of 1906, the Sheppards bade a hard goodbye to their two children in Staunton and headed back to the Congo to continue their work amongst the Bakuba people. They travelled with two black missionaries newly recruited by Mr. Sheppard—Annie Taylor from Tuscaloosa and Adolphus Rochester from Jamaica. Both were later united in marriage while serving in Congo. They joined the newly married William and Bertha Morrison in London and sailed aboard the same vessel to Matadi from where they took a train to Kinshasa. From Kinshasa, they boarded the newly commissioned APCM steamer, *S.S. Lapsley*, and headed to Luebo. Taking leave of the Morrisons and other missionaries in Luebo, the Sheppards proceeded to their home mission station at Ibanche. Although they deplored the destruction of the beautiful buildings they had put up before they left for the United States on a furlough, they were nevertheless happy with the rebuilding work that Mr. Hawkins, the Edmistons, and other Black American missionaries were undertaking.

Soon after the Sheppards' return to Ibanche, King Kot aPe paid them a visit and apologized on behalf of his people who had indiscriminately directed their anger toward all foreigners and burnt down the mission station. Mr. Sheppard accepted the King's apology. As a courteous gesture of his reassurance of his friendship with the King and his people, Mr. Sheppard presented him with a gift of two peacocks he had brought with him from the United States. The Sheppards then asked the King to send them Kuba girls for the Maria Carey Home and boys for the boys' home. The King, who, by now, had already been convinced of the value of literacy and industrial education as his people faced the colonial onslaught, welcomed the Sheppards' request, and sent them forty girls and fifty boys recruited from different villages across the Kuba land. For the following years, the Sheppards continued the development of the Ibanche station. They set up a local printing press and produced translated school materials and hymnals. They also established a health clinic where Lucy, though not a certified nurse, treated the natives alongside missionaries. While the industrial education flourished year after year, the Sheppards also introduced students to music education. Thanks to the donation of musical instruments they received from a donor in the United States, the Sheppards formed a musical band and taught boys and girls how to play Jazz, spirituals, and local sounds.

As reported by British consul Wilfred Thesiger, by 1909, Luebo and Ibanche had become excellent education centers that attracted students from across the whole Kasai region. The two sites also provided numerous well-paying job opportunities for the educated natives. Following his visit in Luebo, Thesiger wrote:

> As regards to education, the work of the Luebo Mission struck me as having been astonishingly successful, especially among the Lulua and Baluba, who seem to be animated with a passionate desire to learn to read and write. Everywhere I found schools crowded during the work hours, and I must have received a score of petitions during my tour from the smaller villages, asking that I would give them a letter to the mission in order that they, too, might obtain a teacher.[...]Under these circumstances it was not surprising to learn that the mission schools and printing press were unable to keep pace with the demand.[...] A large number of their mission-taught boys find good employment on the steamers, railways, and with the trading companies.[...] As many of the boys are sons of chiefs and headmen, who will ultimately take their fathers' places, the beneficial effects of this branch of the station work can scarcely be overstated.
>
> (*Kasai Herald*, 1/1909:5)

This testimonial is indeed a tribute to the pioneering, empowering postcolonial vision that Mr. Sheppard had conceived for the Congolese natives, and later carried out by Morrison and other missionaries in Luebo and Ibanche. In fact, by 1909, Luebo and Ibanche missionary stations counted a total of 7,705 members.

Anti-colonial activism

In a strong anti-colonial move, Sheppard continued to decry and denounce King Leopold's regime that, in his own words, "mangled bodies, severed hands, devastated villages, terrorized districts [...] for gold." In January 1908, Mr. Sheppard wrote an article for The *Kasai Herald* that strongly condemned the devastation of the Kuba villages, the pillage of their resources, and the exploitation of their labor by the Belgian Rubber company, the C K (Compagnie de Kasai). The short, poignant article was entitled "From the Kuba Country" and consisted of three parts. In the first part, Mr. Sheppard talked about the peaceful, dignified life that the Kuba people, whom he was the first westerner to encounter, lived before the colonial invasion:

> These great stalwart men and women, who have from time immemorial been free, cultivating large crops of Indian corn, tobacco, potatoes, trapping elephants for their ivory and leopards for their skins, who have always had their own king and a government not to be despised, officers of the law, established in every town of the kingdom; these magnificent people, perhaps about 400,000 in number, have entered a new chapter in the history of their tribe. Only a few years since travelers through

this country found them living in large homes, having from one to four rooms in each house, loving and living happily with their wives and children, one of the most prosperous and intelligent of all the African tribes, though living in one of the most remote spots on the planet. One seeing the happy, busy, prosperous lives which they lived could not help feeling that surely the lines had fallen unto this people in pleasant places.

(Sheppard 1996a:281)

In the second part of the article, Mr. Sheppard described how desolate, deserted, and run down the hitherto beautiful Kuba villages had become under the colonial, brutal Free State regime since its aggressive incursion into the Kuba land in 1904:

But within these last three years how changed they [the Kuba people] are! Their farms are growing up in weeds and jungle, their king is practically a slave, their houses now are mostly only half-built single rooms, and are much neglected. The streets of their towns are not clean and well-swept as they once were. Even their children cry for bread.

(281)

Mr. Sheppard then concluded his article by squarely placing the responsibility of the devastation of the Kuba people and their land on the shoulders of the inhuman Free State government officials and their allied Belgian rubber traders:

Why this change? You have it in a few words. There are armed sentries of chartered trading companies, who force the men and women to spend most of their days and nights in the forests making rubber, and the price they receive is so meager that they cannot live upon it. In the majority of the villages these people have not time to listen to the gospel story, or give an answer concerning their soul's salvation. Looking upon the changed scene now, one can only join with them in their groans as they must say: "Our burdens are greater than we can bear."

(282)

As a result of his bold criticism of the ruthless exploitation and ill treatment of the Congolese natives by the Belgian Kasai Rubber Company, Sheppard and his coworker William Morrison were sued for libel by the colonial regime of King Leopold II. Sheppard was tried and acquitted in Leopoldville on September 20, 1909. Expressing their support for Sheppard and Morrison's anti-colonial protests, about thirteen natives led by Chief Njoka willed to act as defense witnesses at their trial but were prevented from doing so. Even so, by their presence and support at the trial, the natives unequivocally lent credence to and endorsed Sheppard and his colleague's positionality as trustworthy allies in their anti-colonial struggle.

Their voices and approval were made louder by their presence. Sheppard continued to advocate for the rights of the Congolese natives after his acquittal until he and his wife Lucy were forced to leave the Congo and return to the United States for good in 1910 (at the advice of Dr. Sims), following his protracted bouts with fever. The Sheppards' vision of a hybrid postcolonial African society did not, however, fizzle out after their departure. It was carried on with intensity by other devoted liberal Black missionaries recruited by them, including Althea and Alonzo Edmiston, Henry Hawkins, Maria Fearing, Lillian and Lucius DeYampert, Joseph Phipps, Adolphus Rochester, Annie Taylor, and Edna Atkinson. Walter Williams's summary of William Sheppard's empowering mission amongst the Congolese natives is to the point:

> Sheppard rejected the view that soul-saving excluded earthly considerations, and he worked hard to aid those Congolese in material ways. Whether giving medical aid, ransoming slaves, or protesting colonial exploitation, Sheppard tried to improve African standards of living. While he did not express a Pan-African ideology, he did feel a closeness to the Kasai peoples that was felt by few white Americans.
>
> (1982:29)

Note

1 Intrigued by Sheppard's proficiency in the Kuba language that he had just learnt prior to his visit to the Kuba Kingdom, the Kuba King Lukengu and his council came to the mythological conclusion that he had to be an incarnation of a previous Kuba royalty. They continued to believe so despite his insistence in telling them that he was an American and not a Kuba. King Lukengu's response to his denial was that Sheppard didn't know.

4 The other allies

The postcolonial activist W.M. Morrison (1867–1918)

Following Samuel Lapsley's death, Mr. William M. Morrison was appointed from Sheppard's presbytery in Virginia to join the APCM in Luebo in 1897. He was warmly welcomed by the Sheppards and quickly became a resourceful member of the team. Mr. Morrison was put in charge of the treasury while Mr. Sheppard was the senior missionary. Unlike the racially biased Dr. Snyder, Mr. Morrison was impressed by Mr. Sheppard's productive rapport with the Congolese natives and encouraged him to establish another station in Kuba land. In a letter addressed to *The Missionary* on June 5, 1897, Morrison, who had just made a trip to the edge of the Kuba land with William Sheppard, wrote that "Mr. Sheppard seemed providentially the man to go to open the mission. He has been there, is known along the road, and speaks the language" (Morrison 1996:109). On July 2, 1897, both of them decided to travel to Mushenge and pay a visit to King Mishaape II, but the latter refused to welcome them after they had passed the town of Ibanche. He sent them a message that he would consider their request to visit only after his coronation. Sensing the danger that they could face at the hands of the new king's men, Mr. Sheppard and Mr. Morrison tactically decided to return to Luebo and wait for another opportunity. However, Mr. Morrison was impressed and encouraged by the warm welcome that both received as they passed through Kuba villages for three days. The villagers certainly remembered Mr. Sheppard's convivial interactions with them during his first exploratory journey to the heart of the Kuba land in 1892 and invited the two missionaries to establish stations in their villages. The news of the development work of the missionaries in Luebo was also reaching the Kuba land, and the villagers there started to make a clear distinction between the cruel *Bula Matadi* (government officials) and the missionaries.

By the midst of August 1897, the missionaries learned in Luebo that King Mishaape's mother had died and that his coronation was being delayed as the Kuba people carried out a series of rituals, including the killing of 600 slaves, in her honor. Anxious to attempt to stop that carnage of death and protect a friendly town, Morrison and Sheppard decided

DOI: 10.4324/9780429322426-7

to come to Ibanj at once, and open a station, and to come with full determination to stay unless actual force were used against us, for we believe this to be the door-way to the whole tribe, and it may be of more importance just now than the king's town itself.

(Morrison 1996a:113)

When Sheppard and Morrison reached the town on September 12, 1897, they were enthusiastically welcomed by the people of Ibanche who not only told them to stay in their town but also promised to rebel against the king, should he threaten them. Morrison further reported: "The king, learning of the possibilities of rebellion in this quarter not only sent us no message to return, but up to this time [December 7th, 1897] has completely ignored our presence here" (Morrison 1996:113).

With the protection of their village allies, Sheppard and Morrison started clearing the ground for their "village." Soon after, they put up temporary houses of sticks and palm fronds. However, after a month in Ibanche, Sheppard had to go back to Luebo in order to make arrangements for his wife's return to America with their daughter, Wilhelmina. Morrison remained behind with a number of their native assistants from Luebo. Like Sheppard and Laplsey, the pragmatic Morrison was quick in establishing a convivial relationship with the villagers. He preached to his assistants in Tshiluba, in which he attained basic fluency after only a few months amongst the natives in Luebo and started to learn Bushong. While Sheppard was away, Morrison also made remarkable progress on the development of the new mission station in Ibanche and offered a friendly overture to the Lukengu by sending him a gift. In November 1897, Morrison reported:

Lukengu, the king, while not showing any special signs of friendship, has accepted a small present from me, and has at least consented to my staying here for the present; the village nearby, and others in the vicinity, have shown marked signs of friendship; my work people who came with me from Luebo have given very little trouble, though representing several conflicting tribes; I am now able to preach to them with some degree of fluency in the Baluba dialect, which they all understand; I hope soon to begin regular services for the Bakuba, among whom I have come to labor; and last, but not least, I had the pleasure two Sundays ago of baptizing four of my work people who had for some weeks been inquirers. I have cleared off about two acres of ground, built houses for the people, and a temporary house for myself of sticks and palm fronds, 12x15, rather close quarters, but it is more than my Savior had.

(Morrison 1996b:114)

The missionaries' relationship with the Lukengu, King Mishaape, took a turn for the better when his power became increasingly threatened by the merciless Free State government. On Friday, April 13, 1899, he received

Sheppard and Morrison in Mushenge and asked them to drive the Free State government soldiers out of the Kuba land. But Sheppard and Morrison reminded him of how he menacingly refused to receive them when they had first approached him with a request to settle peacefully amongst his people in the capital and build a school for Bakuba children. Here is how Morrison recorded Sheppard's conversation with the then desperate king Mishaape on that occasion:

> Sheppard, speaking the language most fluently, acted as chief spokesman. We told him very plainly that a long time ago we had wished to come to him but he had refused; we told him that we had sent him word the state was coming, if he did not put in the feather (his crown) and open the roads for all to come and go. All of these warnings he refused and now the state (*Bula Matadi*) had come, he knew the road, was very strong, and would more than likely come again at some time. We told him plainly that we were no friends of *Bula Matadi*, because we were anxious that he should not confuse us and our missions. We explained that we were people of God and did not fight, and that *Bula Matadi* made fight and plenty of *palaver* and we think we did not wander far from the truth. We also told him that we might wish at some time to stop at his village and make this our home, but he made no reply to this.
> (Morrison 1996c:117)

After visiting with King Mishaape, Morrison reported that they observed with a sense of empathy and anger the desolation and devastation that had befallen the large Mushenge town. The hard working, dignified inhabitants of Mushenge abandoned their houses as they ran away from the brutal state soldiers, on the one hand, and the sanguinary King Mishaape who had been eliminating his opponents (especially his predecessor's sons) and carrying out ritual killings in honor of his deceased mother, on the other hand:

> This afternoon we went into his [king Mishaape's] for the first time. By all odds the largest native village I have ever seen, but the houses are all rotten and falling down and regularly laid off streets are grown up with weeds. It is harrowing to think of the awful tragedies which have been enacted here in the past few years. We are the only missionaries who have ever seen Lukengu's face.
> (Morrison 1996d:117)

This horrible double oppression that the ordinary Kuba people faced at that time led Sheppard and Morrison to side with them and adopt a more activist role against both dark forces: the inhumane, colonial Free State government and the brutal King Mishaape, who at one point threatened to kill Sheppard for harboring Prince Maxamalinge at Ibanche. Through that social and political activism, Sheppard and Morrison hoped to empower the oppressed Congolese natives to develop a postcolonial agency in the intersection of Western modernity and their African values. That was the project that Sheppard and Lapsley had started at the Luebo station and that Sheppard and Morrison were expanding to Ibanche. The project's target was to develop local languages, produce learning materials in them, dispense Western and African knowledges through them, empower women and men, resist Free State government's brutal oppression of the natives, and (with humility and dialogue) introduce the natives over time to Christianity. It is in view of these objectives that as soon as he arrived in Luebo, Morrison advised other missionaries to follow Mr. Sheppard's lead and interact with the Congolese natives respectfully. As Morrison's biographer Thomas Vinson (1921) reports, he constantly reminded other white missionaries that their mission was not to colonize the Congolese people:

> We should remember first and last that the natives should be treated as kindly and courteously as white people. We should always keep in mind that we are their servants and not their masters. Under their black skins they have feelings and sensibilities similar to ours, which ought to be respected. If we laugh at their customs, appearance or fetishes, we destroy their confidence in us and repel them. [...] if you make a mistake it is best to confess it in their presence. Conform to the dignified customs of chiefs and dignitaries where no morals are involved. Be ready to receive the natives without becoming impatient when you are busy.
> (Vinson 1921:135–137)

Realizing the limits of his power in the face of the advancing colonial onslaught into Kuba land and facing his people's disillusionment with his sanguinary reign, King Mishaape approached Mr. Sheppard for reconciliation. Instead of holding a grudge against Sheppard over his protection of Maxamalinge in Ibanche, the Lukengu invited him to his palace at night in order to amicably settle their differences. Sheppard described in detail his frightening encounter and conversation with King Mishaape that night as follows:

> I went to the presence of Lukenga. We sat down, turned face to face, folded our legs, and began talking. He said, "I am glad you have come", and I answered, "I am glad to be here." "Do you not know," he said, "that it is the custom when the crown passes from one family to another to murder all the sons of the old king? Were you not told that you were to be shot with poisonous arrows?" I said I had heard it but did not believe it. The king said, "It is true." Then he added, "Can we settle this thing now?" I said, "I hope so," and I could see murder in his eyes. He called for a man. The man brought a small pouch of leopard skin. The king called another man and asked him for a banana leaf. He put it over the fire to make it pliable. Then he took some strong medicine out

of the leopard skin and put it into the banana leaf. After sitting awhile he had it tied up and gave it to the servant, telling him to throw it into the Lingadi River. The king said, "Do you see that?" I said, "Yes." The king said, "It has gone into the Lingadi, from that to the Ligadi, then to the N'gala. I cannot call it back and it will not come back. Just so everything is gone that was between us which I had in my heart against you. He said, "Now, what are you going to do?" I said, "If you will allow me I will kneel here on the mat with you and pray." After prayers we went to our houses. I stayed with him a week and then went back to Ibanc.

(*Southern Workman*, 4/1905:219–220)

Because of Sheppard's fluency in the Bushong language, his deep knowledge of the Kuba people's cultural practices, and his reconciliation with King Mishaape, Morrison conceded that the Sheppards should settle at Ibanche and oversee the development of the new Presbyterian mission station there. They also agreed that Morrison should be in charge of the already well-established and flourishing Luebo station. When Morrison arrived in Luebo in 1897, he was pleased to find out that Sheppard and his team had already built a large church, several houses for missionaries, an orphanage (run by Miss Maria Fearing with Miss Lillian Thomas' assistance), a school for boys and girls (run by Mrs. Lucy Sheppard), and had also started a mission farm (run by Mr. Hawkins). By that time, the town of Luebo was also teeming with unfriendly Free State government officials, soldiers, and Belgian traders. Morrison's racial (his whiteness) and modern positioning, therefore, made his leadership of the Luebo station strategically important as the missionaries and the natives were constantly harassed by the State officials. He firmly stood against the illegal enslavement of the natives, their ruthless taxing by the State, and the exploitation of their labor (in rubber and ivory collection) by European traders. As Kennedy states, "He [Morrison] was angry about injustices all over the world, and hated the greedy individuals and governments that preyed on the meek" (Kennedy 2002:128).

Morrison's first decisive, activist stance against the oppression of the Congolese people by the Free State government took place when he confronted a callous Belgian officer, Fromont, in 1898. Morrison was appalled by the violence that Fromont and his soldiers unleashed upon the natives as they marched into Luebo in order to steal food and gather slaves. Their brutality prompted Morrison to write Fromont a stern protest letter, reminding him that what he was doing was illegal, but the latter unleashed even more violence on the natives. In defiance of Morrison's protest, Fromont ordered his troops to round up the entire Luba population of Luebo and take them to the State barracks for forced labor. However, instead of giving up his protest, as other missionaries usually did at that time, Morrison threatened Fromont that he was going to contact his friends and the media in London, especially the London *Times*, in order to enlighten the world on the atrocities he was committing in the name of the Free State government. Morrison's threat worked, as the humiliated Fromont and his men freed their captives and left the town alone. From that time, Morrison knew that the situation he had just been involved in (the oppression of the natives by the Free State agents) was not unique to Luebo—it was ubiquitous all over the Congo Free State. Perhaps, taking a cue from George Washington Williams' *Open Letter* to King Leopold II and the media campaign that he had launched against the Congo Free State government back in 1890, Morrison resolved that the Western world had to be further enlightened on the oppression of the Congolese people.

Sheppard's anti-colonial report on the Pianga massacre

Having made peace with the Lukengu King Mishaape, in 1899, Sheppard embarked on an extensive physical development of the Ibanche missionary station. Using the insight he gained from the local architectural know-how, he designed and oversaw the construction of a large church and missionaries' houses, including his own. He was also busy cultivating friendship with the inhabitants of the town, translating English hymns into the Bushong language, and planning a school for boys and girls that his wife was going to start off the ground upon her return from America. It was in that promising atmosphere that in September 1899, an anxious runner from the Kuba region of Pianga brought Sheppard the sad news of the massacre of the natives at the hands of the government-supported militia, the Zappo Zaps. The messenger, who brought with him a number of gifts for Sheppard, sought his immediate intervention, but he regretfully declined to oblige. As much as Sheppard empathized with the natives of Pianga, he felt that with only one hunting rifle at his disposal, there was no way he could effectively face the fire power and brutality of the Zappo Zaps led by the sanguinary cannibal, M'lumba N'kusa. However, a few days after the messenger from Pianga visited Ibanche, another messenger came from Luebo with a letter from Morrison and the Presbyterian Committee urging Sheppard to go, investigate, and stop the raid. Although Morrison knew that Sheppard had no guns to fight the well-armed Zappo Zaps with and stop the raid, he must have counted on his excellent language and diplomatic skills in dealing with the natives. These were the weapons that Sheppard precisely deployed when he arrived in Pianga.

On September 14, 1899, Sheppard and eleven willing Ibanche townsmen embarked on a very risky journey to Pianga. Equipped only with a notebook, a Kodak camera, and a hunting rifle, Sheppard and his men passed through deserted villages as they proceeded cautiously. Sheppard wrote in his diary:

> We have secured a guide, and will make a hard and fast march till within an hour of the Zappo Zap camp, and then proceed slowly and

cautiously, for we don't know what turn the Zaps will take. We may suffer at their hands, but we are going as near as possible, near enough to smell them, if not in the citadel.

(Sheppard 1996b:121)

At one of the deserted villages near the Zappo Zap camp, Sheppard and his company came across a man who was shot in the hand but escaped from the carnage of death that they were going to gaze at soon. The man gave Sheppard a horrible account of the orgy of death perpetrated by the Zappo Zaps at their stockade. The man told Sheppard that M'lumba N'kusa and his men had summoned crowds of villagers to their headquarters and demanded of them sixty slaves, herds of goats, baskets of corn, and 2,500 balls of rubber; and when the villagers refused to comply, M'lumba ordered his men to open fire on them. Many of the villagers died, and only a few, including the narrator himself, escaped when a part of the fence surrounding the headquarters collapsed during the ensuing pandemonium. This information and the man's swollen hand gave Sheppard an idea of the Free State government orchestrated violence against the Congolese natives in Pianga. As they camped at another deserted village much closer to the Zappo Zap camp, Sheppard pondered how he could go about collecting a maximum amount of information from the victims, as well as from the assailants themselves, without endangering his own life and those of his men. The following day, Shepard and his company cautiously progressed toward the center of the carnage, but as they approached another deserted village, they suddenly came under fire by the patrolling elements of the militia. Fortunately, for Sheppard and his men, it happened that the leader of the patrol was a man he had met several times back in Luebo by the name of Chebamba. The latter ordered his fighters to lay down their guns and extended a warm handshake to his old friend Sheppard. Chebamba then promised to assist Sheppard in any way possible. Sheppard took advantage of his offer and asked him to give him a guide who could take him to the Zappo Zap stockade where he had been told most of the killings took place. Chebamba agreed and sent a boy "to the camp to say to M'lumba N'kusa that his big friend was coming" (Sheppard 1996:121). Soon after, M'lumba himself came to meet Sheppard with a big escort of his merciless fighters. Sheppard wrote in his report:

> In the meantime I asked question after question [to Chebamba], and said 'yes' and grinned. In twenty minutes we heard the firing of guns, and beating of drums, the war whoop, and here they came as thick as peas, leaping in the air, firing their guns, throwing spears, shooting arrows, falling on the ground as if to escape a passing arrow. As they drew near, we saw their faces, some marked up with red paint, and others with native flour and so on. Oh such devils! My they could take any country! ... The camp is about 80 yards long and 40 yards broad, and stinks, for the dead are lying at its very doors.
>
> (121)

Mistaken for a Free State government official and deceptively accepting that positioning like a trickster, Sheppard quickly gained the confidence of Chief M'lumba and his fighters. The unsuspecting M'lumba then gloated over the killing of the Kuba people as he took Sheppard to the stockade and agreed to grant him an interview. During the interview, he unreservedly confessed to the crime that his men committed on behalf of the Free State government. M'lumba's account of the carnage of death that took place at the stockade corroborated what Sheppard had been told earlier by one of the victims, the man with a swollen hand, at the nearby village. The interview questions that Sheppard masterly put to M'lumba were designed to establish, among other things, the responsibility of the Free State government in the atrocities, the number of guns supplied to the Zappo Zap fighters by the government, the number and sex of the murdered natives, and other areas of the Kuba land they intended to raid.

When asked whether the State had sent him to settle a "strong palaver" or dispute, M'lumba responded:

> I have been here near two months. I demanded thirty slaves from this side of the stream, and thirty from the other side. Rubber, goats and fowls, two points of ivory, 2,500 balls, thirteen goats, ten fowls and six dogs, some corn chumy. [...] I don't like to fight [...] but the state told me if the villages refused to pay to make fire.
>
> (122)

Sheppard then asked him: "To what villages did the state send you?" and M'lumba responded: "To the Bakete, Bena Pianga and Bakuba, and especially *Lukengu*'s." Sheppard continued with a special interest: "Are you going to *Lukengu*'s?" One of M'lumba's men excitedly responded: "Yes, yes! We are going. Yes we are going to kill them all, for they don't want white men to come to their village."

Turning to the source of supply for the guns used, Sheppard asked M'lumba: "You really killed some people?" And "One legged brute (excuse me) pointed to a big stain on the ground where were hundreds of flies swarming," and responded "Look at that, that is our work, we are strong." Sheppard continued: "Is that so? [...] well, how many guns have you?" M'lumba answered: "We have 130 cap guns and 8 state rifles. [...] And I have plenty of powder, a big box full, which the state gave me, plenty caps, but not many balls, so I have my blacksmith making iron balls." At Sheppard's request, M'lumba produced all the eight rifles. In addition to seeing the rifles, Sheppard and his men also watched the blacksmith make the iron balls.

As for the actual killings of the innocent, peaceful Pianga people, Sheppard asked M'lumba:

> "How did the fight come up?" And he callously described the horrible scene: I sent for all their chiefs, sub-chiefs, men and women, to come on

a certain day, saying that I was going to finish all the palaver. When they entered these small gates (the fence being made of fences brought from other villages, the high native ones), I demanded all my pay or I would kill them, so they refused to pay me, and I ordered the fence to be closed so they couldn't run away. Then we killed them here inside the fence. The panels of the fence fell down, and some escaped.

(123)

Sheppard then asked further: "How many did you kill?" M'lumba responded with an invitation: "We killed plenty, will you see some of them?" Sheppard agreed to his invitation, saying "Oh! I don't mind [....]" And M'lumba added: "I think we have killed between 80 and 90, and those in the other villages I don't know, I did no go out, but sent my people." As they strolled outside the camp, Sheppard was shocked to see three dead bodies "with flesh carved off from the waist down." That prompted him to ask M'lumba: "Why are the people carved so, only having the bones?" He answered promptly: "My people ate them. [...] The men who have young children do not eat people, but all the rest ate them." And when they came across a man's body without a head, Sheppard asked him: "Where is the man's head?" M'lumba answered: "Oh, they made a bowl of the forehead to rub up tobacco and dimba in." That afternoon Sheppard counted 41 bodies.

Sheppard also recorded in his report the practice of the cutting of hands required by the government as proofs of expended bullets. As Sheppard and M'lumba were returning to the camp after the stroll, they came across a young woman shot in the back with one hand severed. When Sheppard asked the reason why the woman's hand was cut off, M'lumba "explained that they always cut off the right hand to give to the state on their return." Sheppard then asked him: "Can you not show me some of the hands?" M'lumba obliged, and as Sheppard reported, "So he conducted us to a frame-work of sticks, under which was burning a slow fire, and there they were, the right hands. I counted them, 81 in all."

Sheppard also stated in his report that he saw no less than 500 guns and 60 women prisoners in Bena Pianga. Most of the Chief M'lumba N'kusa's fighters were from Lualaba, Kabunga, and Zappo Kingonda. Sheppard concluded his explosive report by stating:

> We all [Sheppard and his men from Ibanche] say that we have as fully as possible investigated the whole outrage, and find it was a plan previously made to get all the stuff possible, and to catch and kill the poor people in the 'Death Trap'.

(122–124)

Sheppard also attached to his report a detailed chart of the site of the massacre and the photos of mutilated bodies and severed hands that he took with his Kodak camera. These visual elements gave credibility to Sheppard's

116 *The Congo narrative*

report on the atrocities perpetrated by King Leopold's men in the Congo Free State, and they were subsequently used in many other reports that denounced the Belgian King's deceptive, inhumane enterprise in the Congo.

At the conclusion of his investigation, Sheppard sent his shocking report to Morrison and the APCM Committee in Luebo through a group of runners. Upon receiving it, Morrison personally took the report to the State Headquarters and demanded that the killings of the innocent Congolese natives be stopped immediately. Although the State officials denied giving order for the massacre, they agreed to send Belgian officers to the region. The officers thus went to the village of Chinyama, where the main massacre had been carried out, broke down the fence of the stockade, liberated the imprisoned natives, and arrested M'lumba N'Kusa. The arrest of the latter was, in fact, a face-saving gesture by the Belgian officials, for as he protested his detention to the District Officer DuFour: "You have sent me to do this and yet you have put me in chains" (Benedetto 1996:126). Not satisfied with the arrest of M'lumba, Morrison insisted that DuFour be held accountable for the atrocities. Here again, the State government, afraid of the negative campaign that could be launched by Morrison and Sheppard against them, agreed to conduct a further investigation. But their shoddy investigation was just a face-saving exercise as it exonerated DuFour and solely blamed M'lumba for the massacre.

Following the failure of the colonial Free State justice system to investigate the horrible atrocities committed by the government militia Zappo Zaps and to punish the government officials who ordered them, Morrison decided to publicize Sheppard's report in Belgium, Britain, and the United States. The report was debated in the Belgian parliament, where one of its members, George Lorand, denounced the atrocities. It was particularly well-received in Britain and the United States where many newspapers and other publications featured the atrocities documented in the report between 1899 and 1905.

However, while Sheppard and Morrison unreservedly publicized the misrule and atrocities of the King Leopold's brutal regime to the world, the Executive Committee of Foreign Missions in Nashville urged them to be cautious. On January 9, 1900, its secretary S.H. Chester wrote to the APCM:

> The Executive has received the report of the mission, together with several private letters concerning the difficulty as to securing concessions for our stations, and concerning the outrages being perpetrated by the Zappo Zap tribe in your vicinity. We would first assure the Mission of our sympathy in its troubles, our approval and appreciation of the prompt action taken by the Mission in the investigation of these outrages, and of the courageous and prudent conduct of those members of the Mission by whom the investigation was made. **We can hardly think it necessary to remind the Mission as to the necessity of the utmost caution, in making representations regarding these matters to those in authority,**

or in publishing them to the world, to observe all proper deference to the "powers that be," and to avoid anything that might give any color to a charge of doing or saying things inconsistent with its purely and non-political character.

(Benedetto 1996:127, emphasis added)

The advice of the Executive Committee highlighted in this letter went against the postcolonial vision that Sheppard and Morrison espoused for the APCM. In contradiction to the advice of the mother Church, Sheppard and Morrison continued to confront and expose the brutality of the Congo Free State officials against the Congolese people. This can be observed, for example, in the letter of protest that Morrison wrote to Deschamps, Chef de Zone at Luluabourg, on August 6, 1902, putting to him:

> This is the accusation which I make against you: You came into a peaceable and quiet community; the people were all stopping in their villages; they at first feared no evil from you, for they had learned to trust your predecessor, Commandant de Cock. Suddenly, without warning or reason, your soldiers commenced running through the villages, seizing the men by force.
> (Morrison 1996e:134)

Morrison also continued to appeal to the international community and other Church organizations to denounce the inhumane treatment of the Congolese people by King Leopold's Free State regime and its violations of the Berlin Treaty. In a letter he wrote from Luebo on October 7, 1902 to the *Aborigines Protection Society*, Morrison thanked them for taking up the Congo cause and urged them to relentlessly call for international pressure on the brutal regime:

> As representative of the American Presbyterian Congo Mission, I have the pleasure in writing to you to assure you of our great satisfaction in knowing that you have taken up the situation of affairs here in the Congo Free State, and have made representation to your government. We are glad to know that you have found our report of the atrocities committed near us in 1899 of some service to you. If only missionaries and others here would publish to the world all the shameful injustices of this wicked Congo government, such things as they know to be true, there would soon come, I believe, speedy relief. But unfortunately the government is so absolute in its power and so given up all to all that is wicked, and unjust and shameful, that many are **afraid** to speak out, lest the government take action against them. Some, too, seem, to be able to ease their consciences in the matter by letting the government alone to do what it will, hoping by silence and acquiescence to gain the good-will of the authorities that be.
> (Morrison 1996f:138)

118   *The Congo narrative*

On May 4, 1903, Morrison stopped in Britain on his way to the United States on furlough and issued a strongly worded, consequential statement on the Congo situation. The statement entitled "Statement to His Majesty's Government On Conditions in the Congo" (Morrison 1996:150–157) was given to APS, which submitted it to the then British Foreign Secretary Lord Landsdowne on the same day. Following his statement, Morrison addressed a meeting of philanthropists, church leaders, politicians, and activists (including E.D. Morel) concerned with the Congo question at the Royal United Service Institution, Whitehall, on May 5, 1903. As Benedetto notes: "Through this statement and the meeting at the Whitehall, Morrison was responsible for effectively launching the Congo reform movement in England" (Benedetto 1996:156). At the end of the Whitehall meeting, a resolution was moved by the Right Hon. Sir Charles W. Dilke, Bart, M.P. in honor of Morrison as follows:

> That this meeting, having heard the statement of the Rev. W. M. Morrison, earnestly appeals to His Majesty's government, as one of the signatories to the Berlin and Brussels Acts of 1885 and 1892, to use its influence with the other signatory powers toward securing the humane and equitable treatment of natives in the Congo Basin which was guaranteed by those acts.
>
> (Benedetto 1996:161)

The resolution was seconded by E.D. Morel, who saluted Morrison's courage in revealing to the world the atrocities of King Leopold regime in the Congo.

In addition to the statement and the Whitehall meeting, Morrison also gave an interview to Reuter News Agency in which, to use his own words in a letter he wrote to the protesting Belgian *Chef de Cabinet* M.A. Baerts on May 9, 1903, he gave "some concrete examples of the working of the **forced labor system** which I do now and shall always condemn, simply because it could result in injustices to the natives" (Morrison 1996:170). Morrison also sent copies of this letter to the activist E.D. Morel and the representative of the Presbyterian Church in London Sir H.D. Reid, Robert Whyte.

As a result of Morrison's campaign, the British Parliament held a debate on the Congo Free State situation on May 21, 1903. Following the debate, members present unanimously adopted a resolution condemning the exploitation, brutal treatment, and enslavement of the Congolese natives by the Free State government officials. The resolution was sent to all European powers in August 1903. As expected, the Belgian newspapers and authorities rose against the resolution, defending the Free State government. The Germans welcomed the resolution while the French, fearing the anger of King Leopold, adopted a neutral position (though not contesting the validity of the Sheppard and Morrison's reports).

It took the Belgian legislature many months after the British Parliament's resolution before they decided to table the Congo Free State situation, but Morrison now joined by E.D. Morel and other activists relentlessly carried on with their campaign. The Belgian legislature eventually held a debate on the atrocities committed by the Congo Free State regime from February 20 to March 2, 1904. The debate opposed, on the one hand, the socialist members like Vandervelde, Lorand, and Janson who condemned the Congo State regime, and, on the other hand, the conservatives who supported it, including the Minister of Foreign Affairs de Favereau, the Prime Minister de Smet de Naeyer, and the leader of the Catholic Party Woeste. The debate and public pressure forced King Leopold to set up a three-men commission of inquiry in July 1904. The members of the commission, E. Janssens, Giacomo Nisco, and E. de Schumacher, travelled from Boma to Stanley Falls and Lopori Valley and collected numerous evidence of atrocities. The commission was expected to publish its report in March 1905, but it failed to do so. However, the activists of the Congo Reform Movement could no longer wait. Benedetto reports:

> The Commission's Report was to be ready in March of 1905, but when publication was delayed, E. D. Morel collected copies of the evidence supplied to the commissioners and published the material under the title, *Evidence Laid Before the Congo Commission of Inquiry at Bwembu, Bolobo, Lulanga ... Together with a Summary of Events(And Documents Connected Therewith) on the A.B.I.R. Concession since the Commission Visited that Territory.*
> (Benedetto 1996:178)

While on furlough in the United States in 1903, Morrison continued his public campaign against the Congo Free State brutal regime. On May 27, 1903, he addressed the PCUS General Assembly held in Lexington, Virginia, about their struggles and those of the Congolese natives against the inhumane Congo Free State government. After listening to Morrison's plea for strong interventions by the Presbyterian Church and the United States Government, the General Assembly resolved to send a delegation to President Roosevelt. The latter received Secretary Chester and Morrison on November 7, 1903 and promised to act as soon as he received concrete evidence of acts of hostility against the Americans in the Congo. Earlier on June 20, 1903, before that meeting with President Roosevelt, Morrison had also written a letter to King Leopold II about the atrocities committed on his behalf by Congo Free State officials against the natives and their hostility to the APCM. From 1903 onward, Morrison's and Sheppard's political activism became intensified, and the APCM became a valuable source of information on the Congo situation not only to E.D. Morel's Congo Reform Movement but also to humanitarian organizations and governments in the Western world. In a letter to E.D. Morel on January 1, 1904, Morrison welcomed

Consul Roger Casement's investigation (1903–1904) and expressed his satisfaction with the positive impact that their teamwork with E.D. Morel for the human rights of the Congolese natives was having across Western capitals (especially its impact on the fate of King Leopold's Congo Free State):

> You have old Leopold 'on the hip'; keep smiting him under the fifth rib. You will win and the victory will be more yours than anyone else's. Your splendid fight will simply mean the liberation of 20,000,000 slaves; surely this is worth fighting for.
>
> (Morrison 1996g:195)

Thus, following their first exposure of the Congo Free State government atrocities against the natives to the world in 1899, several investigations were commissioned and damning reports produced by foreign powers and other Christian Church denominations. Sheppard and Morrison's public campaign, therefore, contributed a great deal to the Belgian state's takeover of the Congo Free State in 1908. As Robert Burroughs has lamented, it is indeed surprising that "Morel neglects to mention Sheppard in his *History of the Congo Reform Movement* (1914), though Sheppard's replacement, Morrison, is lauded" (Burroughs 2011:18). By the time Sheppard left Belgian Congo in 1910, he had fully embraced the Congo cause against Belgian colonialism and became a staunch anti-/postcolonial agent until his death in Louisville, Kentucky, on November 25, 1927.

The anti-imperial activist Mark Twain (1835–1910)

Among the allies who never went to the Congo, but nevertheless espoused the Congo cause in denouncing the colonial brutalities of the Congo State regime against the Congolese natives was the progressive American writer Mark Twain. Perhaps, influenced by the wave of anti-imperial radicalism that spread from Europe to the United States and other parts of the world between 1890 and 1920, Mark Twain rose not only against the failure of American postcoloniality and post-civil war reconstruction but also against Western imperialism in the Congo. So, despite being somewhat overshadowed by the colossal successes of his major literary works, Mark Twain's *King Leopold's Soliloquy* (1905) offers a penetrating insight into the colonial encounter at the turn of the century. Its narrative brazenly criticizes both domestic and foreign governmental policies in a fashion that is unparalleled at its time of publication. True to his singularly sardonic prose style, Twain's critique of the Belgian King Leopold's rule in the Congo does not conform to a conventional condemnation of a tyrannical government. Rather, he deploys satire to craftily convey disdain for King Leopold's despotic regime. He effectively moves the reader by enlisting humor as a uniquely subversive tactic against colonial rule. Twain's reconstruction of Leopold's voice, though entirely fictional, places overt emphasis on countless factual instances of barbaric violence perpetrated against the Congolese natives by his ruthless regime. In doing so, Twain clearly aligns himself with the anti-imperialist cause and creates a work of historical fiction that is far ahead of its time in fighting for the rights of marginalized peoples without a voice. More specifically, his overt indictment of both the European rule and his own American government in their overt exploitation of the Congolese natives is an unprecedented stance for a writer to take in those days. While many of his contemporaries can be said to be indirectly complicit in colonial subjugation due to their silence on the issue, Twain embraces in his creative project the writer's primary function as social critic. He wields the sharp literary knife of satirical irony and laughter as a guerrilla technique to effectively combat modern colonialism and imperialism. Stefan Heym is indeed right when he notes in his introduction to the International Publishers edition of *King Leopold's Soliloquy* that:

> Mark Twain took seriously the writer's duty to be the conscience of his time. He risked fortune, success, the applause of the press and the favors of the government; he turned his humor into stinging satire; and the harder certain of his contemporaries attempted to type him a funny man, the angrier he became.
>
> Yes, the man who made millions laugh was an angry man because he was a seeing man. He saw what went on in the world around him, and he refused to blind himself or encrust his heart with complacency. He saw who was enemy and who was friend; he sided with the Filipinos who were butchered by the U.S. Army; with the Chinese massacred by the troops of Russia's Czar and Germany's Kaiser, Britain's King and America's President; with the Negroes lynched by church-going, God-fearing white Southern hypocrites; and with the workers bled and exploited everywhere. He hit and hit hard; nor did he cringe when the stuff started flying.
>
> (1905:11–12)

Mark Twain's *King Leopold's Soliloquy* is a singular and early example of how a literary narrative can help move modern societies toward a true state of decoloniality. Here is an example of Twain's satirical vibe as he makes King Leopold complain about the incorruptibility of photography in exposing his crime against humanity:

> The Kodak has been a sore calamity to us. The most powerful enemy indeed. In the early years we had no trouble in getting the press to "expose" the tales of the mutilations as slanders, lies, inventions of busybody American missionaries and exasperated foreigners who found the "open door" of the Berlin-Congo charter closed against them when they innocently went out there to trade; and by the press's help we got the Christian nations everywhere to turn an irritated and unbelieving ear to

those tales and say hard things about the tellers of them. Yes, all things went harmoniously and pleasantly in those good days, and I was looked up to as the benefactor of a down-trodden and friendly people. Then all of a sudden came the crush! That is to say, the incorruptible *Kodak* – and all the harmony went to hell!

(Twain 1905:73–74)

Thus, Twain's bitter criticism of modern imperialism in *King Leopold's Soliloquy* draws its effectiveness from his unique blending of the metaphoric with the metonymic, the imaginative with the factual as he discursively engages the ubiquitous evil of colonialism, which he physically experienced in Latin America and textually gazed at from the Congo context. As he makes the grotesque figure of King Leopold II own and confess his crime against humanity in the Congo, Twain also gives a subjective voice to the oppressed Congolese natives in his text by including their own testimonies collected by Roger Casement and a number of protestant missionaries. Through King Leopold's monologic quibbles, Twain effectively satirizes and denounces the complicity of Western nations, journalists, public intellectuals, politicians, and creative writers who either remain indifferent to the crimes of Western imperialism against the natives or express their support for the so-called Western civilizing mission in other lands and peoples. In 1900, Mark Twain declared, "I am an anti-imperialist, [....] I am **opposed to** having the eagle put his talons on any other lands" (Twain 1905:16, emphasis added). This way, Twain portrayed himself as an anti-imperial agent and a stranger to the exclusive, intolerant order of Western modernity. Through his activism, one can argue that Mark Twain promoted decoloniality. As Madina Tlostanova and Walter Mignolo (2009:132) have argued, "Decoloniality means here decolonization of knowledge and being by epistemically and affectively de-linking from the imperial/colonial organization of society." What Twain's narrative calls for is a movement from coloniality toward global solidarism, which promotes intersubjective alliances and encourages mutual acceptance of each others' values across nationality, ethnicity, race, class, gender, and sexuality. His message remains valid to today's turbulent world, and it should inspire our action in the new empire (Hardt and Negri 2000). His view of the incorruptibility of Kodak then finds its expression in the incorruptibility of today's cell phone videos which have been exposing brutal killings of unarmed persons by state police and religious extremists worldwide.

So, unlike colonial writers like Joseph Conrad and Arthur Doyle and British protestant missionaries like Rev. George Grenfell, Rev. W.H. Bentley, and Rev. Henry Richards who though condemning King Leopold's colonial brutality in Congo Free State, still remained loyal to the civilizing mission as a project of Western modernity, George Washington Williams, William Sheppard, W.W. Morrison, and Mark Twain asserted their independence from it and deployed themselves through their political activism as anti-imperialist allies of the natives. The marginalization and oppression of African Americans following the failure of the American reconstruction project certainly led Williams and Sheppard to regard the Congolese natives' oppression at the hands of a brutal colonial system in similar terms. Therefore, unlike other white missionaries, Sheppard found a strong subjective affinity with the Congolese natives and fought for their human rights by providing "audacious, detailed accounts of atrocities, which anticipate many themes of the reportage later celebrated in Britain, and at a time when little evidence was available" (Burroughs 2011:18).

George Washington Williams's and William Henry Sheppard's shocking reports on the atrocities committed by King Leopold's Congo Free State regime in the 1890s and early 1990s against the Congolese natives sparked a wave of investigations and other reports by a number of Western strangers. Among the strangers who became allies of the Congolese natives as they faced a callous, colonial onslaught are: the British Consul and Irishman Roger Casement, who compiled and presented to British parliament in 1904 a scathing report on the untold atrocities committed by the Congo Free State officials against the Congolese natives (see O' Siochain and O' Sullivan 2003); British Baptist missionaries like Rev. John Harris and his wife Alice Seely Harris, Rev. John H. Weeks, Rev. A.E. Scrivener, and Rev. Kendred Smith, who also became members of E.D. Morel's *The Congo Reform Association* (1904–1908) that extensively campaigned against King Leopold and his Free State regime's massacres and mutilations of the Congolese natives.

Together, these strangers disrupted Western modernity's discursive othering and ordering of the Congolese people and advocated for their human rights. In order to accurately record and document these atrocities, Roger Casement and the Baptist missionaries mentioned here brought forth the voices of the Congolese victims through their interviews, allowing them to use their languages and par-linguistic methods of communication. That way, they empowered the natives to speak for themselves as subjects. As Robert Burroughs notes:

> Interviews thus helped missionaries to produce on-the-spot statistical analyses, which highlighted their agency and local expertise. But by transcribing and publishing interviews, missionaries such as Harris also joined Casement in depicting individuated Africans as producers of knowledge that the traveler records but does not modify. As a sign of their desire to record African perspectives, moreover, missionaries began to write about or reproduce local methods of recording massacres alongside their own data. Weeks pioneered the collection of tallies of losses to Force Publique raids in the form of twigs presented to him in Yandjali in October 1903. From Bongandanga, Rev. H.S. Gamman wrote of a witness who presented to Leopold's Commission of Inquiry a knotted rope, "each knot indicating a person killed at Nsungamboyo. He also had a packet of fifty leaves, each leaf representing women whom

he knew had been seized by the sentries." Harris likewise notes his informants estimating the age of children murdered in punitive raids in terms of their "height from the ground."

(2011:83–84)

The unifying feature of the narrative that defines these often ambivalent colonial agents within the imperial order, whether Christian missionaries, free-lance explorers, or government officials, is the progressive process of their individual transformation: first, they start as loyal agents of the Western imperial order on a mission to civilize those defined as savages of foreign lands; second, they discover a shared common humanity with the natives, following their interaction with and examination of their socio-cultural, economic, and political systems, even when they strive to introduce them to Christianity, literacy, and western value system; and third, they undertake an introspective journey into their rigidly structured Western modernity, turn against Western colonial brutality, and empower the colonized natives in their struggles against colonialism. In spite of their ambivalent positionality, these agents to a certain extent laid a foundation for productive cultural translations, intersubjective dialogues, and contemporary globalization. By learning multiple Congolese languages, introducing the natives to literacy, industrial education, and translating their folksongs into English and English songs as well as the Bible into native languages (Kuba, Kikongo, Lingala, and Chiluba), Sheppard, Lapsley, Morrison, and Black American Women missionaries empowered them and established the foundation upon which postcolonial agency took root in the late 19th century and early 20th century.

The subjective cultural hybridity resulting from the cultural translation of Western modernity and African traditions encouraged by Sheppard and other Black American missionaries later on informed Simon Kimbangu's religious syncretism and Patrice Lumumba's anti-colonial nationalism. Since a lot has been written about Kimbanguism, I conclude this chapter with a summary of Lumumba's cultural politics.

The anti-colonial Congolese hero Patrice Emery Lumumba (1925–1961)

Patrice Emery Lumumba[1] was born on July 2, 1925 at Onalua, in Katako-Kombe Territory, in the present-day Sankuru Province of the Democratic Republic of the Congo. After an early childhood African homestead education at the hands of his peasant parents Francois Tolenga Otetshima and Julienne Wamato Lomendja, he first enrolled in a Catholic school and then at the age of thirteen moved to a Protestant mission school run by Swedish Methodists. While the homestead education inculcated communal, humane African values in the young Lumumba, the assimilationist Catholic education exposed him to exclusive colonial strictures. As Jean-Paul Sartre states in his introduction to a collection of Lumumba's speeches edited by Jean Van Lierde and entitled *Lumumba Speaks* (1972):

> 'Reverend Fathers' wanted to make him a catechist, and the more practical-minded Swedes wanted to teach him a trade that would enable him to get out of the peasant class and work for a wage and live on his own little plot of ground in one of the little villages that the whites had set up, as a *helper* of the white colonials.
> (Sartre 1972:7)

However, rather than be "a helper of the white colonials," at the age of eighteen, Lumumba left the largely rural Sankuru District for the city of Stanleyville (Kisangani) to live with his maternal uncle Lumumba, a Methodist minister. He started his first job as a file clerk at the Symaf Company in the city of Kindu. While working at that company, the industrious and unusually bright young Lumumba won the admiration of his white bosses and gained an "immatriculation certificate," through which native Congolese could move into European circles and enjoy their amenities. Having thus become an "évolué," Lumumba later moved to Stanleyville (Kisangani), the capital of the present-day Tshopo Province, where he worked as a post office employee for several years. In 1957, Lumumba moved to Leopoldville (Kinshasa), got a job as a sales manager at Bracongo Brewery (a local beer distribution company), and started his political career as a community organizer in 1958.

Not having attended college, Lumumba was largely a self-educated intellectual who learned a lot from his extensive reading of world history and political thought as well as from his keen observation of Belgium's colonial strategies and oppressive practices in the Congo. Drawing from all these experiences and sources, Lumumba later followed the lead of other prominent African political leaders of his time (such as Kwame Nkrumah of Ghana, Modibo Keita of Mali, Sékou Touré of Guinea, and Gamal Abdel Nasser of Egypt) and opted for the affirmative, anti-colonial ideology of Positive Neutralism. He outlined the tenets of this ideology, as he understood and sought to apply it to the Congolese context, in many of the speeches he delivered to both local and international audiences during his short, tumultuous political career (October 1958- January 1961). For instance, at a press conference he held on August 9, 1960, in Leopoldville, he stated:

> Africa will tell the West that it wants the rehabilitation of Africa now, a return to the sources, the reinstitution of moral values; the African personality must express itself; that is what our policy of positive neutralism means. Africa will not be divided into blocs, as Europe has been.
> (Lumumba 1972:320)

This ideology, which is extensively explained in Kwame Nkrumah's booklet entitled *What I Mean by Positive Action* (1949; see also Hountondji

1983:131–140), guided Lumumba's political action as the first Prime Minister of the Democratic Republic of the Congo (June 30, 1960–January 17, 1961) and the President of the country's most popular political party (The Congolese National Movement founded in October 1958). Like Nkrumah, with whom he developed a special relationship during and after the December 1958 Accra Conference of the Assembly of African Peoples, Lumumba consistently advocated the solidarity of the African peoples beyond the boundaries of the concepts of nation, race, culture, class, and gender; encouraged a non-violent struggle against colonialism; and called for intersubjective dialogue between developed and developing nations. Lumumba could therefore be described simultaneously as nationalist, pan-Africanist, and humanist.

As a nationalist, Lumumba stood in sharp contrast to sectarian Congolese leaders like Kasavubu, Tshombe, Kalonji, and others, who fell into the colonialist trap of "divide and conquer" and formed divisive ethnically based political parties (see Kasavubu's ABAKO, Tshombe's CONAKAT, and Kalonji's MNC-KALONJI). Using the organizing skills he had previously developed as a post office employee, trade unionist, and sales manager of the Bracongo Brewery, Lumumba and a number of his followers formed an inclusive national party (the Congolese National Movement; MNC in French) in October 1958 and demanded full independence of the Congo from Belgium's colonialism the following year. As he stated in a speech he delivered in Leopoldville on December 28, 1958, "The objective of the MNC is to unite and organize the Congolese masses in the struggle to improve their lot and wipe out the colonialist regime and the exploitation of man by man" (Lumumba 1972:62). Lumumba played a major role in mobilizing all the Congolese across class, gender, and race lines, successfully pressuring Belgium into granting independence to the Democratic Republic of the Congo on June 30, 1960.

As a pan-Africanist, Lumumba urged Africans to be masters of their own cultural production and history. Addressing the closing session of the International Seminar organized by the Congress for the Freedom of Culture and the University of Ibadan, Nigeria, on March 22, 1959, Lumumba called on emerging independent African states to

> make a serious effort to further African culture. We have a culture all our own, unparalleled moral and artistic values, an art of living and patterns of life that are ours alone. All these African splendors must be jealously preserved and developed. We will borrow from Western civilization what is good and beautiful and reject what is not suitable. This amalgam of African and European civilizations will give Africa a civilization of a new type, an authentic civilization corresponding to African realities.
>
> (Lumumba 1972:74)

As a humanist, Lumumba was keenly aware of the interdependency between nations and the necessity for Africans to develop a subjective agency as they sought to nurture an African modernity:

> We do not want to cut ourselves off from the West, for we are quite aware that no people in the world can be self-sufficient. We are altogether in favor of friendship between races, but the West must respond to our appeal. Westerners must understand that friendship is not possible when the relationship between us is one of subjugation and subordination.
> (Lumumba 1972:72–73)

Lumumba was assassinated by colonialist and imperialist forces on January 17, 1961, but his ideas about nationalism, pan-Africanism, cultural translation, African subjectivity, and globalization have continued to inspire generations of African and African-Diaspora intellectuals and creative writers to this day.

Note

1 Lumumba's birth name was Ésau Okitasombo. When he moved to Kisangani to live with his maternal uncle Jérome Lumumba, a prominent Methodist minister, he decided to adopt the latter's surname.

III
Articulations of postcolonial agency in contemporary African literature

5 The colonial encounter and postcolonial agency in Wole Soyinka's *Death and the King's Horseman* and Dani Kouyaté's *Keita! l'héritage du Griot* (film)

Following Soyinka's warning in his author's note that *Death and the King's Horseman* (1975) should not be read as portraying "the clash between old values and the new ways, between western methods and African traditions" (5), critics like Henry Louis Gates (1981), Eldred Jones (1988), and a host of others have confined themselves to the metaphysical dimension of the play within the Yoruba cultural context. That way, they have located the tragic effect of the play in what they see as Elesin's lack of a strong, moral will to carry out his expected public duty—to commit ritual suicide. However, in this chapter, I argue that in *Death and the King's Horseman*, Soyinka has turned death into a space of power contestation not only between the colonizer and the colonized but also between the essentialist and the syncretist elements within the Yoruba cultural order.

In the same author's note, Soyinka also tells the reader that the play was inspired by historical "events which took place in Oyo, ancient Yoruba city of Nigeria, in 1946. That year, the lives of Elesin (Olori Elesin), his son, and the Colonial Officer intertwined with the disastrous results set out in the play" (5). In his artistic mediation of the actual history, however, Soyinka decided to set the action of his plot back to the time of the Second World War. Soyinka's choice of this temporal setting is significant as the war provided Africans who participated in it with an opportunity to think about their own liberation from European colonization and to map up a new course of action for their future. Following this empowerment, the Oyo people, like other African nations, had then to redefine themselves as postcolonial subjects. In my view, this redefinition, which simultaneously entails postcolonial subjects' rejection of colonial oppression and their reassessment of their relationship with pre-colonial traditional practices, is at the center of the tragic conflict in *Death and the King's Horseman*. This conflict, which, on the one hand, opposes the Oyo people collectively against British colonialism, enforced by Simon Pilkings, the District officer, and the enigmatic Elesin against the conservative masses led by Iyaloja and the praise-singer, on the other hand, enables Soyinka to foreground his idea of culture as an open project marked by indeterminate subject-driven negotiations. In fact, as noted by Samuel Johnson, the Yoruba historian, toward the end of the 19th century, many Yoruba men, in a gesture of cultural revision, started refusing to commit ritual suicide, and they were "never forced to do so" (1921:57; see also Izevbaye 2003:148).

At the time of the play's action, that is, by the mid-1940s, Oyo territory and its people had already undergone deep transformation under British colonial rule. By the time the praise-singer, Iyaloja, and other market women urge Elesin to resolutely march toward his ritual death so as to ensure a smooth transition for the dead King and bring peace to the community, Oyo territory is regarded, in the words of the British Resident in the play, as a part of the larger British empire and a "secure colony of His Majesty" (47). In total disregard of Oyo people's tradition and customs which they term "barbaric" (31), "nonsense" (24), "mumbo-jumbo" (24), and "pagan" (24), Simon Pilkings and the Resident impose colonial strictures on them by adopting and deploying the power strategy that Achille Mbembe calls "the Hegelian tradition" of "commandement." According to this strategy:

> the native subjected to power and to the colonial state could in no way be another "myself." As an animal, he/she was even totally alien to me. His/ her manner of seeing the world, his/her manner of being, was not mine. In him/her, it was impossible to discern any power of transcendence. Encapsulated in himself or herself, he/she was a bundle of drives, but not of *capacities*. In such circumstances, the only possible relationship with him/her was one of violence and domination.
> (Mbembe 2001:26)

Olunde, Elsesin's son who has been to Britain and observed British people's attitudes toward "others," also confirms the validity of Mbembe's analysis when he says to Jane, the naive wife of Simon Pilkings who calls the Oyo people's custom of ritual suicide "barbaric": "You forget that I have now spent four years among your people. I discovered that you have no respect for what you do not understand" (50). It is that lack of respect for the "other" that has led Simon Pilkings to order the arrest of the *egungun*, the spirits of ancestors. The desecration and appropriation of this Oyo cult of the dead with impunity by Simon Pilkings and his wife, as they put on the confiscated costume of the *egungun* for a ball held at the European Club in honor of the visiting Prince, shows how the colonial project has attacked not only the territory but also the soul of the Oyo natives. By giving a different, profane meaning to the *egungun* costume, the Pilkingses have turned death into a space of power contestation between themselves and the natives. The magnitude of this contest over death as an important cultural sign amongst the Oyo people is first signaled by Sergeant Amusa, a native police officer, who on two occasions categorically refuses to talk to his determined master, Simon Pilkings, while he is wearing the *egungun* costume: "Mista Pirinkin, I beg you sir, what you think you do with that dress? It belong to dead cult, not for human being" (24). While Amusa considers the ritual suicide which

Elesin is urged to commit as an outdated practice and in his report to Pilkings terms it a "criminal offence" (26), he does not contest the power that the dead have upon the living in his community. Unlike the colonialist Pilkings, who seeks to displace the totality of Oyo People's view of the transcendental order as articulated in their cultural trope of death, Amusa still shares the essential tenets of that view. He questions the validity of ritual suicide as a method of joining the world of the dead and protecting the people, but does not question the power of the *egungun*, as do Pilkings and Jane. So, while Amusa agrees with Pilkings on the applicability of the colonial law to stop Elesin's ritual suicide and to quell riots, he unflinchingly disapproves the desecration of the world of the dead. The following dialogue between Jane and Pilkings, on the one hand, and Amusa, on the other hand, shows the latter's resistance to the Pilkingses' colonialist attempt to culturally contain, objectify, and subjugate the Oyo people:

> Pilkings: Delicately my...! Look here Amusa, I think this little joke has gone far enough hm? Let's have some sense. You seem to forget that you are a police officer in the service of His Majesty's Government. I order you to report your business at once or face disciplinary action.
> Amusa: Sir, it is a matter of death. How can man talk against death to person in uniform of death? Is like talking against government to person in uniform of police. Please sir, I go and come.
> Pilkings (roars): Now! (Amusa switches his gaze to the ceiling suddenly, remains mute.)
> Jane: Oh Amusa, what is there to be scared of in the costume? You saw it confiscated last month from those *egungun* men who were creating trouble in town. You helped arrest the cult leaders yourself- if the juju didn't harm you at the time how could it possibly harm you now? And merely by looking at it?
> Amusa: (without looking down): Madam, I arrest the ring-leaders who make trouble but me I no touch *egungun*. That *egungun* itself, I no touch. And I no abuse'am. I arrest ring-leader but I treat *egungun* with respect.
>
> (25)

Amusa's resistance from within the colonial system destabilizes the colonial "commandement" and relocates his subjective agency in the interstitial zone created by the cultural translation of Oyo people's tradition through Western modernity. To that extent, Amusa functions as a liminal character who simultaneously undermines the cultural assimilation proposed by the colonial system and the unworkable cultural essentialism maintained by Iyaloja and her followers in the Oyo community. They contemptuously call him a "white man's eunuch" (34) and "the eater of the white left-overs" (39).

Like Amusa, Joseph, the Pilkingses' houseboy, understands that in spite of the violence that has accompanied Western modernity, it has become a part of the native culture. Joseph is a Christian convert, but it is he who is called upon by the Pilkingses to interpret the sounds of Yoruba drums, and to tell them why Elesin should die. Both in the way he tells the story of the ritual suicide custom and in his interpretation of the drums, Joseph acts out his borderline position. Adopting an impartial tone and refusing to pass a value judgment on the native customs, as the Pilkingses have been doing, Joseph tells them: "It is native law and custom. The King die last month. Tonight is burial. But before they can bury him, the Elesin must die so as to accompany him to heaven" (28). Joseph's use of heaven, a Christian concept, to talk about the world of the dead as viewed from the native standpoint shows the effect of the cultural translation on him and his like. His confusion in interpreting the sounds of Yoruba drums also functions as a sign of his interstitial state: "Madam, this is what I am trying to say: I am not sure. It sounds like the death of a great chief. It really mix me up" (30). Olakunle George is therefore right when he maintains that

> [b]eing 'eunuchs' of the white man, as the market women see Amusa, and at times frustrating 'natives' to the Pilkingses, Amusa and Joseph belong to both camps and to none. This liminality emerges in the text as an immanent cultural critique, so to speak.
>
> (2003:211)

It is this society divided under the influence of the colonial "commandement" that Elesin, as horseman of the King, is called upon to protect through the metaphysical act of ritual suicide following the death of his master. For Iyaloja, the mother of the market, her followers, and the praise-singer, Elesin cannot deviate from the ancestral tradition without terrible consequences for the community. In their view, Elesin has no other choice than to sacrifice himself and die for the common good. However, his sense of history and his interpretation of his present duty in the absence of the King suggest another course of action to him. In the absence of the King, the responsibility for the security of the people rests upon Elesin's shoulders, and this fact is also acknowledged by Iyaloja as she reverently calls him "Father of us all" (60) while other market women tell him: "The world is in your hands" (18). But Elesin knows well that Oyo society is no longer what it used to be, that its peace has been "shattered" by the colonizers who now arrest and humiliate the masked spirits of their ancestors with impunity, send children like Olunde away to England without their parents' consent, and recruit their kinsmen like Musa to enforce colonial laws. Indeed, as he confirms it in this statement to Pilkings, the Oyo people's "world is set adrift and its inhabitants are lost. Around them, there is nothing but emptiness" (63). In view of these realities faced by his people, Elesin seems to realize that their security can no longer be ensured solely by metaphysical rituals, like the one he is required to undergo. He therefore has to seek a new way of affirming his people's subjectivity as their values are fused with

Western modernity. He now seeks to relocate his people's struggle for security and dignity at the intersection of the metaphysical sphere and the material world. In this sense, instead of regarding Elesin's resistance to ritual suicide as a lack of moral will to carry out his public duty, I would like to suggest that it be seen as a deliberate attempt on his part to revise what he sees as an inadequate practice. His emphasis on the pleasures of this world—clothes and women—when the public expects him to concentrate on his impending transition to the other world shows that Elesin is questing for a new, syncretic cultural order that takes into consideration contemporary realities. Indeed, as Adebayo Williams remarks, "Elesin's consciousness has been shaped by the dialectic of his material and political circumstances" (2003:190). Elesin's revisionist attitude here is comparable to those of earlier Soyinka's characters, such as Igwezu and the beggar (in *The Swamp Dwellers*, 1964) or Daodu and Segi (*Kongi's Harvest*, 1967).

Although Elesin's revisionist posture rises against his people's expectations, it still finds its justification within the dynamism of their cultural matrix. From the onset, Soyinka associates him with the mythological figure of *Esu*, the Yoruba god of interpretation and mediation, and by so doing invites the reader to see him as a liminal figure working out a syncretic order between two rigid poles. As Izevbaye notes, "*Esu Elegba* [is] the principle of uncertainty, fertility and change, and the one god who makes possible the reconciliation of opposites which we associate with mediation" (2003:141). Elesin signals his intention to make *Esu* his main source of inspiration in the exercise of his leadership role when he tells his unsuspecting praise-singer at the beginning of act one: "That Esu-harassed day slipped into the stewpot while we feasted. We ate it up with the rest of the meat" (9). From now on, Elesin's masterly use of language and uncanny behavior is Esu-like. This can be seen as he implicitly debates the relevance of ritual death with the essentialist forces of his society, on the one hand, and the brutal colonial officials, on the other. Through a skillful use of dramatic irony, Soyinka creates a gap between Elesin's revisionist intention and other characters' misinterpretation of it. For instance, while Iyaloja and the praise-singer regard ritual death as something decreed by the gods and ancestors for the common good and place it outside the power of the individual and history, Elesin subjects it to his own will, saying: "I am master of my Fate" (14), and re-interprets its meaning in the light of human history: "Where the storm pleases, and when, it directs/The giants of the forest. When friendship summons/Is when the true comrade goes" (14).

Although the praise-singer is traditionally regarded as a custodian of knowledge and an excellent teacher, in this play, his limitations are exposed by Elesin's ironic twists. In fact, at times, the praise-singer becomes a pupil rather than a teacher to Elesin, and he admits the fact: "Elesin's riddles are not merely the nut in the kernel that breaks human teeth; he also buries the kernel in hot embers and dares a man's fingers to draw it out" (11). An example of such role reversal can be seen in the case of the riddle of "Not-I bird." Not only is the praise-singer ignorant of the story of the Not-I bird, he is also not sure of the sense in which Elesin deploys it. The Not-I bird is a mythic figure that represents any one in society who acts in a cowardly way by shying away from taking critical decisions when called upon to do so, whether a farmer, a hunter, a courtesan, a pupil, a priest, or a courier. Elesin evokes this figure to indirectly tell the praise-singer and Iyaloja that, no matter what consequences may follow, he is resolved to assert his individuality and change the course of things in his society:

> I, when that Not-I bird perched / Upon my roof, bade him seek his nest again, / Safe, without care or fear. I unrolled / My welcome mat for him to see. Not-I / Flew happily away, you'll hear his voice/ No more in this lifetime- You all know/ What I am.
>
> (9)

However, because of the double-entendre that Elesin's Esu-inspired discourse carries, the praise-singer and Iyaloja (mis)interpret it as a commitment on his part to uphold the tradition and die.

The praise-singer's essentialist view of culture also blinds him to a productive interpretation of historical facts, and as such, he can no longer be seen as a good guide to Elesin, who has a different agenda for himself and his people. For example, while correctly relating that the city of Oyo had to be rebuilt several times in the past by its resilient people after facing "great wars" and "white slavers" who "came and went, they took away the heart of our race, they bore the mind and muscle of our race" (10), the praise-singer does not give us the impression that something new came with that rebuilding. He does not seem to suggest that with each rebuilding there has been a reconstitution of the Oyo people's subjectivity. So, when he says to Elesin: "Our world was never wrenched from its course" (10), the praise-singer means that the validity of a king's man's ritual suicide as a protective custom for the Oyo people is timeless, and that Elesin has no power to change it. However, in responding that the "gods have said No," and that it "did not in the time of my forebears, it shall not in mine" (11), Elesin seems to be referring to his people's sense of subjective resilience and adaptability. In fact, this dynamic combination of resilience and adaptability as a cultural signifier amongst the Oyo people is reflected in the praise-singer's own statement when he tells Elesin: "The city fell and was rebuilt; the city fell and *our people trudged through mountain and forest to found a new home* but—Elesin Oba do you hear me?" (11, emphasis added).

Elesin probably knows that the course of action he has chosen will lead him to another type of death, but he is determined to pursue it. He knows that he has a historical responsibility to change his people's destiny in the face of colonial humiliation, and he must act appropriately. His consciousness of history and his sense of responsibility reflect Frantz Fanon's view that "Each generation must, out of relative obscurity, discover its mission, fulfil it, or betray it" (1967:166). So, realizing that practices like ritual death are no longer capable of ensuring his people's security, Elesin refocuses their attention on the world of the living: "The world I know is good. [...] The world I know is the bounty/Of hives after bees have swarmed. No goodness teems with such open hands/Even in the dreams of deities" (17). Within this context, what appears on the surface to be Elesin's excessive concern with sexual and material self-gratification should be seen at a deeper level as his drive to regenerate life in his community. As Mikhail Bakhtin has noted, such concern with "the lower stratum of the body" does not necessarily lead to a barren degeneration of the self:

> To degrade is to bury, to sow and to kill simultaneously, in order to bring forth something more and better. To degrade also means to concern oneself with the lower stratum of the body, the life of the belly and the reproductive organs; it therefore relates to acts of defecation and copulation, conception, pregnancy, and birth. Degradation digs a bodily grave for a new birth; it has not only a destructive, negative aspect, but also a regenerating one.
>
> (1984:21)

The unborn child that Elesin and his new bride are expecting is a fruit of that regenerative exercise. It is a "seed" that will reshape the consciousness and identity of the Oyo people by bridging the metaphysical and the physical, the supernatural and the material, as well as the traditional and the modern in their lives. Elesin's lapse into a trance while delaying his death not only points to his own liminality, it also demonstrates the syncretic order that he would like the unborn and Olunde to shape their society with. Even the conservative Iyaloja acknowledges the important liminal role that the unborn child will play:

> The fruit of such a union is rare. It will be neither of this world nor of the next. Nor of the one behind us. As if the timelessness of the ancestor world and the unborn have joined spirits to wring an issue of the elusive being of passage.
>
> (22)

In his determination to let the unborn "take root/In the earth of my choice, in this earth/I leave behind" (21), Elesin seems to be hoping that this offspring will team up with Olunde to fight British colonialism while at the same time resisting the Oyo people's unproductive cultural essentialism. Although he had opposed Olunde's departure to Britain at the time Pilkings helped him "escape from close confinement and load him onto the next boat" (28), Elesin now believes that Olunde's knowledge of the colonial system will enable him to destroy it. If we relate this motive to his procrastination to commit suicide (even when the drums suggest that it is time for him

138   *Postcolonial agency in African literature*

to do so), it would be plausible for us to say that Elesin must have had in mind beforehand what he later says about Olunde to Pilkings:

> You may have stopped me in my duty but I know now that I did give birth to a son. Once I mistrusted him for seeking the companionship of those my spirit knew as enemies of our race. Now I understand. One should seek to obtain the secrets of his enemies. He will avenge my shame, white one. His spirit will destroy you and yours.
>
> (63)

Elesin's further confession to Iyaloja that his "will was squelched in the spittle of an alien race, and all because I had committed this blasphemy of thought – that there might be the hand of the gods in a stranger's intervention" (69) confirms that he has all along envisioned the salvation of the Oyo people as lying in the conjugation of their culture with Western modernity. That is the reason why he advises Olunde, who is shocked to see his father shackled like a slave in a former slave holding: "Olunde? (He moves his head, inspecting him from side to side.) Olunde! (He collapses slowly at OLUNDE's feet.) Oh son, don't let the sight of your father turn you blind!" (60).

Olunde is particularly suited to carry out the liminal role that his father wants him to play. Having spent four years as a medical student in England and assimilated the English idiom, Olunde has both experienced the good and the ugly sides of Western modernity. His involvement in the treatment of wounded soldiers from the battle front of the Second World War and his probable interaction with progressive forces in British society have especially enabled him to learn more about the Western world and the working of the colonizer's mind:

> Mrs Pilkings, whatever we do, we never suggest that a thing is the opposite of what it really is. In your newsreels I heard defeats, thorough, murderous defeats described as strategic victories. No wait, it wasn't just on your newsreels. Don't forget I was attached to hospitals all the time. Hordes of your wounded passed through those wards. I spoke to them. I spent long evenings by their bedside while they spoke terrible truths of the realities of that war. I know now how history is made.
>
> (54)

Here Olunde makes a distinction between Western policy makers' hypocrisy and distortions of historical facts to justify their inhumane goals and the sense of honesty displayed by ordinary citizens such as the wounded soldiers. In his view, the soldiers' integrity parallels that of the Oyo community. Olunde certainly sees common ground between his people's humanism and that of English soldiers like the captain who decides to blow himself up with a dangerous warship that would have killed "hundreds of the costal population" (51). In enthusiastically comparing the captain's self-sacrifice and sense of moral responsibility to his father's traditionally defined duty and responsibility as King's horseman, Olunde points out the potential for a positive cultural translation of the values of the two worlds. Moreover, by symbolically associating him with the healing profession, the English idiom and Western suit, Soyinka underlines Olunde's role as a potential healer of his society plagued by colonial brutality and arrogance, on the one hand, and his people's rejection of Western modernity, on the other hand.

Thus, like his father and other liminal characters in the play, Olunde resists colonization but envisions the location of his people's subjective agency within the intersection of African tradition and Western modernity. It is this postcolonial hybrid space fertilized by his controversial death and that of Elesin that will ultimately inspire the action of the "unborn." Even the conservative Iyaloja acknowledges that her society should look up to the unborn for its salvation as she optimistically consoles the expectant mother who mourns over the death of Elesin: "Now forget the dead, forget even the living. Turn your mind only to the unborn" (77).

In the end, though Pilkings can for the moment stop Oyo people's anticolonial protests, desecrate their iconic traditional signs, and imprison their King's Horseman, he does not and will not have the last word for the future of their land and society. Soyinka gives that last word to Iyaloja who represents the collective conscience of the masses, and by so doing, he locates the agency for the development of Nigeria in the collective conscience of its masses.

Keita! l'héritage du Griot

Although set in post-independence Burkina Faso, a former French colony, the main characters of the film *Keita*, directed by Dani Kouyaté, face cultural dilemmas similar to those confronted by Soyinka's characters during British colonial rule in Nigeria (in *Death and King's Horseman*). From the opening scenes of the film, post-independence Burkina Faso is presented to viewers as a country that is struggling to shake off its colonial past and bridge the gap between the rural and urban spaces, the indigenous knowledge system and Western epistemology as well as gender and class divisions. Despite lacking modern amenities, Wagadu, the conservative rural town where the Griot Djeliba Kouyaté (played by Griot Sotigui Kouyaté) lives, appears to viewers in the beginning of the film as free of the socio-cultural pressures that city dwellers experience. Before he travels to the city (Ouagadougou), we see Djeliba comfortably relaxing and having a nap in his hammock in open air at his unfenced compound while his wife and other women are carrying out their daily chores outside their modest thatched house. It is in that propitious atmosphere that a divine hunter of Do appears to him in a dream and sets him on a mission to the city. As the living griot of the Keita family, Djeliba Kouyaté is sent to teach a young Mabo Keita (Hamed Dicko), who is already going to a formal modern school, the meaning of his name or the heritage of his family through the epic story of his 13th-century powerful ancestor, Sundjata Keita, the founding father of the West African medieval empire of Mali.

Through Djeliba's journey and gaze, Dani Kouyaté crafts a frame story introducing viewers to the vicissitudes of life in a post-independence African city: heavy traffic of old cars and impatient drivers' outbursts of rage, streams of motorcycles dangerously zigzagging around cars, and roadside hawkers. As Djeliba arrives at Boacar and Sitan Keita's fenced house and introduces himself, Dani Kouyaté implicitly invites viewers to contemplate the rigidly structured life of a post-independence middle class, modern family reflecting colonial legacy: The French language, siesta at noon, formal table manners and imported foodstuffs, servants, reading leisure (newspapers), school homework for children, public service work, and social outings like weddings at weekends. Absent here are prayer times for adults and storytelling for children.

Following Mabo to school, viewers are made to realize that although the country is independent, the school system still bears all the hallmarks of French colonialism in its curriculum, student discipline, and its enforcement (corporal punishment and military-style drills). The language of instruction is French. Children are taught evolution, mathematics, and Western world history (American and French), but no African history or creation stories. This is the kind of French colonial school that Jean Marie-Medza, the main character of Mongo Beti's novel *Mission to Kala*, describes with resentment as "a kind of giant ogre, swallowing young boys, digesting them slowly, vomiting them up again sucked dry of all their youthful essence, mere skeletons" (Beti 1964:68).

Like Elesin in Soyinka's play, Djeliba understands that the encounter between Western modernity and the African tradition he represents has had a profound effect on his people and that the transition from colonialism to true cultural independence has to be managed carefully. Djeliba therefore stands against mimicry or cultural assimilation, though he is receptive to cultural translation of Western and traditional African values from an African subjective positioning. That is the reason why he encourages Mabo to go to school while telling him the story of his great ancestor Maghan Kon Fatta Konate. Djeliba's openness to a foreign source of knowledge (the school) is consistent with his people's world view, especially their sense of adaptability, and this is seen in the dialogue between the hunter of Do and the King's griot in the main story. When the hunter unexpectedly appears in the King's court, he says: "Honor to you, King of Mande and to all your court. I have killed an antelope on your land. According to your customs, here is your share with all my respects." Accepting the gift on behalf of the King, his griot Doua responds: "You have respected our customs. We are very touched by this in Mande.... The true hunters of Do are rare. **If you wish, we shall learn a lot from you**" (Kouyaté, emphasis added). With all due modesty before the towering presence of King Maghan Kon Fatta Konate, the divine hunter of Do responds positively to Griot Doua's request: "I am not a hunter whose tongue is more agile than his arm. Thanks to the lessons of my master, I shall consult the cowries for you" (Kouyaté). He then goes on to foretell how the destiny of the kingdom will unravel, as revealed by the tossed cowries: the King's marriage to Sogolon (Blandine Yameogo), the daughter of the Buffalo woman Do Kamissa; the mysterious conception and birth of Sundjata (Seydou Boro); and Sundjata's growth and eventual accession to his father's throne as the most powerful king of Mande. Although the King is skeptical about the validity of the hunter's knowledge about the future of his kingdom, Doua reassures him: "It's possible. But let us be on our guard. **The same truth can have several versions**" (Kouyaté, emphasis added). Here the traditionalist underlines the fact that there is no absolutism about knowledge, and that all knowledges, no matter their provenance, have to be tested.

In this dialogue, there is a mutual respect between the stranger (the hunter) who is trusted to be a carrier of new knowledge and his hosts. This is something that did not happen between European colonialists, who saw African pre-colonial life-worlds as barbaric, and African traditionalists like Djeliba, who have vehemently and rightly contested the validity of their assertion. The point that Dani Kouyaté makes here through Djeliba's cultural openness, that nevertheless opposes French assimilation policy, was earlier made by the Senegalese writer Cheikh Hamidou Kane in an interview with Phanuel Egejuru:

> Sometimes the white men who have colonized us, particularly the French, think they have to assimilate us. They say to themselves, 'These people have no culture, no wisdom, no civilization, therefore we shall give them our culture, our wisdom, our civilization. We shall make them French men with black skin.' *L'aventure ambigue* (*Ambiguous Adventure*) was a warning to the Europeans. It was to tell them that what they are thinking is not possible.
>
> (Egejuru 1978:149)

In his interactions with Mabo and his parents, Djeliba also refrains from openly condemning their modern habits even when they appear awkward to him. For instance, when Mabo tells him that Bintou, the housemaid, does all the household chores for her mother Sitan (Claire Sanon), Djeliba is surprised and only indirectly criticizes her by evoking women's positioning in the past: "The World has changed.... In the old days, when a woman didn't know how to do housework, she didn't find a husband. But your mother is marvelous" (Kouyaté). As a sign of respect, Djeliba calls Sitan "Orange Blossom" and tells her that her husband Boacar (Mamadou Sarr) always talks glowingly about her beauty. In response, Sitan politely speaks with Djeliba in Jula, welcomes him with a glass of water, and invites him to the house instead of letting him sleep in his hammock in the open air. Though

142 *Postcolonial agency in African literature*

appreciating her hospitality, Djeliba responds that he prefers to sleep in the open air. That way Djeliba seems to be signaling that he prefers to remain out of the confines of the rigidly regulated modern life represented in this instance by the image of the modern house.

As he enunciates a counter-discourse to the exclusive, colonial Western modernity that has engulfed the city life, Djeliba instantiates his vision by his action. He first starts the process at the table when he is invited to join the family at dinner for which spaghetti (called "white meal") is served as the main course. Consistent with their middle-class habits, Boacar, Sitan, and Mabo comfortably use forks and knives to eat spaghetti, but Djeliba cannot. Even when Mabo offers to teach him how to eat with modern cutlery, Djeliba declines the offer, saying "I can't." Instead, he asks for a bowl of water and uses his hands to eat the meal. Here, Djeliba symbolically introduces Boacar and his family to the postcolonial process of cultural translation of Western modernity and African practices. When he is presented with spaghetti, he is unable to pronounce it because of the lack of model for the cluster of consonants in that word in the Jula language. Here again, when Mabo repeats the correct pronunciation for Djeliba, he still cannot pronounce it the way the Italians would. He therefore calls it "SPAKTI" and repeats his pronunciation several times as if in an attempt to teach his hosts to accept it as a localized concept. By this linguistic move, Djeliba didactically abrogates the original perception of spaghetti as "white meal" and domesticates it. Having renamed this Western food item, Djeliba also unconventionally decides to eat it using his hands in the manner he would eat other local foodstuffs. That way, he appropriates spaghetti, and it becomes an ordinary African food item. From now on, Djeliba or any other natives can freely eat SPAKTI, drink water, and belch loudly without regards to Western formalities.[1]

After the meal, Djeliba decides to reveal the purpose of his mission to Boacar and his wife, saying that he has come to "do my duty. Mabo must know his history. I come here for that" (Kouyaté). However, while Boacar readily agrees with Djeliba, The "assimilated" Sitan opposes his mission. So, as soon as Djeliba steps out to pray, Sitan angrily questions Boacar: "He's come to initiate Mabo. Is that all right?" And when Boacar asks her "What do you have against that?" Sitan emphatically responds: "Mabo is taking exams. He shouldn't be disturbed. You know that" (Kouyaté). Djeliba's postcolonial vision for his society thus disrupts the colonial order still prevalent in the country after its nominal independence from France. Unlike his mother's objection, Mabo, who has started questioning why the history he is being taught at school does "not explain my name," is now eager to learn the history of his ancestor and his people from Djeliba. As in the case of Olunde in Soyinka's *Death and the King's Horseman*, here, Mabo's mind also becomes a space of power contestation between the assimilationist Western modernity represented by the school and the African memory represented by the griot Djeliba Kouyaté.

Colonial encounter and postcolonial agency 143

For his pedagogy, Djeliba chooses a relaxing, open air homestead setting (Mabo's parents' home), free of modern strictures and rules that the school requires (tight time schedule, military-style drills before class begins, corporal punishment when a student fails to give the right response to a question, and intolerance for students' questions). Here, over several days, after school time Mabo learns the history of the founding of the 13th-century Empire of Mali narrated through the Sunjata epic. He attentively follows Djeliba's contextual narration of the events in the epic, including the following: the dangerous hunting down and killing of the Buffalo woman Do Kamissa by two hunters-brothers from Do, their reward from her nephew Do-Samo for killing her in the form of the ugly crippled maiden Sogolon, their journey with Sogolon to King Maghan Kon Fatta Konate, the King's struggle to make her pregnant, her pregnancy that lasts more than nine months (outside the calendar that Mabo knows), the mysterious circumstances surrounding Sundjata's birth, his struggle as he grows with disability, the jealousy of the King's first wife Sassouma Berete toward Sogolon and Sundjata, the King's death, Sunjata's time to overcome disability and stand on his feet following Sassouma Berete's insults to him and his mother, the delivery of the rod prepared by the blind blacksmith Noumoufari who earlier on assured the King that Sundjata would walk, the breaking of the rod as Sundjata attempts to stand with its help, the intervention of the divine hunter of Do who advises Sogolon to bring a branch of 'sun-sun' to her son, Sundjata's triumphant standing on his feet with the help of the branch, Bella Fasseke proclamation: "Men of Mande! Women of Mande! Sundjata Walks!," the uprooting of a giant baobah tree by Sundjata, Dankaran Touman, and Sassouma Berete's violent threat to Sundjata and his mother, the cruel separation of Sundjata from his Griot Bella Fasseke by his half-brother Dankaran Touman, and his departure to exile in obedience to his mother's plea with a promise to return.

In the course of his narration of the epic story, Djeliba pauses from time to time to contextualize its events and allows Mabo to ask probing questions in the manner that the formal school would not permit. As a result of the conviction that Djeliba brings to the story, Mabo starts revaluating the validity and relevance of the knowledge that he and his classmates are acquiring at school, especially Darwin's theory of evolution. He now prefers to spend more time with Djeliba than his teacher and is daydreaming during class lessons. However, concerned about what he sees as Mabo's lackluster performance at school (despite the corporal punishment that he inflicts upon him), Teacher Fofana decides to seek the boy's parents' intervention rather than diagnose the real problem himself. But the family being divided over Djeliba's mission, Teacher Fofana only finds an ally in Sitan while Boacar remains firmly on the side of the griot's mission. That family division ensures Mabo's movement toward a liminal position that Djeliba's action and the story that he is telling suggest. Sitan and Teacher Fofana therefore fail in their attempts to persuade Mabo to detach himself from Djeliba and be exclusively anchored in Western modernity—the school.

144 *Postcolonial agency in African literature*

Having failed to persuade Mabo to solely devote attention to his schoolwork rather than listen to Djeliba's story, Teacher Fofana decides to approach Djeliba himself directly. But through his responses to Djeliba's probing questions during their conversation, Teacher Drissa Fofana unwittingly exposes his colonized mind. The first question that Djeliba asks Fofana is his name, for the name can tell him the history of his family. Fofana responds that his name is "Drissa Fofana." Djeliba compliments him and asks another question: "That's a nice name. Do you know what it means?" Fofana responds "No." Surprised by his ignorance, Djeliba laments: "Pity you don't know. What can you teach to children without knowing your own origin?" Fofana's excuse is "I don't have a griot in my service." But Djeliba rejects his frivolous excuse out of hand, saying: "The griots are in the service of everyone. If you wish I can explain your origin." Exposed and disarmed by Djeliba, Fofana recoils and asks Djeliba to come to an "agreement" with him about Mabo. However, Djeliba seizes the opportunity of their conversation to debunk the theory of evolution and Western modernity's absolute claim to truth. He emphatically tells Fofana:

> Then I will listen to you. But first it is you who will listen to me. There are 124,000 beings between the sky and the earth, who breathe like you and me. Of all these 124,000 beings I am only ignorant of two things: sheep and sorghum. **So don't tell Mabo any more that his ancestor was a gorilla! He was a king! Maghan Kon Fatta Konate, King of Mande.**
>
> (Kouyaté, emphasis added)

Without disputing the validity of Djeliba's history and way of knowing, Fofana tacitly puts the responsibility for the flaws in the post-independence school system on the shoulders of the country's neocolonial elite. He tells Djeliba: "Ok, but if Mabo wrote this on his examination, he would fail. For your knowledge and mine are different." For Fofana and the government, Western knowledge that he imparts to children is a finished project and therefore cannot be contested as the African World view articulated by Djeliba suggests. But Djeliba rejects that colonial monopoly of knowledge, saying to him: "My son, knowledge is heavy with sense. Knowledge is ungraspable, complex. It might be in the breath of ancestors, in millet, in sand. It passes from spirit to man, from the man to the spirit…" (Kouyaté). In the end, Fofana proposes that Djeliba let Mabo concentrate on his schoolwork at the moment and come back during the school vacation to tell him the rest of the story. Djeliba flatly rejects his suggestion and advises him: "Teach your things during the vacation and leave him to me now. I'll have soon finished. I'll return him to you afterwards. I wish you a long life." And when Fofana tells Djeliba that he does not determine the school calendar, the government does, Djeliba responds: "In that case, I have nothing to do with you, if you don't determine anything. Bring them here (the government) … yes, if you can. I am here, I am waiting for them" (Kouyaté). Deflated by Djeliba's powerful postcolonial posture, Fofana leaves Djeliba and Mabo to continue with their story. It is at that point that Mabo tells Djeliba that he does not want to return to school because "the master is angry," but Djeliba looks up to a bird flying over them and encourages him: "Lift your head, look at that bird up in the sky, it's my totem.... He has promised me that he will watch over you." Apart from being Djeliba's totem, the bird here symbolically signals Mabo's freedom from an oppressive and confining school system that does not resonate with the totality of his people's life-world and lived experiences.

Djeliba's convincing talk with Fofana in the presence of the attentive Mabo further encourages the latter to move toward the liminal postcolonial critical zone that Walter Mignolo has called "border thinking." According to Mignolo, "Border thinking becomes, then, the necessary epistemology to delink and decolonize knowledge and, in the process, to build decolonial local histories, restoring the dignity that the Western idea of universal history took away from millions of people" (2000:x). Mabo returns to school with this vision and fearlessly invites two of his classmates to a neutral setting on a tree to tell them the story of the making of the great empire of Mali that the school or Western modernity has been hiding from them. Mabo tells his classmates in French the epic story that Djeliba has told him in Jula and by so doing abrogates and appropriates the French language. Mabo's enlightenment of his classmates with their country's suppressed history threatens the dominance of the Western knowledge system and the assimilationist positioning of the neocolonial post-independence elite. Fofana not only punishes Mabo and his classmates for skipping class but also enlists the assistance of the boys' "assimilated" parents to end Djeliba's decolonial mission.

In the end, Fofana dismisses Mabo from school and takes the other boys' parents to confront Mabo's parents and Djeliba. However, though they cause a stir at Boacar and Sitan's home and Djeliba decides to leave, Fofana and the boys' mentally colonized parents do not have the last word. Just as in the case of Soyinka's play with Iyaloja, here also, it is the traditionalist Djeliba who has the last authoritative word. When Sitan emotionally asks Mabo if he no longer wants to return to school or if he could tell Djeliba to stop the story, Mabo emphasizes his critical liminal positioning by responding: "**I want to go to school, but I want the story to continue**" (emphasis added). Soon after, Djeliba decides to leave but tells the distraught Sitan and the stunned Boacar "All right, I'm going. But I must speak to Mabo." He then turns to Mabo after Fofana and the boys' parents have left, and advises him:

> Do you know why the hunter always beats the lions in stories? It's because it's the hunter who tells the stories. If the lion told the stories, he would occasionally win. It's valuable for you. Think of it and be confident in the future. **Always remember that it's an old world and that the future emerges from the past. Farewell.**
>
> (Kouaté, emphasis added)

Djeliba's lesson to Mabo here reminds us of David Diop's poem "Africa," in which the persona responds to the searching question of "an impetuous child" about his/her positioning vis-à-vis Africa and its history in a similar way:

> Africa, tell me Africa,
> Are you the back that bends
> Lies down under the weight of humbleness?
> The trembling back striped red
> That says yes to the sjambok on the roads of noon?
> Solemnly a voice answers me
> 'Impetuous child, that young and sturdy tree
> That tree that grows
> There splendidly alone among white and faded flowers
> Is Africa, your Africa. It puts forth new shoots
> With patience and stubbornness puts forth new shoots
> Slowly its fruits grow to have
> The bitter taste of liberty.' (Diop 1967:111)

The new shoots here are the anticipated independent, postcolonial generation of the "unborn" in *Death and the King's Horseman* and Mabo Keita in the film *Keita*. One could conjecture with reference to African history that in the works mentioned here, Diop, Kouyaté, and Soyinka have in mind the generation of early anti-colonial revolutionary leaders who envisioned the future of postcolonial Africa to be shaped at the decolonized intersection of African values and Western modernity. Such political leaders include Ahmed Sékou Touré (Guinea), Modibo Keita (Mali), Obafemi Awolowo (Nigeria), Kwame Nkrumah (Ghana), Jomo Kenyatta (Kenya), Julius Nyerere (Tanzania), Kenneth Kaunda (Zambia), Patrice Lumumba (Democratic Republic of Congo), and Agostinho Neto (Angola).

Note

1 For more on the postcolonial process of language abrogation and appropriation, see Bill Ashcroft, Griffiths and Tiffin (1989:38–77).

6 Postcolonial conjunctive consciousness in the literature of the new African diaspora

Chris Abani's *The Virgin of Flames,* Chimamanda Ngozi Adichie's *Americanah,* Leila Aboulela's *The Translator*

In his assessment of the African writer's positionality vis-à-vis his/her public in *Hopes and Impediments*, Chinua Achebe stated that "[E]very literature must seek the things that belong unto its peace, must, in other words, speak of a particular place, evolve out of the necessities of its history, past and current, and the aspirations and destiny of its people" (Achebe 1988:50). And commenting on the same issue several decades later from the new diasporic space, Chris Abani states in an interview with Ron Singer:

> I'm in a generation that's lucky. Chinua Achebe, Wole Soyinka, and others have built [a] foundation for us. We no longer have to represent Nigeria. There's a clear picture of it, a very positive picture. It allows us new writers to have this aesthetic freedom, privilege, the aesthetic moment, the moment of making art over any kind of political insurgency.
> (Singer 2015:2)

Thus, while the first generation of African writers who emerged during the colonial period sought to deliver a counter-narrative to colonial writers' negative representation of Africa and its peoples, the second generation that emerged after the independence of many African countries from the 1960s to the 1980s focused mainly on Africa's post-independence malaise marked by political violence, civil wars, class division, gender disparity, corrupt military dictatorships, and neocolonialism. In this chapter, I would like to argue that the so-called third generation or new African Diasporic writers have also reflected Achebe's aesthetic creed in their writings, but in a different way. As interpreters of their publics' experiences and historical moment, new African Diasporic creative writers occupy a "third space" (Bhabha 1994:37) from where they cast a critical gaze upon three life-worlds—the African societies they originate from, the Western world they presently live in, and the diasporic consciousness they articulate. In so doing, new African Diasporic writers' writings draw their effectiveness and conviction from the authors' sophisticated use of language, cultural objects, and social media as

DOI: 10.4324/9780429322426-10

narrative techniques. Instead of merely providing a survey of the works of such writers, I have chosen to use three representative novels, Chris Abani's *The Virgin of Flames* (2007), Chimamanda Adichie's *Americanah* (2013), and Leila Aboulela's *The Translator* (1999), to discuss the emergence of a global, postcolonial conjunctive consciousness in the writings of the new African Diasporic authors around issues like race, gender, sexuality, disability, religion, politics, nationality, coloniality, and transnational identities. These global issues and the imaginaries they condition have not only become the main themes of the literature of the new African diaspora but also that of other diasporic constellations in North America and Europe. As noted by Kavita Daiya, this

> [G]rowing archive of writing explodes our traditional national frames of American literature, British literature, and even world literature. This new literature offers us postcolonial stories unconstrained by national boundaries and often undone by nationalism. They are American and Nigerian, Pakistani and British, Sri Lankan and Canadian, Indian and Bangladeshi, Dominican and American.
>
> (Daiya 2017:154)

In his reflections on the transnational identity of the new African Diasporic subjects, Paul Zeleza has defined diaspora as "[S]imultaneously a state of being and a process of becoming, a kind of voyage that encompasses the possibility of never arriving or returning, a navigation of multiple belongings, of networks of affiliation" (Zeleza 2009:32). Also enlisting Edward Said's idea that there is a kind of exile that "exists in a median state, neither completely at one with the new setting nor fully disencumbered of the old" (qtd. in Okpewho 2009:13), Isidore Okpewho has candidly stated: "Honestly, I admit that many of us first-generation immigrants of the new African diaspora fit that description, and I doubt that the kinds of coding often conceived for us are likely to put us at ease" (Okpewho 2009:13). Whether writing in English, French, or other European languages, many new African Diasporic writers including Chris Abani, Chimamanda Adichie, Tess Onwueme, Helen Oyeyemi, Teju Cole, Taiye Selasi, Imbolo Mbue, NoViolet Bulawayo, Alain Mabanckou, Abdourahman Waberi, Tshisungu wa Tshisungu, and a host of others have time and again articulated this sense of what I can call transnational, postcolonial conjunctive consciousness in various interviews about their lives and in their respective creative projects. Most of them have refused to be narrowly zoned and labeled African writers. For example, when asked the question whether she would describe herself and her writing as "African" in an interview with Aminatta Forna, Adichie responds:

> Being labeled an 'African writer' is something I am uncomfortable with but also proud of. Proud because it's a heritage that I embrace; uncomfortable because it's a loaded term and often one that's given to you by

somebody else. If it didn't come with baggage, then it would be fine, but it does and because of that there is some discomfort.

(Forna 2006:6)

In the same interview, Helen Oyeyemi also expresses the same discomfort, stating that the label "African writer" can "pigeonhole you because when you walk into bookshops you often see a lot of great Nigerian or African writers being put into categories such as 'Black Interest' or 'African Interest'... That is annoying" (Forna 2006:6). Chris Abani has also described the new African diasporic writer's creative project as transnational and liberated from the cultural nationalism found in the writings of the earlier generations of African writers. In an interview with Yogita Goyal, Abani states:

> The third generation is doing exciting work. About my work, it is in many ways post-national and global not only in its reach, but in its attempts to locate a very specific African sensibility without attempting to limit it with certain kinds of arguments about essentiality and so forth.
>
> (Goyal 2014:229–230)

As Goyal has remarked, Abani "has resisted various labels of an Igbo writer, a British writer, a Los Angeles writer, black writer, African writer, or a Nigerian writer" (234). In an interview with Claire Chambers, Leila Aboulela has also resisted being narrowly defined by one cultural site stating that there are "three things that [together] make up my identity, Sudan, Egypt and Britain" (Chambers 2009:91). Ahmed Wahab is therefore right when he points out that the transnational consciousness that informs Aboulela's creative writing emanates from her conjunctive diasporic positioning:

> Daughter of an Egyptian mother and Sudanese father and at the same time brought up at a Westernized environment of a private American school, Aboulela has always been tuned to cultural negotiations across heterogeneous geographies, ethnicities, and languages in Cairo, Khartoum, Jakarta, Abu Dhabi, Dubai, London, and Aberdeen.
>
> (Wahab 2014:225)

Thus, although coming from different constellations of postcoloniality, new African Diasporic writers like Adichie, Abani, and Aboulela are unified by their articulation of a transnational, postcolonial conjunctive consciousness which promotes what Gayatri Spivak calls "a collective rearrangement of desires" (Spivak 2008:4), a condition of possibility of "cosmopolitan conviviality" (Gilroy 2005:8) in the "New Empire," to use Michael Hardt and Antonio Negri's apt characterization of our contemporary world (Hardt and Negri 2000:xii–xiii, see also Losambe 2017:837). In fact, the main characters of the novels under discussion here are largely modeled after their creators' transnational lived experiences. So, like his bi-racial creator Abani whose mother is English and father Igbo, and who has lived in Nigeria, Britain, and the United States, Black, the main character of the novel *The Virgin of Flames* (2007), is a bi-racial artist whose father is Igbo and mother Salvadorian. Black also lives in the United States. Adichie's main character in *Americanah* (2013), Ifemelu, also mirrors the life-trajectory of her creator. Both are creative Igbo women who immigrated to the United States to pursue university studies after spending their early formative years in post-independence Nigeria. Sammar, the main character of Aboulela's novel *The Translator* (1999), is also, like her creator, a Muslim Sudanese woman who has lived in Khartoum in Sudan and Aberdeen in Scotland. Through their respective professional activities, whether painting (Black), or writing and moderating blogs (Ifemelu), or translating Arabic texts into English (Sammar), these African diasporic subjects reject the notion of rigid originary cultural totality and bring to the consciousness of their multiple publics the hidden structure of negative attitudes that hinders the emergence of a new humanism that cherishes difference, whether corporeal or social—gender and sexuality, body size, race, class, ideology, religious belief, ethnicity, and nationality.

The Virgin of Flames

In *The Virgin of Flames*, the focalizer through whom Abani articulates this diasporic, postcolonial conjunctive consciousness is the thirty-six-year-old Black, whose Igbo name is Obinna, which means "his father's heart." His Catholic mother, Maria, named him Black because she conceived him before her Christian marriage to Frank Anyanwu and, as such, believed that her son was cursed. Just as Maria invoked a Catholic doctrine to sanction her son's problematic entry into the symbolic world by naming him Black, so did his father also associate him with an Igbo curse under which all male children in his family lived before the age of seven. In order to protect their child from these negative metaphysical influences, Frank Anyanwu cross-dressed Obinna like a girl until the age of seven, and Maria later subjected him to a ruthless regimen of atoning prayers to Virgin Mary from the age of eight. Here is how Black later explains to June, another visionary artist in the novel, the reason why he was dressed like a girl in the photo that is inside the plastic pouch, a kind of relic from his dead father, that he is carrying around his neck:

> My father told me that there is a curse on our family, that a malevolent spirit kills all the male children before they turn six. So all the boys are dressed as girls and sometimes even given girl's names until they turn seven. Then the dress comes off and we become boys again.
>
> (Abani 2007:100)

This partially explains the origin of his present desire for cross-dressing. As for the origin of his name Black, his mother constantly reminded him:

> You are my punishment from God. Do you know why? Because I got pregnant before I married your father. Against my family's wishes, I dated that Moreno. And now I have to live with you. You are my living sin, m'ijo. Pray, pray that God forgives you.
>
> (107)

These spiritual influences thus shaped Black's process of cultural hybridization early in life and are manifested in his desire to see Los Angeles become a postcolonial multicultural and convivial society. Black lost his father, who went to fight on behalf of the United States in Vietnam, at the age of seven and his mother, who died of cancer, at the age of fifteen. However, as a thirty-six-year-old artist, their conjunctive influence still shapes his transformative creative vision. Although the Virgin of Guadalupe (his late mother's spiritual idol) is his creative muse, Black's artistic vision is simultaneously informed by a voice from his father's Igbo cultural memory which urges him to "Grow strong and make our name proud" (164). As the omniscient narrator in the novel says:

> He was having trouble these days separating the real from the imagined. Like the words he could hear now, as clearly as if someone stood next to him, voice soft on the blue light. Don't Forget Me. But the words were in a different language, all music. Echefulam. A language he hadn't heard since his childhood, but one he knew was Igbo, as sure as if he had been born to it.
>
> (45)

This conjunction of memories enhances Black's liminality as he seeks to bring to light through his painting and carnivalesque corporeal engagements the repressed inequities and shortcomings of the contemporary world, represented by Los Angeles. As Abani has remarked in an interview with Kate Durbin, "There is no authentic LA, that's kind of what my book argues. There are only multiple cities within it, each as valid as the next" (Durbin 2007:4). Los Angeles is therefore like Lagos in Nigeria and other postmodern cities around the world (Ouma 2011:90) that, as suggested by Paul Gilroy, need new "multicultural ethics and politics [...] premised upon agonistic, planetary humanism capable of comprehending the universality of our elemental vulnerability to the wrongs we visit upon each other" (Gilroy 2005:4). These are the wrongs that Black gazes at from his spaceship simulacrum and dilapidated mobile home he nicknamed "Blackmobile"; that he personally experiences in LA streets, bars, stores, the riverside, and public places; and that he seeks to cure through his artistic intervention.

Black outlines the transformative aim of his public, outdoor artistic installation (murals) in LA when he tells his enigmatic psychic companion Iggy:

> I figured that racism and sexism had retreated from the overtly public to the private, you know, all the jokes and so forth that people only feel safe telling in the confessional space of toilets, but ones that still reveal the soul of this country to be racist and sexist, and I want to point that heart of darkness.
>
> (89)

Black, therefore, sets out to produce a critical art form, whose aim, to use Jacques Rancière's words, is "to produce a new perception of the world, and therefore to create a commitment to its transformation" (Rancière 2015:150).

Much of *The Virgin of Flames* depicts the transformative power of the imagination, the way in which the mirror of art transforms the world. Black, the protagonist of the novel, takes his artistic power to extremes, going out in the midst of day with his face painted white, so that Bomboy, a Rwandan immigrant, is compelled to say that Black looks "more like the undead in a Japanese horror movie" (8). For Black, art is that which has the potential to transcend the ugly vicissitudes of life. The world is for him a canvas, something which through transformative artistic powers he hopes to give an uncanny meaning. As the novel's omniscient narrator observes, "Black, as a painter, lived in a world of composition—shade, angle of light, perspective—one in which things blurred into one another even as they stood out in sharp relief." This is unlike Bomboy who "lived in a world of statements—often contradictory, but no less rigid and clear each time" (24). Here, Abani contrasts Black's transcendent, unsettling artistic vision of what contemporary world should be with Bomboy's passive acceptance of its problematic, present certainty.

As stated above, the Virgin represents in a significant way the core of Black's artistic mission—the reconciliation of high and low, fragment, and whole in terms of class, race, gender, sexuality, ethnicity, and nationality. She is the very thing of artistic sublimation, an object which, in Black's view, mediates the threshold between high and low, life and art:

> The Virgin was important to the people here. Not only as a symbol of the adopted religion of Catholicism, but because she was a brown virgin who had appeared to a brown saint, Juan Diego. She was also a symbol of justice, of a political spirituality.
>
> (41)

Black's emphasis here is not on the traditional, redemptive symbolic role of the Virgin, but rather on the Virgin's color, which symbolizes her closeness to the people—the poor, the homeless, the addicted, as well as the racially and sexually marginalized. In contrast to traditional conceptions of the

Virgin where her whiteness is a direct marker of her purity or her distance away from the material reality of actual life, Black's Virgin is indeed nothing more than an iconic embodiment of multiple colors or diverse races. That way, the masses or "multitudes" (Hardt and Negri 2000:60–61) can witness her epiphany in Nigeria, America, and presumably, all over the world. So, rather than following traditional depictions of the Virgin as the infinitely distant creator of life beyond life, Black's vision of the Virgin is one that is intertwined with his experience of the quotidian as he observes the LA multitude restlessly questing for a collective and just rearrangement of desires, to echo Spivak:

> The Virgin appeared here often, to reassure her people no doubt. In the Winchells donut shop on Fourth and Soto, hovering in the window for the longest time, transforming the tasty local treat into the most sought after cure for every ailment and malaise. In the law office of Tomas Alarcon, who was the most expensive and dishonest immigration lawyer in the whole area, but who, since the night he saw her shadow burned into the glass frame of his office door, had taken to not charging for his cases, accepting only whatever donations his clients could manage. [...] Rumors of these apparitions spread by word of mouth and fast. The news was wrapped in Big Macs and passed over counters, it filled buckets of KFC, was whispered in the hush of washing machines in the Laundromat, passed out on the street between passerby and even between the dealers and their clients. Black heard it from Bomboy who heard it from Pedro who owned the taco stand opposite The Ugly Store.
> (41–42)

I would like to emphasize here the way in which the news of the Virgin's apparitions—the Virgin in her phenomenological form—emanates and spreads from capitalist garbage: it comes from cheap foil and bulk fried chicken. There is therefore an acknowledgement in Black's imagination that the Virgin is not a being beyond the experience of the everyday, but rather one that resides within the very fabric of the quotidian, within the non-cohesive, multitudinous composite of city life. The Virgin, as a symbol of religious salvation, is not an escape from garbage, but is found within it. But it is not sufficient to say that, as represented by Black, the Virgin is merely a piece of garbage; she is rather projecting the convivial consciousness and new humanism that the multitudes seem to be yearning for.

Abani's invocation of Wallace Stevens' poetic vision in the novel shows his conjunctive consciousness in his creative project. Indeed, his articulation of the transformative power of the art agrees with Stevens' view of the transformative power of poetry. Like Abani, Stevens as a poet was interested in the dialectical contact between the ordinary and the transcendent. Like Stevens, Abani through Black demonstrates a resistance to the established official and consensual order as he seeks to push beyond the world of mere appearances, to find something in his immediate world that is "dissensual" (Rancière 2015) and transformative. Black's concern is not what the popular image of Los Angeles means. He rather uses the chaotic world of Los Angeles to create a space that is meaningful to him and other marginalized or injured individuals in society. Black wants Los Angeles to become a space of conviviality where different peoples, different languages, and different ways of thinking are brought together rather than sequestered and stratified. Black (and by extension Abani) prefers the Los Angeles of the contingent and the random. Indeed, he prefers the Los Angeles of "The Ugly Store" where the normalized marginalization of its inhabitants on the basis of race, class, gender, sexuality, body size, and originary identity is subverted. Abani's artistic vision here is not coincidentally prevalent throughout a wide range of ethnically diverse, postcolonial artistic articulations. And it is prevalent because this type of creative heteroglossia provides the perfect "third space" in which to reflect on the pitfalls of the normalized arrangement of desires in contemporary world.

Abani's other marginalized, injured but otherwise transformative carnivalesque characters in *The Virgin of Flames* include the illegal Rwandan Hutu immigrant Bomboy Dickens, the lonely transgendered stripper Sweet Girl, the Jewish psychic Iggy, and the African American little person and drug-addict Ray-Ray. They team up with Black as they seek to bring to the open through their carnivalesque actions their hurt and the iniquities of the society they live in, in particular, and those of the postcolonial, globalized world, in general. Randy Newman's song that Black plays as he drives through the streets of LA, "I Want You to Hurt Like I Do" (16), captures the essence of his "aesthetics of politics." As Rancière has argued, this kind of

> Politics consists in reconfiguring the distribution of the sensible which defines the common of a community, to introduce into it new subjects and objects, to render visible what had not been, and to make heard as speakers those who had been perceived as noisy animals.
> (Rancière 2009:25)

Bomboy came to LA after running away from Rwanda where he was forced to participate in the genocide of thousands of the Tutsi. His participation in the genocide, committed by the Hutu in 1994, still haunts his conscience while in exile. Unable to officially secure residency in the United States, he buys forged immigration papers, assumes different identities, lives in a dilapidated apartment building, and illegally owns an abattoir in LA. However, just as Black is haunted by the ghosts of the dead, "[C]rowding in, singing, begging, crying, and dying all over again, every night" (10) in old parts of Los Angeles, so is Bomboy also haunted by the ghosts of those who died in the Rwandan genocide in Kigali. Much as both seek a temporary relief from these pains by smoking pot, Black and Bomboy do not give up on the idea of a search for a new "planetary humanism and global multiculture"

(Gilroy 2005:80) that would prevent such unnecessary deaths. Bomboy is therefore determined to go back to Rwanda to seek atonement for the genocide and "celebrate the peace," but he first needs "to buy some fake papers" with Black's assistance (8) in order to be able to return to the United States. Their action here undermines national boundaries and projects their postcolonial, transnational desires. In fact, through their frequent conversations about language and identity, often marked by mutual light invectives, Black and Bomboy reinforce in one another the new diasporic, multicultural consciousness which resists the notion of a static cultural totality or confinement to a narrow originary identity. For example, when Black reproaches Bomboy for not speaking Spanish after spending several years in LA, he fires back by asking why he does not speak any African languages. Black then derogatively calls African languages "chingado," but Bomboy, as a postcolonial subject, disabuses his mind and ironically teaches him that African languages are "rich chingado" and that "Africans are very ambitious and progressive" (9). On another occasion, Bomboy tells Black: "Your father was African, and so therefore, you are African. Simple logistics." However, Black responds ambiguously, saying "I don't know" (195). By this response, Black affirms his diasporic liminality and conjunctive consciousness and teaches Bomboy not to be held captive by a narrow nativism, such as the one that led him and his Hutu ethnic group to massacre innocent Tutsi in Rwanda. A strong marker of this conjunctive positioning is Black's interpolation of both Spanish and Igbo words and imaginaries into the structure of his English speech.

Abani's conjunctive consciousness has also led him to cast a critical gaze upon the contemporary world's lack of conviviality regarding sexuality. In *The Virgin of Flames*, under intolerant societal pressure, Black is seen repressing his sexual desire as homosexual and engaging instead in an unproductive and unfulfilling heterosexual intercourse with a woman called Brandy. Regardless of this action, however, the enabling and reassuring gaze of the Virgin, the symbol of a perfect humanity for Black, interpolates his conscience to openly affirm his sexual identity and disrupt the consensual, faulty societal normativity about sexuality. Black's encounter with Sweet Girl, a Mexican transsexual and transvestite stripper, at Charlie's strip bar finally enables him to "feel safe" (77) and come out of his self-denial as gay and as a transvestite. Sweet Girl tells him: "I know you wanted to be a woman. I knew it from the moment you walked into Charlie's" (284). With that frank talk, Sweet Girl boldly pursues Black to his hideout (an obscure place with unlisted number), draws him out of his invisibility, teaches him to embrace his sexual identity as she has done, and gives him very fulfilling oral sex—sex that fulfills his previously contained and disregarded sexual desires. From this point onward, Black becomes obsessed with Sweet Girl as she leads him toward full self-discovery through many more sexual acts. In the end, Sweet Girl also becomes a source of inspiration for his transformative creative project as Fatima has been.

Though she is rejected by her family in Mexico because of her different sexual orientation and is unable to find work permit in the United States because of discriminatory national boundaries, Sweet Girl nevertheless finds comfort, love, and humanity in the company of other borderline, injured people in LA like Black, Bomboy, and Iggy. In a conversation with Black, Sweet Girl condemns her family's inhumanity and intolerance for sexual difference, bitterly stating: "They betrayed me when I needed them most, because I was different. They disagreed with my life choices, said I was unnatural and threw me out. What is more unnatural than throwing your child away, cutting yourself from yourself?" (271). Black accepts Sweet Girl as a soulmate and can now confidently invite her to his spaceship simulacrum—his creative altar—so that she can have a planetary view of LA with its inequities and appreciate his transformative and corrective creative project—the murals. From here, both can hear the cries and yearnings of the masses—the illegal immigrants, the homeless, the drug addicts, the poor, the delusional rich, students, teachers, and even the tortured dogs—as they search for justice and love in their society through the mediation of the Virgin whose supposed epiphany is actually Black in a white wedding dress on top of a building. Through this confusion, Abani makes Black and his muse, the Virgin, "objective correlative" (to use T.S. Eliot's words), and underscores the transformative and conscientizing power of his art.

The transformative power of Black's art is also confirmed by his other companion and inspirational character, the psychic and tattoo artist Iggy, who includes his indoor mural—*American Gothic: The Remix*—as an important part of her healing psychic apparatus at the Ugly Store. Iggy, the daughter of Jewish immigrants, is another carnivalesque character who seeks to undermine any discrimination based on class, race, nationality, and sexual orientation in LA by bringing deluded celebrities down to earth and encouraging the socially marginalized like Black, Sweet Girl, Bomboy, and Ray-Ray to assert themselves as vibrant, transformative subjects:

> As a fakir-psychic, she suspended her body in midair from meat hooks in order to induce a trance. Black still thought it was a strange practice for a lapsed white Jew from East LA, but she'd had a lot of success with it as she now had a celebrity client list. The Ugly Store had one rule and that was that to gain entry, clients had to be scarred. Psychic scars, mental scars, and general eccentricities were welcomed, but as it took some time and observation to determine these, visible scars were like gold and guaranteed an appointment. He'd seen Jennifer Garner and Uma Thurman in line scratching desperately but discreetly at their faces to ensure entry.
>
> (31)

Apart from Black's unsettling mural (a collage of confessional racist and sexist graffiti collected from men's bathroom stalls all around LA), other

Postcolonial conjunctive consciousness 157

objects which adorn Iggy's psychic chamber and reflect her planetary vision of humanity as well as her postcolonial conjunctive consciousness include:

> [B]roken toys, voodoo dolls, fetishes from Java, Africa, New Zealand, Australia and Papua New Guinea, sour-faced-Annies (dolls with heads made from desiccated apples, that looked like the shrunken heads of cannibal cultures), and flowerpots that could only look at home on a balcony in the lower sixth circle of hell.
>
> (31)

Here, Iggy's desire to heal deluded class-captured subjects in LA is shared by Black who, also aspiring to become a preacher or spiritual healer to the same subjects, wishes he could approach the lonely businesswoman wandering on the beach in Santa Monica and save her:

> Her sadness seemed absolute. He was riveted, as though she and he were the last people left on earth. He wasn't attracted to her, but to her absolute aloneness; this was what had drawn him to Sweet Girl. He wanted to approach her, this stranger on the beach. He wanted to save her. He knew he could do it. He could make up the rituals.
>
> (18)

Black wishes he could lead her to a humbling expiatory process by showering her with sand and water, thus reminding her of the planetary kinship of humanity that she and other upper-class people in LA are oblivious to. With sand, he would say to her: "*This is our body. The one true home. Feel the fall of it. Feel the wind carry it. This is the ancient way. Do this in memory of us. Don't forget*" (18–19); and washing her head "[G]ently with the salty water of the ocean, fetched in his cupped hands, with the tenderness of a woman washing a child in a long-ago gathering of shadows," he would say to her: "*This is water [...]. This is mother. The path. Taste the salt of it. Feel the flow. This is the ancient way. This is dread. This is freedom. Do this in memory of us. Don't forget*" (19). With this reminder, the upper-class businesswoman would have appreciated and shared the pain of the melancholic homeless and the depraved drug addicts who flock to the beach "to escape the dangers of down town LA." However, unlike Iggy who physically marks the healing process of her delusional, class-captured subjects by tattooing their bodies, Black can only seek to heal them by transmuting their hidden delusion into public art—his consciousness-raising murals that adorn the bank of the LA river, the wall of Bomboy's illegal abattoir, and the wall of the Ugly Store.

Iggy confirms the transformative power of Black's art when she states that he is always "[C]ooking up the magic of his murals and threatening the people passing above with his art. Just like love" (190). Black's murals, especially the one exuding a deep sense of compassion, love, and justice emanating from the gaze of the Virgin of Fatima, threaten the official order or societal consensus enforced by public policing (see Rancière 2015:108). It is because of their fear of the dissensual threat posed by Black's critical art that the LA City Council and the police seek to shield school children and teachers from its influence by ordering him to take down the Fatima mural and by hiring a contractor to sandblast it. However, for Black and Iggy, the repressive efforts of the City Council and the state police are in vain because the children and other multitudes have already become "[I]nfected by the desire for Fatima. And even though they would never remember the name of it, this desire, it would fill every pore of their body and drive them crazy" (238–239). Black further confirms the enduring and transformative nature of his art when he tells Iggy: "Everyone who saw that painting will always carry it with them. [...] It will haunt that wall for ever" (239). Here, Abani makes a distinction between the lingering effect of Black's critical art on society and his personal vulnerability as an individual or ephemeral member of the same society. In this way, neither Black himself, Iggy, Bomboy, Ray-Ray, the Sweet Girl nor any other members of the LA society are exempted from the call for a profound self-examination and a collective rearrangement of desires advocated by Black's art. The in-and-out slippages that the reader observes as these characters interact with one another and expose their personal ambiguities about race, sexuality, gender, body size, ethnicity, nationality, and identity make them oxymoronic figures through whom Abani effectively casts a critical gaze upon the structure of negative attitudes that impede conviviality in our global world.

Americanah

Like Abani, Chimamanda Adichie also occupies a third space from where she casts a critical gaze upon contemporary Nigerian and American societies through her enigmatic oxymoronic main characters. For example, in her latest novel *Americanah*, Ifemelu is the expressive agent of her postcolonial conjunctive consciousness and third space critical gaze. Refusing to be confined to, or monolithically defined by, any national and ideological boundaries, Ifemelu inhabits an independent diasporic space from where she boldly brings to light repressed melancholic and anachronistic attitudes about race, gender, sexuality, body size, class, ideology, ethnicity, coloniality, and globalization in Nigeria, the United States, and Britain. Like Abani's Black and his satirical murals in *The Virgin of Flames*, in *Americanah*, Ifemelu adopts a planetary humanist approach by creating a public cyber space—her blogs—where readers and writers from a diverse societal spectrum, including herself, can independently voice their struggles, prejudices, frustrations, and observations as they interact with "others" in America and Nigeria. She gets a planetary view of the world around her as "Often, she would sit in cafés, or airports, or train stations, watching strangers, imagining their lives, and wondering which of them were likely to have read her blog" (Adichie 2013:5). One of the blog's contributors, Sapphic Derrida, pointedly acknowledges the critical impact and educational value of Ifemelu's "[A]nonymous blog called *Raceteenth or Various Observations About American Blacks (Those Formerly Known as Negroes) by a Non-American Black*," when he says: "You've used your irreverent, hectoring, funny and thought-provoking voice to create a space for real conversations about an important subject [race]" (5). Through Ifemelu's blogs, Adichie creatively repackages world history from enslavement and colonial encounters and delivers it in a simple, day-to-day language to the common multitudes. She does so as she deconstructs the underlying structure of attitudes around which contemporary American and Nigerian life-worlds are built. Adichie takes the reader from Nigeria to America and back countless times through Ifemelu's relationships and memories in both locations. She shows that while Nigerians and other Africans disappointed with the failure of post-independence political leadership in their countries generally look at America or the Western world with an idealized gaze, believing that it is a land of opportunities for all, Americans and Europeans view Africa as "having a single story," a continent of poverty and exotica. Both gazes certainly find their origin in the early construction of blackness and Africa as figures of lack (to use a Lacanian term) that justified the enslavement and colonization of Africans by Europeans, and Adichie effectively chronicles this enduring (often hidden) structure of anachronistic attitudes in her innovative novelistic art in order to stimulate its transformation and a movement toward a new convivial humanism. These innovative narrative techniques include her characters' in-and-out slippages, her use of cultural interpolation through language and memories, her harmonious blending of the metaphorical with the metonymic, her use of grotesque realism to depict societal excesses, and her effective use of cyber network—blog and e-mails.

When she arrives in America, Ifemelu is quickly struck by the sharp contrast between the America of her (and Nigerians') dreams, which she calls "the real America" and the America she discovers. Unlike the largely utopian image of America marketed worldwide by films and sitcoms, as well as capitalist multinational establishments, she discovers that America is a divided and ordered society in terms of race, class, gender, body-size, national origin, and sexuality. She also discovers that it is a society that represses transformative, "real conversations" about the same issues. Apart from her disappointment over seeing dilapidated buildings side by side with Manhattan affluence (a reminder of the Lagos situation), Ifemelu is also surprised by the subduing effect that America has had on her mentor Aunty Uju, who back in Nigeria advised her to always be herself, and by her biracial Nigerian-American childhood friend, Ginika, who now advises her to embrace the American idea of beauty. Now, Aunty Uju has become an "Americanah" who does not want her son Dike to speak Igbo, mimics American accent, accepts the mispronunciation of her name by Americans, and advises Ifemelu to impersonate another person, Ngozi Okonkwo, by fraudulently using her social security card for work. Ginika also advises Ifemelu that in America,

"You're supposed to pretend that you don't notice certain things" (128). It is indeed an America that expects African immigrants, like Ifemelu, to normatively "become black" with its historical burden and repress their difference in terms of hairstyle, English accent, language choice, body size, and other cultural markers in order to find jobs and acceptance. So, as she embarks on a dystopian reimagining of America, Ifemelu sarcastically advises African immigrants in her early blog post: "To My Fellow Non-American Blacks: In America, You Are Black, Baby. [...] When you make the choice to come to America, you become black. Stop arguing. Stop saying I'm Jamaican or I'm Ghanaian. America doesn't care" (222). Imagined this way, all blacks (Black Americans and other non-American blacks) are then simply and surreptitiously ordered as inferior to whites in American society. However, because of the inevitable historical guilt that this unjust racial ordering entails, it is hardly voiced in various social and other transactional interactions. To a large extent, most of the conversations about race and racism regrettably remain confined to academic sites. It is here that Ifemelu and other members of the new African Diaspora in the United States are initiated into the discourse of being black and its baggage of prejudice in America, something she later on voices in her blog:

> We all have our moments of initiation into the Society of Former Negroes. Mine was in class in undergrad when I was asked to give the black perspective, only I had no idea what that was. So I just made something up. And admit it—you say 'I'm not black' only because you know black is at the bottom of America's race ladder.
>
> (222)

From now on, whether in her intimate love relationships with the white upper-class Curt and the socialist African American Yale academic Blaine, or in conversations with the latter's racially and sexually diversified circle of academic friends, Ifemelu will feel a sense of discomfort about their reluctance to bring the issue of race and racism to public debate, as it affects not only blacks but also other racial minorities in the United States. As she writes in her blog post entitled "Understanding America for the Non-American Black: What Do WASPs Aspire To?," "[T]here is an oppression Olympics going on. American racial minorities—blacks, Hispanics, Asians, and Jews—all get shit from white folks, different kind of shit, but shit still" (207). So, although Paula (Blaine's ex-girlfriend and colleague who hid her lesbian identity from him until she fell in love with another woman) tasks her students at Yale University to read Ifemelu's blog in order "[T]o push them out of their comfort zone" (326), Ifemelu still tells Blaine that "[A]cademics were not intellectuals; they were not curious, they built their solid tents of specialized knowledge and stayed securely in them" (325). She further laments at a dinner with Blaine's liberal friends who have gathered in Manhattan to celebrate Obama's nomination as Democratic Party candidate for

President of the United States of America: "[W]hen we come to nice liberal dinners like this, we say that race doesn't matter because that's what we're supposed to say, to keep out nice liberal friends comfortable. It's true. I speak from experience" (293).

As noted by Ifemelu in the same blog post, the oppressed minorities also seem to acquiesce to the white-constructed racial ordering and perpetuate it further, as many of them "[H]ave a conflicted longing for WASP whiteness or, more accurately, for the privileges of WASP whiteness" (207). Even amongst blacks, who are ordered as inferior to other oppressed minorities in the United States, there is a preference for light skin, something that reminds Ifemelu of the Nigerian context where, owing to its colonial legacy, light skin or whiteness is often anachronistically associated with power and ideal beauty. Though race is not a major defining factor in Nigeria as it is in the United States, it still exists as a remnant of colonial racial ordering. The preference for fair skin can be seen in the cases of the half-caste Ginika, who was crowned beauty queen (at the expense of another more deserving black girl) at high school because of her light skin, and Obinze's wife Kosi who is often admired and praised for her light skin color. The association of whiteness with power in Nigeria is also depicted in the novel when Obinze, who is trying to start an estate business, is advised by his cousin Nneoma that in order to succeed he would need to

> [F]ind one of your white friends in England. Tell everybody he is your General Manager. You will see how doors will open for you because you have an oyinbo General Manager. [...] That is how Nigeria works. I'm telling you. Even Chief has some white men that he brings in for show when he needs them. That is how Nigeria works. I'm telling you.
> (27)

Thus, Adichie's depiction of contemporary American, British, and Nigerian societies in *Americanah* allows for a clear understanding of the postcolonial melancholic impediments (societal fear about difference or desire to appear superior in terms of race, gender, sexual orientation, national or cultural origin, language, and ideology) to global consciousness that Gilroy outlines in his *Postcolonial Melancholia* (2005). As Adichie depicts in the novel, denying difference in order to assert equality actually encourages institutionalized inequality. Ifemelu understands this, and so after a period of passive slippage into the Americanah way (with respect to American accent, Igbo language, hairstyle, body-size, and being black in America) under the influence of Aunty Uju, Ginika, and her American school advisers Cristina Tomas and Ruth, she eventually regains the independent critical gaze that back in Nigeria shaped her critical attitude toward gender relation, women's often carnivalesque deployment of their bodies for material gains, perverted religious practices based on material and power lust, class division, poor language politics, and the ineptitude of post-independence leadership.

The period of depression she goes into following her shameful and remorseful sexual encounter with a manipulative, nameless tennis coach for desperately needed rent money enables her to undertake an introspective journey into her past and present and reassess her role as a new diasporic subject. This temporary isolation marks the beginning of the emergence of her conjunctive consciousness as she asserts her independence from Obinze and the Nigerian cultural memory that he represents as well as from the American normativity described above. From now on, she will reclaim control of her body and mind and will deploy both for the betterment of humanity. Ifemelu therefore decides to revert to her Nigerian English accent, her natural hairstyle, her freely flowing linguistic code-switching (English-Igbo-English when talking with other Igbo speakers), and by so doing moves toward a third space and develops a postcolonial conjunctive consciousness that seamlessly straddles contemporary America's and Nigeria's differentiated constellations of hybridity as she critically points out the pitfalls of both societies. Rather than continuing to heed the assimilationist advice of the Americanahs like Aunty Uju and Ginika, Ifemelu finds a new ally in Wambui (another third-space new diasporic subject from Kenya and president of The African Student Union at her college), who refers her to a website for black people's hair called "HappilyKinkyNappy.com" (211). Wambui tells her that "[R]elaxing your hair is like being in prison. You're caged in. Your hair rules you [...] you're always battling to make your hair do what it wasn't meant to do" (210). On that website, Ifemelu discovers a world of self-assertive black women who cherish their difference and refuse to relax their hair with what they call "creamy crack": "They sculpted for themselves a virtual world where their coily, kinky, nappy woolly hair was normal. And Ifemelu fell into this world with a tumbling gratitude" (214). In the process of her self-transformation as a humanistic activist, Ifemelu is also inspired by the childhood innocence of her cousin Dike whose desire to develop a sense of convivial humanity is constantly hindered by his culturally self-loathing mother, Aunty Uju, his mother's chauvinistic Nigerian boyfriend, Bartholomew, and the racism he experiences at school in Warrington, Massachusetts. To a certain extent, Dike functions as Ifemelu's muse for her transformative blog as the Virgin Mary does for Black's murals in Abani's *The Virgin of Flames*. Ifemelu has thus tapped into the hidden cultural melancholic desire of the Western world as it reifies the accepted notion of ranked difference while maintaining inequality and the structure of power, and her blog can be said to be an instance of a dissensual counternarrative to it.

Having acquired through books and personal experiences deep knowledge of what she calls "America's mythologies," especially "America's tribalism—class, ideology, region, and race" (137, 186), and having "returned her voice to herself" (182) and retaken control of her body, Ifemelu resolves to create a blog, a public, independent space where real conversations about these America's mythologies can take place. From this point,

Ifemelu's relationships with men are characterized by uncertainty or what she calls "borderlessness" (6). Thus, when the upper-class Curt asks her to give up her babysitting job at his sister Kimberly's so that they can have more time together, Ifemelu emphatically responds, "I have to have a job" (202); when Curt wants to own her body and claim her as "the fucking love of your life" (226), Ifemelu breaks away from his capture and sleeps with someone else, a working-class musician Rob; when "Often, naked beside him [Curt], she found herself thinking of Obinze" (197); and when Curt brushes aside her concern about racial ordering in America, preferring to be color-blind, Ifemelu takes their discussions to her blog (293). Similarly, when the liberal academic Blaine tries to shape the tone of her blog ideologically and give her what he calls "more depth," Ifemelu emphatically responds: "It has enough depth" (313); and when Blaine wants to own her love completely, saying "You are the absolute love of my life," she felt that "there was cement in her soul" (6). Also, when Obinze tries to reclaim her as his own on her return to Nigeria, Ifemelu sees another man, Tunde Razaq, against his objection, and reconnects with the former lovers she left behind in America, Curt and Blaine (475); and finally, at the level of national boundaries, when Nigeria attempts to totally reclaim her, the "blue American passport in her bag" acts as an ever-present refusal (390).

Returning to Nigeria, Ifemelu is confronted with family and friends who question her decision to come back to Nigeria, and who by so doing, like Aunty Uju and members of the African Diaspora at Mariama hair salon in America, want to locate her firmly and totally in the American cultural site. They wonder whether she would adjust successfully to Nigerian hectic life after being gone for so long (thirteen years). Upon her arrival, the change in Ifemelu or her conjunctive consciousness is immediately noted and commented on by Ranyinudo, a childhood friend of hers, who while calling her "Americanah," also says: "You are looking at things with American eyes. But the problem is that you are not even a real Americanah. At least if you had an American accent we would tolerate your complaining!" (385). What she fails to notice is the fact that Ifemelu has a different agenda as she critically gazes at the Nigerian life-world and imagines the condition of possibility of its transformation for the benefit of all. In fact, Ifemelu relates to and treats her fellow returnees or Americanahs at the Nigerpolitan Club with sarcasm and irony. Unlike these ostentatious and corrupt Americanahs, Ifemelu's new sense of self is one that is both Nigerian and American, and from this perspective, she begins a new blog, "The Small Redemptions of Lagos" after she quits the confinement of the unproductive "Zoe Magazine" of the sycophantic Aunty Onenu. Through this blog, Ifemelu hopes to initiate a consciousness-raising, dissensual public discourse on issues that negatively affect Nigerian society, including the Nigerian colonized mind that prefers Western education (English and French schools) and whiteness to Nigerian schools and black skin, Nigerian women's dependence on men for their success in society, male chauvinism, class division, Western-modeled beauty

164 *Postcolonial agency in African literature*

magazines and reading tastes, religious fanaticism, poor infrastructure, and corrupt political leadership.

The Translator

In *The Translator* (1999), Leila Aboulela, like Abani and Adichie in their respective novels discussed above, also creates a third space from where her main characters, the Scottish Rae Isle, "a Middle-East historian and lecturer in Third World Politics" (Aboulela 1999:5) at Aberdeen University, and Sammar, his Sudanese Arabic translator, critically examine the structure of attitudes that exists in Britain and the Middle Eastern or Muslim world. They examine how these attitudes generate fear of one another and impede acceptance of multicultural conviviality amongst the British and the Muslims. Although not a member of the new African diaspora (because of his country of origin—Britain), Rae shares the same critical postcolonial conjunctive consciousness that refuses to be monolithically defined by one cultural site or national identity. Through his character, Aboulela effectively universalizes the presence of this consciousness and its different articulations in the new borderless "empire" (Hardt and Negri 2000:xiv). Having been brought up in a conservative Christian circle in Scotland and having lived in North Africa (Egypt and Morocco) and learned a lot from and about Muslims and Islamic religion as a young man, Rae (now an informed scholar) is well suited to critically bring to light the misunderstandings that shape the mutual negative attitudes or prejudices that the West and the Muslim world hold toward each other.

Rae's postcolonial conjunctive consciousness started being shaped at an early age after he heard and read about the experiences of his uncle David, who went to Egypt with the British army during the Second World War, converted to Islam, left the army, changed his name, married an Egyptian woman, and had children with her. David was treated as defector and traitor at home, but the letters he wrote to Rae's culturally anchored mother (who never responded to them) inspired Rae's interest in Islam, in particular, and critical thinking about self and others, in general. So, while studying at a conservative Christian school in the 1950s, he defiantly (and perhaps naively as he went further than his uncle's balanced view of Islam and Christianity) wrote a controversial class essay (partly plagiarizing his uncle's letter) "entitled Islam is better than Christianity" (17). The essay earned him expulsion from school. However, Rae who was then excited about having "Egyptian cousins, relatives in Africa," was not deterred by this punishment. He later "[W]ent looking for him [David] for five years, between 1976 and '81 when I was in Cairo teaching at the UUC, but I couldn't find him" (18). Rae's connection with post-independence Africa and the Muslim world and his unhomeliness in terms of identity became deeper when he lived for an extended period of his early adult life (after graduating from university in Britain) in Morocco in the 1960s. Staying behind in Fez, after his two former university friends, Chris and Steve, who travelled there with him on a flaneurial trip left for home, Rae took a job "in a craft shop, owned by a local scholar and his French wife," and it became an important learning site for him. There, Rae met "foreign journalists, Westernized Moroccans, French diplomats [...]. He listened to their conversations: Palestine, what Fanon said, what Sartre said...Nasser closed the Straits of Tiran...Six days of war, six days!... Israel took Sinai, the West Bank..." (59). As the narrator says, in Fez, "Rae learnt what he had not learnt in university nor in the debating society he had been so active in. Things more important than anger, more important than an argument cleverly expressed" (59). In addition to the craft shop, which can be regarded as a secluded upper-class intellectual site, Rae also connected with ordinary Moroccans with the help of three Air Maroc pilots who shared an apartment with him, and learned a lot about their quotidian preoccupations:

> While the pilots were his link with the locals, his employers were the link with the International community. In small expatriate communities, social integration is as fast as the judgement passed on a newcomer. Those his age and older decided they did not like him much. He was cheeky and somewhat secretive. He did not have the straightforward charm they admired; he did not have the cool, self-determined look that they favoured. In some shadows, according to the ladies, he looked exactly like an Arab. Rae got along better with the young who had grown up in Morocco, a minority of privileged lives. He did what the young did not do: he read newspapers, he was learning Arabic. Wandering into mosques, living with Moroccans. This was subversive enough for the young ones. They liked him.
>
> (60)

It is his interest in the lives of the ordinary Moroccans that also led Amelia, the rebellious daughter of an upper-class English father and Spanish mother who lived in Morocco, to fall in love and marry Rae against her parents' objection. As the narrator says:

> There was something *Arab* about this young Scottish man. Something Arab that Amelia had wanted for years. For she had grown up in the splendid villa of her parents, secretly and guiltily eyeing the house-boys, fancying the gardener from Fez.
>
> (61)

In fact, the still-born son that Amelia and Rae had and that is buried in Morocco has become an important solid link uniting Rae with Africa. However, unlike his uncle David who chose to convert to Islam, change his name, and remain statically anchored in Egypt, Rae returned to Scotland. There, through his politically and culturally committed scholarship about Islam and third world, he has sought to remove the fear of one another that the Western and Middle Eastern worlds have in the 20th century. Here is how he explains his detached and critical positioning to Sammar who wants him to convert to Islam so that she can marry him:

> I studied Islam for the politics of the Middle East. I did not study it for myself. I was not searching for something spiritual. Some people do. I had a friend who went to India and became a Buddhist. But I was not like that. I believed the best I could do, what I owed a place and people who had a deep meaning for me, was to be objective, detached. In the middle of all the prejudice and hypocrisy, I wanted to be one of the few who was saying what was reasonable and right.
>
> (126)

With his bold and insightful book entitled *The Illusion of an Islamic Threat* and his controversial interventions on public TV and radio, Rae turns scholarship and public media into sites of activism against the Western world's "post-colonial melancholia" (Gilroy 2005) and the Muslim world's politicization of religion. On a radio discussion program, he does not hesitate to remind his British listeners that Muslim extremism is "not the biggest threat facing the Western world. If we look at real terrorist damage, Muslim extremists have caused much less of it than the IRA, the Red Brigade, the Baader-Meinhof gang, the Basque separatist ETA..." (35). At the same time, he does not spare Muslim extremists' misuse of Islam either. In a conversation with Sammar, Rae disapproves of their collective Manichean hostile gaze at the West, saying that "They are shooting themselves in the foot. There is no recourse in the Sharia for what they're doing, however much they try and justify themselves" (26). He further describes terrorist organizations like *Al-Nidaa* in Egypt, whose manifesto he has asked Sammar to translate into English, as detached from the people they claim to represent:

> They are protest movements, and they do have plenty to protest about. Israel's occupation of the West Bank, the mediocrity of the ruling party which has no mass support and which are in the main client states to the West. These groups appeal to people's anger, anger against class divisions, but do people really believe them to be a viable alternative? I don't think so.
>
> (27–28)

Because of his critical views directed at both sides, Rae's Western detractors call him a "disgrace" and "a wog bastard" (100), while essentialist Muslims like Sammar's friend Yasmin call him "orientalist." Also, "When he appeared on TV or was quoted in a newspaper he was referred to as an Islamic expert, a label he disliked because, he told Sammar, there could be no such monolith" (5).

Thus, attracted by his liminality and an unusual sense of convivial humanism, the nomadic Sammar disagrees with Yasmin's essentialist assessment of Rae's character, stating that "Rae looked like he could easily pass for a Turk or a Persian" (6) and that "He's sort of familiar, like people from back home [Sudan]" (21). Born in Britain of Sudanese parents, Sammar grew up in Sudan, and her simultaneous attachment to these two cultural locations makes her unhomely or nomadic and shapes her postcolonial conjunctive consciousness. Aboulela gives the reader a hint at Sammar's rhizomic character through the meaning of her name as she tells Rae, "It means conversations with friends, late at night. It's what the desert nomads like to do, talk leisurely by the light of the moon, when it was no longer so hot and the day's work was over" (5). Throughout the novel, Sammar exists in a liminal space, in-between two languages and two countries, and often takes on the image of a floating ghost through her dreams and hallucinations. On one occasion at her apartment in Aberdeen, she wonders during a telephone conversation with Rae, "Where was she now, which country? What year? She climbed the stairs into hallucination in which the world had swung around. Home and past had come here and balanced just for her" (41). This seamless straddling of the past and present, Sudan and Britain shapes Sammar's postcolonial conjunctive consciousness, and it enables her to have a planetary view of both societies, their potentials, as well as their pitfalls. United by the act of translation, the in-between critical third space of interpretation of experiences, Rae regards Sammar as a potential ally for his transformative vision of the Western and Muslim worlds. And Sammar appreciates the fact Rae "[K]new she was heavy with other loyalties, full to the brim with distant places, voices in language that was not his own" (29). From Sammar's gaze, Rae has a deep, unique, and convivial sense of appreciation of others that many people in British society do not have:

> In this country, when she spoke to people, they seemed wary, on their guard as if any minute she would say something out of place, embarrassing. He was not like that. He seemed to understand, not in a modern, deliberately non-judgmental way but as if he was about to say, 'This has happened to me too'.
>
> (6)

And in a reciprocal way, Rae also feels reassured and humanized by Sammar's nomadic character when he says to her: "But I trust you [...]. You make me feel safe. I feel safe when I talk to you" (51, 64).

By contrasting Sammar's nomadic character with Yasmin's essentialist posture, Aboulela effectively shows the unproductivity of cultural or nativistic essentialism in our global time while foregrounding the necessity of globalectic solidarism. As enunciated by Ngugi wa Thiong'o, "Globalectics embraces wholeness, interconnectedness, equality of potentiality of parts, tension, and motion. It is a way of thinking and relating to the world, particularly in the era of globalism and globalization" (Ngugi 2012:8). Going against this globalectic perspective, Yasmin reductively sees the world through a normative, totalizing, monolithic Islamic lens (as Western colonialists did with their sense of modernity), and she would like Sammar to do the same. So, taking advantage of Sammar's vulnerable state of mind following the death of her husband Tarig, Yasmin seems for a moment to have a strong influence on her as she discourages her from getting romantically involved with the non-Muslim Rae whom she dubs "an agnostic if not atheist" (92). Yasmin is Rae's secretary and Sammar's only friend in Scotland besides Rae. Although born and raised in Britain, Yasmin prefers to locate herself exclusively within a putative, originary Middle Eastern Muslim identity. She therefore advises Sammar: "Go home and maybe you'll meet someone normal, someone Sudanese like yourself. Mixed couples just don't look right, they irritate everyone" (93). Here is how the novel's omniscient narrator describes Yasmin's essentialist character:

> Yasmin's parents were from Pakistan but she was born and had lived all her life in different parts of Britain. She had a habit of making general statements starting with 'we,' where 'we' meant the whole of the Third World and its people. So she would say, 'We are not like them,' or 'We have close family ties, not like them.'
>
> (11)

Here, Aboulela treats Yasmin's static view of identity with irony as she does Sammar's temporary slippage into it as she now selfishly tries to convince Rae to abandon his detached positioning and convert to Islam so that they can get married. However, Rae, who has seen in Sammar a potential third space critical ally with a postcolonial conjunctive consciousness, refuses to see their relationship be statically defined by a fundamentalist Islamic view. Thus, though bitter, their temporary separation before Sammar's return to Sudan enables her to undertake a productive introspective journey into herself as she reassesses her vision of Islam and society in both Britain and Sudan. This moment of isolation from Rae, her detachment from upper-class, modern desires of her misogynistic mother-in-law Mahasen and her brother who want her to return to Scotland, as well as her critical gaze at the failures of the post-independence Sudanese political leadership catalyze Sammar's unhomeliness and subjective movement toward a third space critical gaze. At the same time, Rae's temporary physical separation from Sammar, who has returned to Sudan after he angrily shouted at her "Go away...Get out of here...Get away from me" (129), is salutary. It enables him to independently undertake a deep exploration of Islamic faith at a personal level, as suggested by his Palestinian activist and journalist friend Fareed. Here, just as Sammar finally realizes that she needs to explore the possibility of a detached public mission of Islam when she is in Sudan, so does Rae find personal faith in Islam while in Scotland. Their separate explorations or reassessments of their personal engagements with Islam logically lead to their total reunion (spatial and emotional). United in love and Islam, Rae and Sammar give an activist meaning to their faith:

> Ours isn't a religion of suffering,' he said, 'nor is it tied to a particular place.' His words made her feel close to him, pulled in, closer than any time before because it was 'ours' now, not hers alone. And because he understood. Not a religion of pathos, not a religion of redemption through sacrifice.
>
> (198)

From now on, both Rae and Sammar will critically gaze at both the Sudanese and British societies from a third space of translation and scholarship. Like Black in Abani's *The Virgin of Flames* and Ifemelu in *Americanah*, both will work to promote "a collective rearrangement of desires" in our global time. As Kaiama Glover has rightly pointed out, for "both characters, love means having someone to tell their stories to, without fear. It means effacing the boundaries of language, of nation, of religion. [...] in other words, love translates" (2006). So, like Abani, Adichie, and other New African Diasporic writers, Aboulela has articulated a postcolonial conjunctive consciousness through her transformative critical art form.

CODA
Francis Abiola Irele and the African imagination

In his early formulation of the concept of *the African Imagination*, Irele focused on African literature and defined it as "a conjunction of impulses which can be said to have been given a unified expression in a body of literary texts" (Irele 1990:50). Because of this integrative conjunctiveness, he also insisted:

> I should like to emphasize that I am not making a case for a unique essence of African literature but consider in fact that our literature needs to be related to other areas of literary expression, and has a significance for human experience beyond our continent.
>
> (Irele 1981:9)

With that understanding, Irele expanded the scope of the concept of the African Imagination as a generative matrix to include African diasporic (or the whole of black) literary production. Thus, works by African or African descent writers who have either lived and created in Africa or have invoked African memory in various African diasporic constellations are part of the African Imagination. Taken together from this perspective, the writings of the early black authors such as Phillis Wheatley and Olaudah Equiano can be said to have enunciated a counter-discourse within a Western modernity that placed Africans or black subjects outside history while subjecting them to enslavement and colonialism. Despite what has been described as their mild responses to the Western colonial ordering of the African or black otherness (see, e.g., Jeyifo 2011:ix), Irele has maintained that these early writings shaped the counter-discourse that has characterized African and African diasporic writings up until now.

Considering the fact that cultural nationalist movements that rose against enslavement and colonialism also conditioned African authors' imaginaries and their anti-colonial tone, Irele included critical and philosophical writings of their periods in the concept of the African Imagination. Among such early cultural and spiritually syncretic or "messianic" movements which sought to assert Africans' place in the world and affirm their humanity are Edward Blyden's "African personality" (Sierra-Leone), Simon Kimbangu's

DOI: 10.4324/9780429322426-11

Kimbanguism (Democratic Republic of Congo), Peter Lobengula's resistance in Southern Africa, and Samory Touré's resistance in Guinea. In the African context, these early nationalist, anti-colonial movements, to use Irele's words "form an essential part of the stock of symbols that have nourished the nationalist strain of Negritude" (Irele 2011:3). The Kenyan Mau Mau revolt against British rule that took place in the mid-1950s is also a part of the same anti-colonial messianic movement. As Irele has pointed out, "The messianic movements presented in bold relief certain traits which were to figure in the more sophisticated reaction to colonial rule, Negritude. In other words, Negritude had a popular precedent in Africa" (2011:5). In the African diaspora, similar movements in Haiti (vodoun), Guadeloupe (slave revolt), Brazil (candomblé), and the United States (Negro spirituals) served as springboards for black "nationalist" cultural movements like Negritude, Negrismo (Cuba and Brazil), and the Negro Renaissance or Harlem Renaissance in the United States. These black cultural movements therefore set the tone for what has evolved as contemporary African and African diasporic literatures, African philosophy, and African history.

Having outlined the origin and the scope of Irele's concept of the African Imagination, I now turn to the position of his critical thought within it. Assessing the state of African critical discourse some five years ago, Biodun Jeyifo deplored what he saw as an unnecessary "acrimonious, enervating controversies between these two particular camps of 'transnationalism' and 'cosmopolitanism' on one side, and 'nativism' and 'localism' on the other side." He further added:

> But the reified notion of cosmopolitanism is objectionable, as repressive and obfuscating as the reified conception of the localism and autochthony. In the real world, especially in the performed, enacted negotiations of actual, lived conditions of existence, all of these notions are never encountered as pure or ideal forms; they are considerably intertwined and commingled, even as there are constant eruptions of violent expressions of their reified, fundamentalist forms.
> (Jeyifo 2011:xv)

Irele's position as a literary and cultural critic is in line with what Jeyifo has stated here, for, in his critical practice, he has consistently mediated between these two extreme positions, though not without occasional slippages in his emphasis here and there.[1] Considering the role of the African literary critic as "a middleman[...] in the cultural life of the community," Irele has argued that:

> The position of the critic in this whole process of giving our literature audience on its home ground is an important one and must be seen in the broader context of the cultural evolution in our societies at the heart of which I believe literature today is situated.
> (Irele 1971:11–12)

Here, Irele reiterates the double role of literary criticism as T.S. Eliot also saw it: "the elucidation of works of art and the correction of taste" (Eliot 1972:78). To be sure, Irele's conception of taste goes beyond the formalistic literariness of a work of art. It embraces the totality of complex cultural values that are emerging in and shaping African societies following their colonial encounter with the Western world. He, therefore, reminds us that, as "our writers are groping implicitly, through the imagination, towards the creation of a new order in Africa," the African literary critic must also be an active participant in the same cultural activity. For him, "Criticism cannot be pure scholarship and is not simply an intellectual exercise. I believe the best criticism implies an affective and intense participation in the creative act" (Irele 1971:10–14). It is in the light of this conviction that he has insistently advocated for a sociological approach, which takes into consideration the totality of African experience (orality, literacy, and creativity in African languages and European languages, and all other socio-political aspects that are shaping the African life-world) in the criticism of African literature. According to Irele, this approach is the most appropriate to the context of African literature because it undermines extreme nativism and its assimilationist opposite while critically examining all aspects of African cultural hybridity (see Losambe 2005). Irele's defining critical assessment of the evolution of African literature and society is well summarized in this quote:

> [w]e all tend to forget that the dichotomy between traditional and modern, as applied to Africa, expresses itself not as an opposition of two worlds but as unity, as an entity which is more unified than our distinctions are wont to make clear. Traditional African culture and society are in fact contemporary, and traditional literature is all around us, alive, growing, and transforming itself and still, therefore, available to our modern writers. Its impress on their works is far from negligible. It shows itself both directly in their conscious assimilation of its forms and of its conventional symbols, and indirectly in the way it influences the manner in which our writers construct their works, in the way in which they give a formal pattern to their sensibilities, and present a certain order of the imagination. It seems to me then legitimate to assume that in a fundamental and significant way, a continuity of form and reference exists between oral literature of Africa and the modern literature written in the European languages.
>
> (Irele 1971:18)

These views about African literature, its criticism and society, first presented by Irele to a conference on "African writing in English," held at the University of Ife (now Obafemi Awolowo University) in 1968, subsequently became very influential and were expanded in the 1970s and 1980s by critics like Bernth Lindfors, C.L. Innes, Bill Ashcroft, Gareth Griffiths, Ngugi wa Thiong'o, D.S. Izevbaye, Simon Gikandi, and a host of others. Especially, since the publication of Ashcroft, Griffiths, and Tiffin's *The Empire Writes Back* (1989), African writers' "abrogation" and "appropriation" of the English language and their harmonious integration of proverbs, riddles, and untranslated words or phrases from African languages in the formal structure of their works have been appreciated and lauded as subjective, innovative, postcolonial narrative strategies. Indeed, as Irele has remarked, the main distinguishing feature of modern African imaginative writings is their producers' skillful blending of oral literature materials with modern novelistic forms through transliteration, transfer, reinterpretation, and transposition (Irele 2001:58).

As I have noted elsewhere (Losambe 1996:xi), following a steady development in the past six decades or so, African literature has certainly established itself as a solid literary tradition out of which many paradigms have emerged. This tradition includes both oral and written literature produced in diverse languages used in Africa. The lesson we learn from Irele's critical engagement with African literature is the view that any serious attempt to work out a genealogy of the African literary tradition must start from its oral source before moving on to consider the conjugation of orality and literacy as a paradigm shift within the tradition. It is indeed surprising that while acknowledging the influence of African oral literature on its written counterpart, a number of critics still undermine its importance and prefer to attribute the source of modern African literature mainly to European writings. It is a mistake for Kenneth Harrow, for example, to maintain that "For African literature, 'patriarchal texts' can be located in the colonial novels-travelogues, and their fictional counterparts, exotic literature or ethnography, adventure concoctions, or testimonials by expatriates" (Harrow 1994:10). Assumptions such as this inevitably imply that African oral poetry, drama, and prose do not have sophisticated literary qualities generally associated with the same genres in the written medium and take us back to the era of early European ethnographers who naively or cunningly treated the whole of African oral literature as a body of simplistic didactic stories. One has only to read Isidore Okpewho's, Ruth Finnegan's, Isabel Hofmeyr's, and other scholars' numerous contributions to the study of African oral literature to be convinced of its complexity. Gerald Moore is indeed right when he states on this subject:

> Much of the exaggerated surprise which greeted the flood of African novels and poems published in the years from 1956 onwards would have been avoided if critics had paused to reflect that their authors were not starting from scratch, even if the activity of writing, or of writing in a foreign language, was relatively new.
>
> (Moore 1980:7)

Consistent with his "view of orality as a matrix of the African imagination" (Irele 2001:58), Irele has identified two broad diachronic paradigms in the development of modern African literature: "aesthetic traditionalism" and "new realism." Aesthetic traditionalism, which he defines as "a poetics of indigenism that shapes the formal structure of much of the imaginative literature" (2001:70–71), arose from first-generation African writers' need for cultural affirmation and, to use Irele's own words, "compulsion to recast their linguistic medium as well as the conventions taken from the Western literate tradition in order to reflect more adequately the African inspiration and reference of their works" (2001:57). This is the paradigm initiated and well executed through the "abrogation" and "appropriation" (Ashcroft et al. 1989:38–39) of foreign languages and defamiliarization of Western literary forms by writers like Chinua Achebe, Christopher Okigbo, Flora Nwapa, Wole Soyinka, Amos Tutuola, Gabriel Okara, J.P. Clark-Bekederemo, Kofi Awoonor, Ama Ata Aidoo, Okot p'Bitek, Thomas Mofolo, Ahmadou Kourouma, and Amadou Hampaté Ba, among others.[2] The new realism emerges in the writings of the second generation of African writers who skillfully blend aspects of aesthetic traditionalism with Western modern and postmodern artistic experimentation. Most of these writers combine the grotesque and the magical in their art as they bitingly satirize the absurdities and failures of post-independence politics in Africa. The most prominent representatives of this radical paradigm are Sembene Ousmane, Ngugi wa Thiong'o, Ayi Kwei Armah, Femi Osofisan, Niyi Osundare, Festus Iyayi, Tanure Ojaide, Ben Okri, Syl Cheney-Coker, Kojo Laing, Nuruddin Farah, Jack Mapanje, Tsitsi Dangarembga, Chenjerai Hove, and Sony Labou Tansi. Here is how Irele pointedly describes the formal concerns and the radical tone of this generation of African writers:

> The project of the new realism is to lay bare the stresses that weave through the fabric of the contemporary African situation and to explore this situation in its full range of moral significance and in its most profound human implications, those inner tensions that the conventional novel seems inadequate to fully encompass. The specific moral objective of the new African fiction is thus bound up with general and resolute experimentation with form, based largely upon the application of the procedures of European modernism in the creation of what are manifestly parables of the African condition.
>
> (2001:64)

The neohumanism or the transnational consciousness articulated in the writings of third-generation African writers (the Afropolitans) reflects Irele's idea of African literature as a conjunction of creative impulses refracting local and global issues of our time. This new trend should be acknowledged as the latest paradigm in the African literary tradition, though Irele does not mention it.[3] As stated above in the previous chapters of this book, these writers occupy a "third space" from where they cast a critical gaze upon three life-worlds, the African societies they originate from, the Western world they presently live in, and the humanistic or globalist consciousness they project. Their writings draw their effectiveness and compelling vitality from the authors' masterful combination of aspects of aesthetic traditionalism (cultural interpolation and metonymic gap [Ashcroft 2001:71]), the new realism (which combines the grotesque, the magical, the metonymic, the metaphoric, and shifting points of view in an episodic narrative structure), and the neohumanist aesthetic (which enlists analepsis, textual collage, social media, and cyberspace—especially the blogosphere—as important narrative techniques). This sophisticated, complex arsenal of narrative techniques makes the writings of the third-generation transformative as they bring to the surface globally repressed anachronistic and melancholic attitudes about class, race, gender, sexuality, disability, religion, nationality, ethnicity, migrancy, transnational identities, and the environment. Their art is to a certain extent akin to the "new poetics," which, to quote Rancière:

> frames a new hermeneutics, taking upon itself the task of making society conscious of its own secrets, by leaving the noisy stage of political claims and doctrines and delving to the depths of the social, to disclose the enigmas and fantasies hidden in the intimate realities of everyday life.
>
> (Rancière 2015:135)

As indicated in the last chapter of this book, Chris Abani has cogently described the creative project of this generation of African writers that I call African *neohumanists* as transnational and liberated from the cultural nationalism found in the writings of the early generations. One can argue that these African neohumanists are, in fact, giving a contemporary expression to the humanistic project that Olaudah Equiano initiated in his abolitionist slave narrative. This is what Irele spent decades chronicling and, to a great extent, shaping through his incisive critical interventions up until his death on July 2, 2017.

Commenting on the state of cultural studies and on his own critical practice in his book *Culture and Imperialism*, Edward Said states:

> My principal aim is not to separate but to connect, and I am interested in this for the main philosophical and methodological reason that cultural forms are hybrid, mixed, impure, and the time has come in cultural analysis to reconnect their analysis with their actuality.
>
> (Said 1994:14)

Said's advice to cultural critics in 1994 was, in fact, anticipated by Irele in 1968 in his comments on African writers' refraction of the cultural hybridity that had then been shaping their societies since the colonial encounter: "It is rather in their appropriation of the European language and tradition, and the adaptation of both to an imaginative mode upon which each one imparts an individual stamp, that their Africanness is revealed" (Irele 1971:17).

Notes

1 For example, while acknowledging the nationalist and anti-colonialist stance of the so called "messianic movements," Irele surprisingly terms them "regressive" just as Bronislaw Malinowski also calls them "re-crossing" (Irele, *The Negritude* 4–5). Another instance of slippage in his critical discourse can be seen in his reaction to the extreme nativism advocated by the *Bolekaja* group (Chinweizu et al. 1980). In what appears to be an equally extreme response, Irele states: "we have no choice besides Western culture and civilization" (Irele, *In Praise of Alienation* 59).
2 For more details about the categorization of African writers into first, second, and third generations, see Ojaide (2015).
3 I am using the concept of neohumanism here as conceived by the Indian philosopher Prabbat Ranjan Sarkar in his landmark book, *The Liberation of the Intellect: Neohumanism* (1982). It is a progressive, holistic, post-national philosophical theory which promotes justice, equity, interconnectedness, and respect for all human and environmental diversities.

Bibliography

Abani, Chris (2007), *The Virgin of Flames*. London: Penguin. Print.
Aboulela, Leila (1999), *The Translator*. New York: Black Cat. Print.
Achebe, Chinua (1978), *Things Fall Apart*. London: Heinemann. Print.
Achebe, Chinua (1988), *Hopes and Impediments: Selected Essays 1965–87*. London: Heinemann. Print.
Adichie, Chimamanda Ngozi (2013), *Americanah*. New York and Toronto: Alfred A. Knopf. Print.
Ashcroft, Bill (2001a), *Post-Colonial Transformations*. London: Routledge. Print.
Ashcroft, Bill (2001b), *On Post-Colonial Futures: Transformations of Colonial Culture*. London and New York: Continuum. Print.
Ashcroft, Bill, Griffiths, Gareth and Tiffin, Helen (1989), *The Empire Writes Back: Theory and Practice in Post-colonial Literatures*. London and New York: Routledge. Print.
Bâ, Mariama (1980), *So Long a Letter*. London: Heinemann. Print.
Baker, Houston A. Jr (1988), *Afro-American Poetics: Revisions of Harlem and the Black Aesthetic*. Madison: The University of Wisconsin Press. Print.
Bakhtin, Mikhail (1984), *Rabelais and His World*, trans. Helene Iswolsky. Bloomington: Indiana UP. Print.
Bauman, Zygmunt (1991), *Modernity and Ambivalence*. Malden, MA: Polity Press. Print.
Bendinger, Robert Dabney [and Edmiston, Althea Brown] (1937), "Althea Brown Edmiston," in Winsborough, Hallie Paxson and Sarah Lee Vinson Timmons, eds., *Glorious Living*. Atlanta, Georgia: Committee on Woman's Work PCUS, 263–286. Print.
Benedetto, Robert (1996), ed., *Presbyterian Reformers in Central Africa: A Documentary Account of the Presbyterian Congo Mission and Human rights Struggle in the Congo, 1890–1918*. Leiden and New York: E.J. Brill. Print.
Beti, Mongo (1964), *Mission to Kala*, trans. Peter Green. London: Heinemann. Print.
Bhabha, Homi (1994), *The Location of Culture*. London: Routledge. Print.
Bignall, Simone (2010), *Postcolonial Agony: Critique and Constructivism*. Edinburgh: Edinburgh University Press. Print.
Boehmer, Elleke (2005a), *Colonial and Postcolonial Literature: Migrant Metaphors*. Oxford: Oxford University Press. Print.
Boehmer, Elleke (2005b), *Empire, the National, and the Postcolonial 1890–1920*. Oxford: Oxford University Press. Print.

Blyden, Edward W. (1994), *Christianity, Islam and the Negro Race*, introduction by the Hon Samuel Lewis. Baltimore: Black Classic Press. Print.

Brathwaite, Edward Kamau (1999), *Conversations with Nathaniel Mackey*. Staten Island, NY: We Press. Print.

Burroughs, Robert M. (2011), *Travel Writing and Atrocities*. New York and London: Routledge. Print.

Butler, Judith (1987), *Subjects of Desire*. New York: Columbia University Press. Print.

Byrne, Paula (2014), *Belle: The True Story of dido Belle*. London: William Collins. Print.

Carretta, Vincent (2005), *Equiano the African: Biography of a Self-Made Man*. Athens: University of Georgia Press. Print.

Chambers, Claire (2009), "An Interview with Leila Aboulela." *Contemporary Women's Writing* 3:1, 86–102. Print.

Chinweizu, O. Jemie, and Madubuike, I. (1980), *Toward the Decolonization of African Literature*. Enugu: Fourth Dimension. Print.

Conrad, Joseph (1946), *Heart of Darkness*. London: Dent. Print.

Cooper, Julia (2014), "Sankofa: The Deed of Memory." *Phylon* 51:1, https//www.worldcat.org/issn/0031-8906.

Cullen, Countee (2004), "Tableau," in Henry Louis Gates, Jr. and Nellie Y. Mckay, eds., *The Norton Anthology of African American Literature*. New York: Norton, 1341. Print.

Daiya, Kavita (2017), "The World after Empire; or, Wither Postcoloniality?" *Publications of Modern Language Association* 132:1, 149–155. Print.

DeLoughrey, Elizabeth (2010), *Routes and Roots: Navigating Caribbean and Pacific Island Literatures*. Honolulu: University of Hawaii Press. Print.

Diop, David (1967), "Africa," in Donatus I. Nwoga, ed., *West African Verse*. Harlow, Essex: Longman, 111. Print.

Durbin, Kate (2007), "Guest Interview- Chris Abani." *The Elegant Variation: A Literary Blog*, April 4, http://Marksarvas.Blogs.Com/elegvar/2007/04/Guest Interview. Html.

Edmiston, Althea Brown (1937), "Maria Fearing: A Mother to African Girls," in Winsborough, Hallie Paxson and Sarah Lee Vinson Timmons, eds., *Glorious Living*. Atlanta, Georgia: Committee on Woman's Work PCUS, 291–318. Print.

Egejuru, Phanuel Akubueze. (1978), *Black Writers: White Audience*. New York: Exposition. Print.

Eliot, Thomas Stearns (1972), "The Function of Criticism," in David Lodge, ed., *Twentieth Century Literary Criticism*. London and New York: Longman, 77–84. Print.

Equiano, Olaudah (1995), *The Interesting Narrative and Other Writings*. London: Penguin Books. Print.

Fanon, Frantz (1967), *The Wretched of the Earth*. London and New York: Penguin Books. Print.

Forna, Aminatta (2006), "New Writing and Nigeria: Chimamanda Ngozi Adichie and Helen Oyeyemi in Conversation with Aminatta Forna." *Wasafari* 21:1, 1–16. Print.

Franklin, John Hope (1998), *George Washington Williams: A Biography*. Durham and London: Duke University Press. Print.

Gates, Henry Louis, Jr. (1981), "Being, the Will, and the Semantics of Death." *Harvard Educational Review* 51:1, 163–173. Print.

Gates, Louis Henry Jr. (1988), *The Signifying Monkey: A Theory of Afro-American Literary Criticism*. New York: Oxford University Press, 1988. Print.
George, Olankule (2003), "Cultural Criticism in Wole Soyinka's *Death and the King's Horseman*," in Simon Gikandi, ed., *Wole Soyinka, Death and the King's Horseman, Background and Sources*. New York: Norton & Company, 207–222. Print.
Gikandi, Simon (2011a), "On Afropolitanism," in J. Warzinek and J. Makokha, eds., *Negotiating Afropolitanism*. Amsterdam: Rodopi, 9–11. Print.
Gikandi, Simon (2011b), *Slavery and the Culture of Taste*. Princeton and Oxford: Princeton University Press, 2011. Print.
Gilroy, Paul (2005), *Postcolonial Melancholia*. New York: Columbia University Press. Print.
Giroux, Henry (1993), "Living Dangerously: Identity politics and the New Cultural Racism—Towards a Critical Pedagogy of Representation." *Cultural Studies* 7:1, 1–27. Print.
Glover, Kaima (2006), "Love's Language." *The New York Times*, November 12, http://www.nytimes.com/2006/11/books/review/Glover.t.html. Accessed May 1, 2017.
Goyal, Yogita (2014), "A Deep humanness, a Deep Grace: Interview with Chris Abani." *Research in In African Literatures* 45:3, 227–240. Print.
Guinness, H. Grattan (1890), ed., *Congo Recollections: Edited from Notes and Conversations of Missionaries*. London: Hodder and Stoughton. Print.
Hardt, Michael and Negri, Antonio (2000), *Empire*. Cambridge, MA and London: Harvard University Press. Print.
Harrow, Kenneth (1994), *Thresholds of Change in African Literature: The Emergence of a Tradition*. London: James Currey and Heinemann, 1994. Print.
Harrow, Kenneth W. (2013), *Trash: African Cinema from Below*. Bloomington and Indianapolis: Indiana University Press. Print.
Hochschild, Adam (1998), *King Leopold's Ghost*. Boston and New York: Houghton Mifflin Company. Print.
Hountondji, Paulin J. (1996), *African Philosophy: Myth and Reality*, trans. Henri Evans. Bloomington: Indiana University Press. Print.
Huggan, Graham (2013), ed., *The Oxford Handbook of Postcolonial Studies*. Oxford:Oxford University Press. Print.
Hughes, Langston (1994), "Mulatto," in David Levering Lewis, ed., *The Portable Harlem Renaissance Reader*. New York: Penguin Books, 263. Print.
Hughes, Langston (2004), "The Negro Artist and the Racial Mountain," in Henry Louis Gates, Jr. and Nellie Y. Mckay, eds., *The Norton Anthology of African American Literature*. New York: Norton, 1311–1314. Print.
Hume, David (1997), "Negroes...Naturally Inferior to the Whites," in Emannuel Chukwudi Eze, ed., *Race and the Enlightenment*. Malden, MA: Blackwell, 29–34. Print.
Huntington, Collis (1890), "To George Washington Williams, New York, January7, 1890." Huntington Papers, Syracuse University Library. Print.
Kandé, Sylvie and Karaganis, Joe (1998), "Look Homeward, Angel: Maroons and Mulattos in Haile Gerima's 'Sankofa'." *Research in African Literatures* 29:2, 128–146. Print.
Kanza, Thomas (1972), *The Rise and Fall of Patrice Lumumba: Conflict in the Congo*. London: Penguin African Library. Print.

Kellersberger, Julia Lake (n.d.), *Lucy Gantt Sheppard: Shepherdess of His Sheep on Two Continents*. Atlanta, Georgia: PCUS. Print.

Kumar, Rhea (2007), "The Golden Stool and the Porcupine." *Adaptation* 21:2, https://globalist.Yale.edu.

Irele, Abiola (1971), "The Criticism of Modern African Literature," in Christopher Heywood, ed., *Perspectives on African Literature*. London: Heinemann, 9–24. Print.

Irele, Abiola (1981), *The African Experience in Literature and Ideology*. London: Heinemann. Print.

Irele, Abiola (1987), *In Praise of Alienation*. Ibadan: Ibadan University Press. Print.

Irele, Abiola (1990), "The African Imagination." *Research in African Literatures* 21, 49–67. Print.

Irele, Abiola (2001), *The African Imagination: Literature in Africa and the Black Diaspora*. Oxford: Oxford University Press, 2001. Print.

Irele, Abiola (2011), *The Negritude Moment: Explorations in Francophone African and Caribbean Literature and Thought*. Trenton: Africa World Press, 2011. Print.

Izevbaye, Dan (2003), "Mediation in Soyinka: The Case of the King's Horseman," in Simon Gikandi, ed., *Wole Soyinka, Death and the King's Horseman, Background and Sources*. New York: Norton & Company, 141–151. Print.

Jacobs, Sylvia (1982), ed., *Black Americans and the Missionary Movement in Africa*. London: Greenwood Press. Print.

Jeal, Tim (2007), *Stanley: The Impossible Life of Africa's Greatest Explorer*. New Haven and London: Yale University Press. Print.

Jeyifo, Biodun (2011), ed., *Africa in the World and the World in Africa: Essays in Honor of Abiola Irele*. Trenton: Africa World Press. Print.

Johnson, Samuel (1921), *The History of the Yoruba*. Lagos: CMS. Print.

Johnson, Sylvester (2015), *African American Religions, 1500–2000: Colonialism, Democracy, and Freedoms*. New York: Cambridge University Press. Print.

Jones, Eldred Durosimi(1988), *The Writings of Wole Soyinka*. London: James Currey.

Kapchan, Deborah and Strong, Pauline Turner (1999), "Theorizing the Hybrid." *The Journal of American Folklore* 112:445, 239–253. JSTOR. Web. 22 Feb 2013.

Kennedy, Pagan (2002), *Black Livingston, A True Adventure in the Nineteenth-Century Congo*. New York and London: Viking. Print.

Kilberd, Declan (1997), *Inventing Ireland: The Literature of the Modern Nation*. London: Random House. Print.

Landry, Donna and MacClean, Gerald M. (1996), eds., *The Spivak Reader*. New York and London: Routledge. Print.

Lapsley, Samuel N. (1891), "[To the Editor] Missionary." *The Missionary* 2, 34. Print.

Lapsley, James W. (1893), ed., *Life and Letters of Samuel Norvell Lapsley*. Richmond, VA: Whittet and Shepperson. Print.

Losambe, Lokangaka (1996), ed., *Introduction to the African Prose Narrative*. Pretoria: Kagiso. Print.

Losambe, Lokangaka (2005), *Borderline Movements in African Fiction*. Trenton: Africa World Press. Print.

Losambe, Lokangaka (2017), "The Colonial Stranger and Postcolonial Agency: The Congo Narrative." *Interventions: International Journal of Postcolonial Studies* 19:6, 837–854. Print.

Losambe, Lokangaka (2020), "The Local and the Global in Francis Abiola Irele's Critical Thought." *Journal of the African Literature Association* 14:1, 58–71. Print.

Losambe, Lokangaka (2021), "Post-Hybrid Conjunctive Consciousness in the Literature of the New African Diaspora," in Olakunle George, ed., *A Companion to African Literatures*. Hoboken, NJ: Wiley Blackwell, 367–380. Print.

Losambe, Lokangaka and Maureen Eke (2011), eds., *Literature, the Visual Arts And Globalization In African and Its Diaspora*. Trenton: Africa World Press. Print.

Lumumba, Patrice Emery (1972a), "African Unity and Nationalism," in Jean Van Lierde, ed., *Lumumba Speaks: The Speeches and Writings of Patrice Lumumba: 1958–1961*, trans. Helen R. Lane. London: Frederick Muller Limited, 69–75. Print.

Lumumba, Patrice Emery (1972b), "Press Conference in Leopoldville," in Jean Van Lierde, ed., *Lumumba Speaks: The Speeches and Writings of Patrice Lumumba: 1958–1961*, trans. Helen R. Lane. London: Frederick Muller Limited, 308–331. Print.

Lumumba, Patrice Emery (1972c), "Speech at Leopoldville," in Jean Van Lierde, ed., *Lumumba Speaks: The Speeches and Writings of Patrice Lumumba: 1958–1961*, trans. Helen R. Lane. London: Frederick Muller Limited, 59–68. Print.

Magee, Carol (2012), *Africa in the American Imagination: Popular Culture Racialized Identities, and African Visual Culture*. Jackson: University Press of Mississippi. Print.

Mbembe, Achille (2001), *On the Postcolony*. Oakland: University of California Press. Print.

Mbembe, Achille (2007), "Afropolitanism," in S. Njami and L. Duran, eds., *Africa Remix*. Johannesburg: Jacana Media. Print.

Mignolo, Walter D. (2000), *Local Histories/ Global Designs: Coloniality, Subaltern Knowledges, and Border Thinking*. Princeton, NJ: Princeton University Press. Print.

Moore, Gerald (1980), *Twelve African Writers*. London: Hutchinson. Print.

Morel, Edmund Dene (1904), *King Leopold's Rule in Africa*. London: Heinemann. Print.

Morrison, M. William (1996a), "To the Missionary [Luebo, 5 June 1897 and Ibanj, 7 December 1897]," in Robert Benedetto, ed., *Presbyterian Reformers in Central Africa: A Documentary Account of the American Presbyterian Congo Mission and the Human Rights Struggle in Congo, 1890–1918*. Leiden and New York: E.J. Brill, 109–114. Print.

Morrison, M. William (1996b), "Diary: 1 January-12 October 1899," in Robert Benedetto, ed., *Presbyterian Reformers in Central Africa: A Documentary Account of the American Presbyterian Congo Mission and the Human Rights Struggle in Congo, 1890–1918*. Leiden and New York: E.J. Brill, 117. Print.

Morrison, M. William (1996c), "On the Borders of Bakuba Land," in Robert Benedetto, ed., *Presbyterian Reformers in Central Africa: A Documentary Account of the American Presbyterian Congo Mission and the Human Rights Struggle in Congo, 1890–1918*. Leiden and New York: E.J. Brill, 112–114. Print.

Morrison, M. William (1996d), "To E.D. Morel [Lexington, Va., 1 January 1904]," in Robert Benedetto, ed., *Presbyterian Reformers in Central Africa: A Documentary Account of the American Presbyterian Congo Mission and the Human Rights Struggle in Congo, 1890–1918*. Leiden and New York: E.J. Brill, 195–197. Print.

Morrison, M. William (1996e), "To M.A. Baerts, Chef de Cabinet [Royal Mail Steamship Etruria, 9 May 1903]," in Robert Benedetto, ed., *Presbyterian Reformers in Central Africa: A Documentary Account of the American Presbyterian Congo Mission and the Human Rights Struggle in Congo, 1890–1918*. Leiden and New York: E.J. Brill, 169–171. Print.

Bibliography

Morrison, M. William (1996f), "To the Aborigines Protection Society [Luebo, 7 October 1902]," in Robert Benedetto, ed., *Presbyterian Reformers in Central Africa: A Documentary Account of the American Presbyterian Congo Mission and the Human Rights Struggle in Congo, 1890–1918*. Leiden and New York: E.J. Brill, 138–143. Print.

Morrison, M. William (1996g), "To the Chef de Zone at Luluabourg [Luebo, 6 August 1902]," in Robert Benedetto, ed., *Presbyterian Reformers in Central Africa: A Documentary Account of the American Presbyterian Congo Mission and the Human Rights Struggle in Congo, 1890–1918*. Leiden and New York: E.J. Brill, 134–137. Print.

Morrison, M. William (1996h), "Statement to His Majesty's Government on Conditions in the Congo," in Robert Benedetto, ed., *Presbyterian Reformers in Central Africa: A Documentary Account of the American Presbyterian Congo Mission and the Human Rights Struggle in Congo, 1890–1918*. Leiden and New York: E.J. Brill, 150–157. Print.

Neal, Larry (1972), "Any Day Now: Black Art and Black Liberation," in Woodie King and Earl Anthony, eds., *Black Poets and Prophets*. New York: Mentor, 152–160. Print. Ngugi wa Thiong'o (1993), *Moving the Centre*. London: James Currey. Print.

Ngugi wa Thiong'o (2012), *Globalectics: Theory and Politics of Knowing*. New York: Columbia University Press. Print.

Nkrumah, Kwame (1949), *What I mean by Positive Action*. Accra (Ghana): Convention People's Party. Print.

Ojaide, Tanure (2015), *Indigeneity, Globalization, and African Literature: Personally Speaking*. New York, Palgrave Macmillan. Print.

Okpewho, Isidore and Nkiru Nzegwu (2009), eds., *The New African Diaspora*. Bloomington: Indiana University Press. Print.

O'Siochain, Seamus and Michael O'Sullivan (2003), eds., *The Eyes of Another Race: Roger Casement's Congo Report and 1903 Diary*. Dublin: University College Dublin Press. Print.

Ouma, Christopher E.W. (2011), "'In the Name of the Son': Fatherhood's Critical Legitimacy, Sonhood and Masculinities in Chris Abani's Graceland and The Virgin of the Flames." *English in Africa* 38:2, 77–93. Print.

Ousmane, Semebene (1960), *God's Bits of Wood*. London: Heineman. Print.

Phipps, William E. (2002), *William Sheppard: Congo's African Livingstone*. Louisville, KY: Geneva Press. Print.

Pieterse, Jan Nederveen (1992), *White on Black: Images of Africa and Blacks in Western Popular Culture*. New Haven: Yale University Press. Print.

Rancière, Jacques (2009), *Aesthetics and Its Discontents*, trans. Steven Corcoran. Cambridge, Malden, MA: Polity Press. Print.

Rancière, Jacques (2015), *Dissensus: On Politics and Aesthetics*, trans. Steven Corcoran. London: Bloomsbury. Print.

Sabino, Robin and Hall, Jennifer (1999), "The Path Not Taken: Cultural Identity in the Interesting Life of Olaudah Equiano." *MELUS* 24:1, 5–19.

Said, Edward W. (1979), *Orientalism*. New York: Vintage Books. Print.

Said, Edward W. (1994), *Culture and Imperialism*. New York: Vintage Books. Print.

Sarkar, Prabhat Ranjan (1982), *The Liberation of the Intellect: Neohumanism*. Kalkata: Amanda Marga Publications. Print.

Sartre, Jean-Paul (1972), "Introduction: The Undertaking," in Jean van Lierde, ed., *Lumumba Speaks: The Speeches and Writings of Patrice Lumumba, 1958–1961*. London: Frederick Muller Limited, 3–52. Print.

Selasi, Taiye (2005), "Bye-Bye Babar." *The LIP.* http://thelip.robertsharp.co.uk/?p=76.
Senghor, Leopold Sédar (1985), "Prayer to Masks," in Isidore Okpewho, ed., *The Heritage of African Poetry*. Harlow, Essex: Longman, 134. Print.
Sharp, Jenny and Spivak, Gayatri (2003), "A Conversation with Gayatri Chakravorty Spivak: Politics and the Imagination." *Signs: Journal of Women in Culture and Society* 28:2, 609–624. Print.
Sheppard, William (1905a), "[To the Editor]." *Southern Workman* 4, 219–200. Print.
Sheppard, William (1905b), "[To the Editor]." *The Missionary* 2, 600. Print.
Sheppard, William (1917), *Pioneers in the Congo*. Louisville, KY: Pentecostal Publishing Company. Print.
Sheppard, William (1980), "[To the Editor]." *The Missionary* 9, 335. Print.
Sheppard, William (1996a), "From the Bakuba Country," in Robert Benedetto, ed., *Presbyterian Reformers in Central Africa: A Documentary Account of the Presbyterian Congo Mission and Human Rights Struggle in the Congo, 1890–1918*. Leiden and New York: E.J. Brill, 281–283. Print.
Sheppard, William (1996b), "Reports of Atrocities, Forced Labor, and Denial of Land Concessions," in Robert Benedetto, ed., *Presbyterian Reformers in Central Africa: A Documentary Account of the Presbyterian Congo Mission and Human rights Struggle in the Congo, 1890–1918*. Leiden and New York: E.J. Brill, 121–126. Print.
Singer, Ron (2006), "Interview with Poet and Fiction writer Chris Abani." *Poets and Writers Magazine*, June 1. Pw.org.
Snyder, Dewitt C. (1996a), "To Arthur Rowbotham [Luebo, January 13, 1894]," in Robert Benedetto, ed., *Presbyterian Reformers in Central Africa: A Documentary Account of the Presbyterian Congo Mission and Human Rights Struggle in the Congo, 1890–1918*. Leiden and New York: E.J. Brill, 98. Print.
Snyder, Dewitt C. (1996b), "To Joseph Hawley [Luebo, September 5, 1894]," in Robert Benedetto, ed., *Presbyterian Reformers in Central Africa: A Documentary Account of the Presbyterian Congo Mission and Human rights Struggle in the Congo, 1890–1918*. Leiden and New York: E.J. Brill, 100–102. Print.
Snyder, Dewitt C. (1996c), "To Mr. Phillips [Luebo, January 13, 1894]," in Robert Benedetto, ed., *Presbyterian Reformers in Central Africa: A Documentary Account of the Presbyterian Congo Mission and Human rights Struggle in the Congo, 1890–1918*. Leiden and New York: E.J. Brill, 97–99. Print.
Soyinka, Wole (1964), *The Swamp Dwellers*. Oxford: Oxford University Press. Print.
Soyinka, Wole (1967), *Kongi's Harvest*. Oxford: Oxford University Press. Print.
Soyinka, Wole (1975), *Death and the King's Horseman*. New York: Hill and Wang. Print.
Spivak, Gayatri (2003), *The Death of a Discipline*. New York: Columbia University Press. Print.
Spivak, Gayatri (2008), *Other Asias*. Malden, MA: Blackwell. Print.
Stanard, Matthew (2011), *Selling the Congo*. Lincoln, NE and London: University of Nebraska Press. Print.
Stanley, Henry (1885), *The Congo and the Founding of Its Free State*. 2vols. New York: Harper. Print.
Thesiger, Wilfred (1909), "[To the Editor]." *Kasai Herald* 1:5. Print.
Tlostanova, Madina and Mignolo, Walter (2009), "Global Coloniality and the Decolonial Option." *Kult* 6:(Special Issue), 130–146. Print.
Twain, Mark (1961), *King Leopold's Soliloquy*. New York: International Publishers. Print.

Van Lierde, Jean (1972), ed., *Lumumba Speaks: The Speeches and Writings of Patrice Lumumba:1958–1961*, trans. Helen R. Lane. London: Frederick Muller Limited.
Vansina, Jan (2010), *Being Colonized: The Kuba Experience in Rural Congo, 1880–1960*. Madison: University of Wisconsin Press. Print.
Vinson, Thomas (1921), *William McCutchan Morrison*. Richmond: Presbyterian Committee of Publication. Print.
Wahad, Ahmed Gamal Abdel (2014), "Counter-Orientalism: Retranslating the 'Invisible Arab' in Leila Aboulela's *TheTranslator* and *Lyrics Alley*." *Arab Studies Quaterly* 36:3, 220–241. Print.
Williams, Adebayo (2003), "Ritual and the Political Unconscious: The Case of Death and the King's Horseman," in Simon Gikandi, ed., *Wole Soyinka, Death and the King's Horseman, Background and Sources*. New York: Norton & Company, 187–195. Print.
Williams, George Washington (1874a), "Early Christianity in Africa," Unpublished Commencement Address delivered at Newton Theological School. Andover, New Hampshire: The Library of Newton Theological School. Print.
Williams, George Washington (1874b), *History of the Twelfth Baptist Church: 1840–1874*. Boston, MA: S.N. Print.
Williams, George Washington (1875), "To Henry Wadsworth Longfellow, July 24, 1875." Longfellow Papers. Houghton Library, Harvard University. Print.
Williams, George Washington (1890a), "To Collis Huntington, Boma, April 14, 1890." Huntington Papers, Syracuse University Library. Print.
Williams, George Washington (1890b), "To Collis P. Huntington, Las Palmas, February 6, 1890." Huntington Papers, Syracuse University Library. Print.
Williams, George Washington (1998a), "An Open Letter to His Serene Majesty Leopold II, King of the Belgians and Sovereign of the Independent State of Congo, by Colonel the honorable Geo. W. Williams of the United States of America" (Appendix 1), in John Hope Franklin, ed., *George Washington Williams*. Durham and London: Duke University Press, 243–254. Print.
Williams, George Washington (1998b), "A Report on the Proposed Congo Railway, by Colonel the Honorable Geo. W. Williams, of the United States of America" (Appendix2), in John Hope Franklin, ed., *George Washington Williams*. Durham and London: Duke University Press, 255–263. Print.
Williams, George Washington (1998c), "A Report Upon the Congo-State and Country to the President of the United States of America, by Colonel the Honorable Geo. W. Williams" (Appendix 3), in John Hope Franklin, ed., *George Washington Williams*. Durham and London: Duke University Press, 264–279. Print.
Williams, George Washington (2016), *History of the Negro Race in America from 1619 to 1880 As Slaves, as Soldiers, and as Citizens*. 2 vols. New York: Create Space. Print.
Williams, Walter (1982), *Black Americans and the Evangelization of Africa: 1877–1900*. Madison: The University of Wisconsin Press. Print.
Winsborough, Hallie Paxson and Timmons, Sarah Lee Vinson (1937), *Glorious Living*. Atlanta, Georgia: Committee on Woman's Work PCUS. Print.
Wright, Assanta E. (1994), "A Return to the Past." *Black Film Review* 8:1, 24–28.
Young, Robert J.C. (2015), *Empire, Colony, Postcolony*. Malden, MA: Wiley Blackwell. Print.
Zeleza, Paul (2009), "Diaspora Dialogues: Engagements between Africa and Its Diaspora," in Isidore Okpewho and Nkiru Nzegwu, eds., *The New African Diaspora*. Bloomington and Indianapolis: Indiana University Press, 31–58. Print.

Filmography

Asante, Amma (2013), *Belle*. London: DJ Films. 105min.
Calmettes, Joël (2010), *Berlin 1885: The Division of Africa*. Brooklyn, NY: Icarus Films. 84 min.
Gerima, Haile (1993), *Sankofa*. Washington, DC: Mypheduh Films, Inc. 125 min.
Kouyaté, Dani (1995), *Keita: L'héritage du Griot*. Paris and Ouagadougou: Sahelis Productions. 94 min.

Index

Note: Page numbers followed by "n" denote endnotes.

Abani, Chris 2, 7, 147–169, 175; *The Virgin of Flames* 148, 150–158
Abolitionist Movement 33
Aborigines Protection Society 117
Aboulela, Leila 2, 7, 147–169; *The Translator* 148, 150, 164–169
Achebe, Chinua 6, 11, 174; *Hopes and Impediments* 147; *Things Fall Apart* 13
Adichie, Chimamanda Ngozi 2, 7, 147–169; *Americanah* 148, 150, 158–164
"aesthetic traditionalism" 174
Africa: beliefs 18, 23, 25; counteracting negative western representations of 83–90; cultural memory 19–20; orality 16; unlearning western invention of 58–63
"Africa" (Diop) 146
African Americans 21, 26, 38–39, 123
African diaspora 2, 11, 21, 26; creative writers 147; intellectuals 127; writers 147–149, 169
the African Imagination 7; Irele and 170–176
African life-worlds 6
African memory 12, 20, 22–25, 142, 170
African modernity 127
Africanness 19, 176
"African personality" 18, 125, 170
"the Agencies of Race Organization" 39–40
Aidoo, Ama Ata 6–7, 174
Al-Nidaa 166
America: pastoring for racial justice in 37–40; pastoring for social justice in 37–40
Americanah (Adichie) 148, 150, 158–164
American postcoloniality 5, 120

American Presbyterian Congo Mission (APCM) 68, 84, 93, 95, 97, 100–101, 103, 107, 116–117, 119
American Reconstruction project 39
American Southern Church 57
Anderson, Galusha 38
Anglo-African identity 16
anti-colonial: activism 104–106; Congolese hero Patrice Emery Lumumba (1925–1961) 124–127; messianic movement 171, 176n1; nationalism 124; "Ngunzism" 53; report on the Pianga massacre 112–120; strike in French West Africa 4
anti-enslavement abolitionist movement 12
Arab Spring 2
Armah, Ayi Kwei 6, 174
Asante, Amma 2, 11–33, 26
Ashcroft, Bill 70–71, 146n1, 172–173; *The Empire Writes Back* 173
Associated Literary Press 40, 53n1
Atkinson, Edna 106
Awoonor, Kofi 174

Ba, Amadou Hampaté 174
Bâ, Mariama 4–5, 7; *So Long a Letter* 4
Baker, Richard 14
Bakhtin, Mikhail 137
Baldwin, Mary 82
Baring, Sir Evelyn 52
Bauman, Zygmunt 5
Bedinger, Robert 99
Belgian colonialism 120, 126
Belgian Kasai Rubber Company 53, 105
Belle (film) 26–33
Benedetto, Robert 118–119
Bentley, W.H. 122

Berlin Treaty 5, 48
Beti, Mongo 7; *Mission to Kala* 140
Bignall, Simone 3
Black American missionaries 6, 87–90, 93, 95, 98, 102–103, 124; women missionaries 90–106
Black Americans 24, 39, 41, 58, 72, 86–87, 99, 103, 160
Black Christian missionaries 18
Black Lives Matter 1
black people's enslavement, crusading against 41–43
Blyden, Edward Wilmot 55, 170; *Christianity, Islam and the Negro Race* 18
Boehmer, Elleke 57
"Boko Haram" 7n1
"border thinking" 7n2
Brathwaite, Kamau 2
British colonialism 131, 137
British Parliament 118–119
Brown, Althea 98, 100; *Grammar and Dictionary of the Bushonga or Bakuba Language* 100–101
Bulawayo, NoViolet 7, 148
Burroughs, Robert 120, 123
Butler, Judith 4
Byrne, Paula 33, 33n1

Calmettes, Joel 5
Casement, Roger 43, 53
Castle, Elmina 21
Césaire, Aimé 6
Chambers, Claire 149
Cheney-Coker, Syl 174
Chester, S.H. 56, 116
Christianity 16, 18, 23, 25, 38, 56, 64, 66, 69, 71–72, 89, 110, 124, 164
Christianity, Islam and the Negro Race (Blyden) 18
Churchill, Randolph 53n1
The Cincinnati Commercial 40
Clark-Bekederemo, J.P. 174
Clarkson, Thomas 33
Cleveland, Grover 85
CODA 170–176
Cole, Teju 7, 148
Coleridge, Samuel 33
Coles, John J. 41
colonial brutality, crusading against 41–43
colonial encounter: in *Death and the King's Horseman* (Soyinka) 131–146; in *Keita! l'héritage du Griot* (film) 139–146

colonialism 1, 19, 170; Belgian 120, 126; British 131, 137; European 5; French 140; modern 121; struggles against 124, 126; ubiquitous evil of 122
Colored Protective Association 40
"commandement" 3
The Commoner 39
"common notions" 4
Congo Free State 5, 6, 41–43, 49–51, 58, 62, 67, 74, 86–87, 112, 116–120, 122–123
Congo Reform Association 53, 123
Congo Reform Movement 119
Conrad, Joseph 46, 60, 122; *Heart of Darkness* 46, 53, 61
counteracting negative western representations of Africa 83–90
Cowper, William 33
critical regionalism 2
Crummel, Alexander 41
crusading: against Black people's enslavement 41–43; against colonial brutality 41–43
Cugoano, Ottobah 33
Cullen, Countee 15, 17
cultural hybridity 14, 71, 124, 175; postcolonial 74–83
cultural translation 11, 16, 18, 22, 67, 69, 71, 89, 102, 124, 127, 133–134, 139–140, 142
Culture and Imperialism (Said) 1, 175

Dadié, Bernard 7
Daiya, Kavita 2, 148
Damas, Léon 6
Dangarembga, Tsitsi 7, 174
Darwin, Charles 84
Death and the King's Horseman (Soyinka) 7, 131–146; colonial encounter in 131–146; postcolonial agency in 131–146
decolonialism 2
decolonial solidarism 122
Deleuze, Gilles 71
DeLoughrey, Elizabeth 2
Denham, Sir Thomas 16
Derrida, Sapphic 158
Dewey, John 92
DeYampert, Lillian 106
DeYampert, Lucius 106
diaspora, defined 148
Dilke, Sir Charles W. 118
Diome, Fatou 7
Diop, David 6; "Africa" 146
Douglass, Frederick 27, 37, 39

Doyle, Arthur Conan 53n1, 122
Duah, Alexandra 22
Durbin, Kate 151

Edmiston, Alonzo 101, 106
Edmiston, Althea 106
Ekotto, Frieda 7
Eliot, T.S. 172
Emecheta, Buchi 6
The Empire Writes Back (Ashcroft, Griffiths, and Tiffin) 173
Enlightenment thinking 19
enslavement 2, 11, 13, 16–17, 19–20, 22–25, 33, 38–39, 41–43, 47, 51–52, 67, 111, 118, 159, 170
Equiano, Olaudah 2, 170; *The Interesting Narrative of the Life of Olaudah Equiano, or Gustavus Vassa, the African* 11–33
European colonialism 5

Fanon, Frantz 1, 4, 136
Farah, Nuruddin 7, 174
Farmer, Thomas 17
Fearing, Maria 86, 89, 91–93, 95, 106, 111, 118
Felton, Tom 28
forced labor system 118
Forna, Aminatta 148
Fox, William 33n1
Franklin, John Hope 37, 53
"free our girls" protest 7n1
French colonialism 140
Frissel, H.B. 55

Gadon, Sarah 28
Gantt, Eliza 85
Gantt, Lucy 82, 84–85
Gates, Henry Louis 131
Gerima, Haile 2, 11–33, 18
Ghanaba, Kofi 19
Gikandi, Simon 24, 172
Gilroy, Paul 2, 5; *Postcolonial Melancholia* 161
Giroux, Henry 19
globalectics 2
globalectic solidarism 122
global solidarism 122
God's Bits of Wood (Ousmane) 4
Goode, Matthew 27
Goyal, Yogita 149
Grammar and Dictionary of the Bushonga or Bakuba Language (Brown) 100–101
Grenfell, George 43, 60, 84, 122

Griffiths, Gareth 172–173; *The Empire Writes Back* 173
Grimes, Leonard 38
Guattari, Félix 71
Gurnah, Abdulrazak 7

Hall, Jennifer 16
Hampton Institute 85
Hardt, Michael 1, 149
Harlem Renaissance 15, 22, 171
Harris, Alice Seely 123
Harris, John 123
Hawkins, Henry 86, 106
Heart of Darkness (Conrad) 46, 53, 61
Hebdo, Charlie 7n1
Henkel, S.H. 54
History of the Congo Reform Movement (Sheppard) 120
History of the Negro Race in America from 1619 to 1880: Negroes as Slaves, as Soldiers, and as Citizens (Williams) 40
A History of the Negro Troops in the War of the Rebellion, 1861–1865 (Williams) 40
Hoar, George Frisbie 43
Hochschild, Adam 5
Hopes and Impediments (Achebe) 147
Houston, James 12
Houston, M.H. 69
Hove, Chenjerai 174
Hughes, Langston 15, 27, 39; "The Negro Artist and the Racial Mountain" 22
Hume, David 12
Huntington, Collis P. 41
hybridity 2; cultural 14, 71, 124, 175; postcolonial cultural 74–83

Ibo culture 13
imperialism 1; modern 121–122; Western 19, 120, 122
Innes, C.L. 172
The Interesting Narrative of the Life of Olaudah Equiano, or Gustavus Vassa, the African (Equiano) 11–33
Inventing Ireland: The Literature of the Modern Nation (Kiberd) 3
Irele, Francis Abiola 7, 11; and the African imagination 170–176
Islam 18, 164–166, 168–169
Iyayi, Festus 174
Izevbaye, D.S. 172

James, Henry 53n1
Janssens, E. 119

190 *Index*

Jeal, Tim 5
Johnson, Samuel 131
Johnston, Sylvester 56
Jones, Eldred 131
justice: racial 37–40; social 37–40

Kandé, Sylvie 21
Kane, Cheikh Hamidou 7, 11, 141
Kapchan, Deborah 71
Karaganis, Joe 21
Kasai Herald 97, 104
Keita! l'héritage du Griot (film) 7; colonial encounter in 139–146; postcolonial agency in 139–146
Kellersberger, Julia 85, 86
Kennedy, Pagan 63
Kiberd, Declan: *Inventing Ireland: The Literature of the Modern Nation* 3
Kimbangu, Simon 53, 124
King, Robert 11, 17
King Bope Mekabe 81
King Kot aMbweeky 77, 79, 82, 90, 94–95
King Kot aMbweeky II 95
King Kwete Mabintshi 100
King Leopold II 6, 41–43, 46, 50–51, 58–59, 62, 73–74, 105, 112, 119
King Leopold's Soliloquy (Twain) 6, 53, 120–121
King Mishaape 111
King Mishaape II 107
Kipling, Rudyard 53n1
Kourouma, Ahmadou 174
Kouyaté, Dani 2, 7, 131–146
Kuba Kingdom 106n1
Kuba King Lukengu 106n1
Kuba land and postcolonial cultural hybridity 74–83
Kumar, Rhea 22

Lady Hardy 33
Laing, Kojo 174
Landsdowne, Lord 118
Langston, John Mercer 39
Lapsley, Samuel 6, 56–74, 80, 84, 86, 97–98, 107, 110, 124; postcolonial 68–73
Lapsley, Sara Pratt 57
Laye, Camara 7, 11
Le Temps 52
Lewis, Samuel 18
The Liberation of the Intellect: Neohumanism (Sarkar) 176n3
Lincoln, Herman 38
Lindfors, Bernth 172
Linnaeus, Carl: *Systema Naturae* 19

Livingstone, David 84
London Times 111
Longfellow, Henry Wadsworth 39
L'Ouverture, Toussaint 40, 44
Lumumba, Jérome 127n1
Lumumba, Patrice Emery 124–127, 127n1
Lumumba Speaks 125

Mabanckou, Alain 7, 148
Malinowski, Bronislaw 176n1
Manichaeism 4
Mapanje, Jack 174
Martin, J. Sella 37
Martin, Sarah Frances 54
Mary-James, Bethan 28
Maximilian, Emperor of Mexico 37
Mbembe, Achille 3–4, 132
Mbue, Imbolo 7, 148
McClure, S.S. 40, 53n1
Medley, Nick 23
middle-passage memory 12
Middleton, Lady Margaret 33
Mignolo, Walter 2, 7n2, 122, 145
Milton, John 16
The Missionary 58, 60, 107
Mission to Kala (Beti) 140
modern colonialism 121
modern imperialism 121–122
Mofolo, Thomas 174
Moore, Gerald 173
More, Hannah 33
Morel, E.D. 53, 118–120, 123
Morrison, William 6, 105
Morrison, W.M. 107–120
Mphahlele, Es'kia 6
Mudimbe, V.Y. 7
Musambu wa Nzambi (Songs of God) 95

nativism 2, 155, 171, 172, 176n1
Ndiaye, Marie 7
Neal, Larry 24
Negri, Antonio 1, 149
Negrismo 171
Negritude movement 6, 171
"The Negro Artist and the Racial Mountain" (Hughes) 22
Negro Renaissance 171
neohumanism 174, 176n3
new African diaspora: postcolonial conjunctive consciousness in literature of 147–169
New National Era 37, 39
"new realism" 174
New World 21–23, 86
Ngal, Georges 7

Ngugi wa Thiong'o 1, 2, 6, 167, 172, 174
"Ngunzism" 53
Nisco, Giacomo 119
Nkrumah, Kwame: *What I Mean by Positive Action* 125
Norton, James 28
Nwapa, Flora 174

Obama, Barack 160
"Occupy Wall Street" 1
Ogunlano, Oyafunmike 20
Ojaide, Tanure 174
Okara, Gabriel 174
Okigbo, Christopher 174
Okpewho, Isidore 148
Okri, Ben 174
Onwueme, Tess 148
An Open Letter to His Serene Majesty Leopold II, King of the Belgians and Sovereign of the Independent State of Congo, By Colonel the Honorable Geo. W. Williams, of the United States of America (Williams) 43–44, 50, 53, 87, 112
Osofisan, Femi 174
Osundare, Niyi 174
Ousmane, Sembene 4–5, 7, 174; *God's Bits of Wood* 4
Oyeyemi, Helen 7, 148, 149

p'Bitek, Okot 174
Phillips, R. Cobden 52
Phipps, Joseph 67, 106
Phipps, William 58
Pianga massacre 112–120
planetarity 2
planetary humanism 2
postcolonial agency 2, 4, 6–7, 25, 33, 71, 110, 124; in *Death and the King's Horseman* 131–146; in *Keita! l'héritage du Griot* (film) 131–146
postcolonial conjunctive consciousness: critical 164; in literature of new African diaspora 147–169
postcolonial cultural hybridity 74–83; and Kuba land 74–83
postcolonialism 3
Postcolonial Melancholia (Gilroy) 161
postcolonial outpost: turning luebo into a 63–68
postcolonial pragmatism 54–106
postcolonial pragmatist 54–106
post-hybrid conjunctive consciousness 2
Presbyterian Pioneers in the Congo (Sheppard) 54, 56

Prince, Mary 33
protest open letter and reports 43–53
public square movements 1

Queen, Daniel 16–17
Queen Victoria 84

racial justice 37–40
Ramsay, James 33
Rancière, Jacques 56, 175
Rawlings, J.J. 21
Reid, Sam 28
Reid, Sir H.D. 118
A Report upon the Congo-State and Country to the President of the Republic of the United States of America, by Colonel the Honorable Geo. W. Williams 51
Richards, Henry 122
Rochester, Adolphus 106
Roosevelt, Franklin D. 102, 119
Ropes, E.D. 52
Rouse, Ellen 37
Rowbotham, Arthur 84
Rowbotham, Margaret 84

Sabino, Robin 16
Sagay, Misan 28
Said, Edward 7n2, 148; *Culture and Imperialism* 1, 175
Salih, Tayeb 7
Sancho, Ignatius 33
Sanford, Henry S. 41, 57
Sankofa (film) 18–26
Sarkar, Prabbat Ranjan: *The Liberation of the Intellect: Neohumanism* 176n3
Sartre, Jean-Paul 124
Sayyid Ali, Sultan of Zanzibar 52
de Schumacher, E. 119
Scrivener, A.E. 123
Second World War 138
Selasi, Taiye 7, 148
Senghor, L.S. 6
Sharp, Granville 33
Sheppard, William, Sr. 54
Sheppard, William Henry 2, 5, 6, 54–106; anti-colonial activism 104–106; anti-colonial report on Pianga massacre 112–120; Black American women missionaries' contributions 90–106; counteracting negative western representations of Africa 83–90; expanding postcolonial cultural hybridity to Kuba land 74–83; *History of the Congo Reform*

Movement 120; postcolonial Samuel Lapsley 68–73; *Presbyterian Pioneers in the Congo* 54, 56; subverting racialized order of Southern Presbyterian Church 56–58; turning luebo into postcolonial outpost 63–68; unlearning western invention of Africa 58–63
Singer, Ron 147
Smith, Kendred 123
Smith, Sir Charles Euan 52
Smythies, Charles Alan 52
Snyder, Dewitt C. 84
Snyder, Margaret 84
social justice 37–40
So Long a Letter (Bâ) 4
Southern Presbyterian Church 55; and Henry Hawkins 86; subverting racialized order of 56–58
Soyinka, Wole 2, 6, 131–146
Spinoza, Baruch 4
Spivak, Gayatri 2, 7n2, 149
Standard, Mathew 5
Stanfield, James 33
Stanley, Henry Morton 43, 45, 84
Sterretts, Sarah A. 37
Stevens, Wallace 153
Stevenson, Robert Louis 53n1
"strategic essentialism" 7n2
"strategic location" 7n2
Strong, Pauline 71
Systema Naturae (Linnaeus) 19

Tansi, Sony Labou 174
Taylor, Annie 106
Terrell, Robert H. 43, 51
Thesiger, Wilfred 103–104
Things Fall Apart (Achebe) 13
Thomas, Lillian 86
Thys, Albert 41
tidalectics 2
Tiffin, Helen 146n1; *The Empire Writes Back* 173
Tlostanova, Madina 122
The Translator (Aboulela) 148, 150, 164–169
transnational consciousness 7, 149, 174
Trotter, James M. 37
Tshisungu wa Tshisungu 148
Tutuola, Amos 174
Twain, Mark 5, 6, 53, 53n1, 120–124

Union Baptist Church 40

Van Kerckhoven, Guillaume 62–63
"Van Kerckhoven Expedition" 62
Van Lierde, Jean 125
Vinson, Thomas 110
The Virgin of Flames (Abani) 148, 150–158

Waberi, Abdourahman 7, 148
Wahab, Ahmed 149
Washington Post 21
Weeks, John H. 123
Weissmann, Baron Major 52
Western colonial brutality 124
Western imperialism 19, 120, 122
Western literacy 16
Western memory 12
Western modernity 2, 5–6, 18–20, 22–23; and African cultural memory 19–20; and African life-worlds 6–7; and African memory 22, 24; and American postcoloniality 5; colonial "structure of attitudes" 72; cultural translation of 102, 142; and European colonialism 5; rigidly structured 124; self-contradiction of 5
What I Mean by Positive Action (Nkrumah) 125
Wheatley, Phillis 170
Wilberforce, William 33
Wilkinson, Tom 28
Williams, George Washington 2, 5–6, 37–53; crusading against Black people's enslavement 41–43; crusading against colonial brutality 41–43; *History of the Negro Race in America from 1619 to 1880: Negroes as Slaves, as Soldiers, and as Citizens* 40; *A History of the Negro Troops in the War of the Rebellion, 1861–1865* 40; *An Open Letter to His Serene Majesty Leopold II, King of the Belgians and Sovereign of the Independent State of Congo, By Colonel the Honorable Geo. W. Williams, of the United States of America* 43–44, 50, 53, 87, 112; pastoring for racial and social justice in America 37–40; protest open letter and reports 43–53
Williams, Thomas 37
Williams, Walter 55
Wilton, Penelope 28
Women's March 2
Wright, Assata 26

Zeleza, Paul 148